JIM BUTCHER'S

STORM FRONT

VOLUME ONE: THE GATHERING STORM

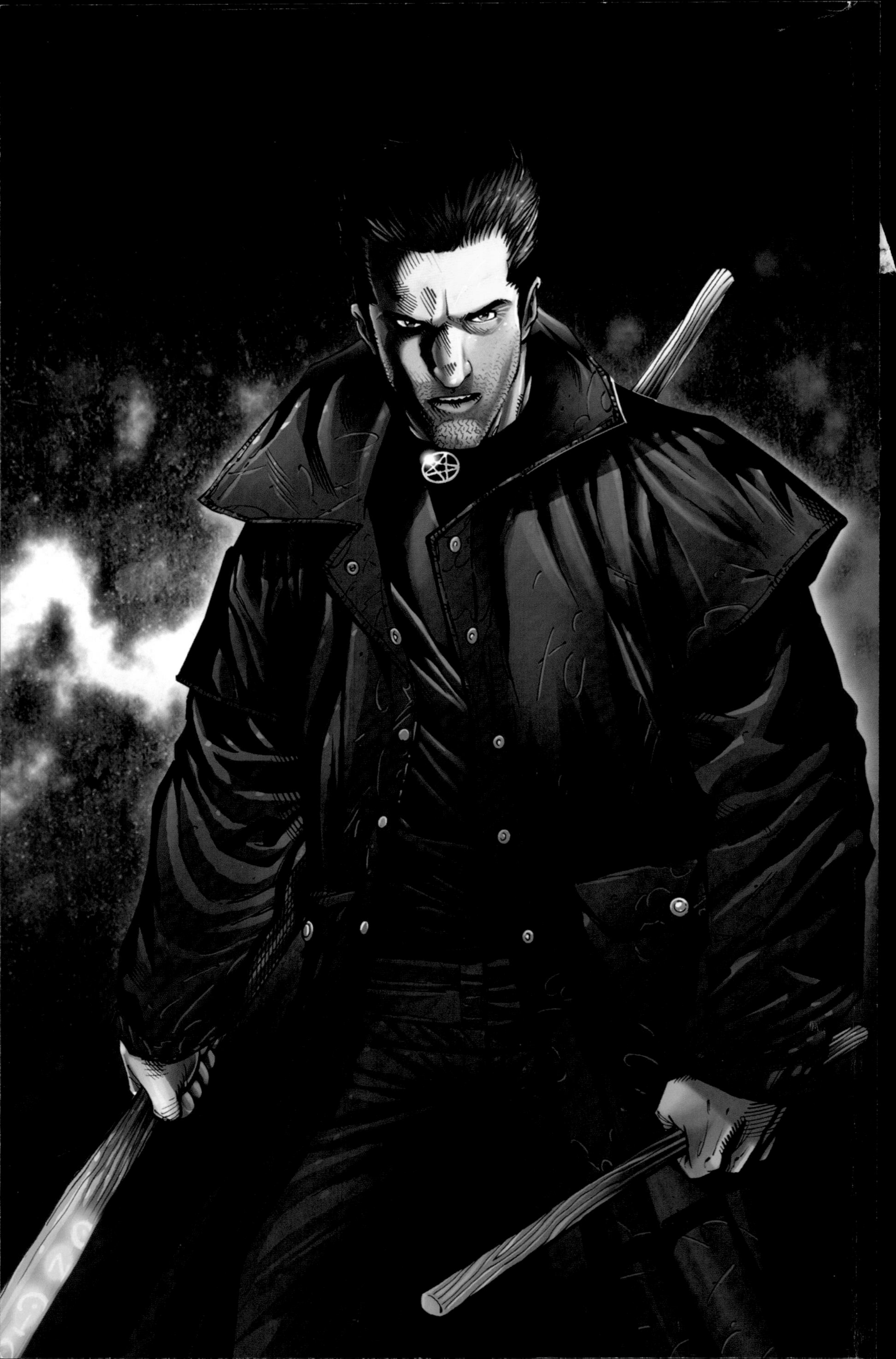

JIM BUTCHER'S The DRESDEN FILES

STORM FRONT

VOLUME ONE: THE GATHERING STORM

adaptation by
MARK POWERS

based on the novel *Storm Front* by
JIM BUTCHER

pencils by
ARDIAN SYAF

inks by
RICK KETCHAM

colors by
MOHAN

lettering/design by
BILL TORTOLINI

edited by
DAVID LAWRENCE

DEL REY

BALLANTINE BOOKS · NEW YORK

Thanks to thematic consultants
PRISCILLA SPENCER, MICHAEL FINN, and **FRED HICKS.**

Published in the United States by Del Rey, an imprint of The Random House Publishing Group, a division of Random House, Inc., New York.

DEL REY is a registered trademark and the Del Rey colophon is a trademark of Random House, Inc.

Originally published as *The Dresden Files: Storm Front*, volume 1, issues 1–4 by Dabel Brothers Publishing in 2008 and 2009.

ISBN 978-0-345-50639-9
ISBN 978-0-345-51539-1 (direct market edition)

Printed in the United States of America on acid-free paper

www.delreybooks.com
www.dabelbrothers.com

9 8 7 6 5 4 3 2 1

First Edition

publisher
ERNST DABEL

v.p. business operations
LES DABEL

business development
RICH YOUNG

project manager
DEREK RUIZ

consulting editor
DAVID LAWRENCE

special projects
DAVID DABEL

marketing/street team
NEIL SCHWARTZ

Introduction by Jim Butcher

I remember the first comic book I ever bought with my own money. It was 1978, and I was seven. My family was on vacation in Acapulco, and I got myself the kind of sunburn that leaves you lying on your stomach for a day or two while you heal up. Being seven, and speaking no Spanish (and thus unable to understand the TV), I was bored out of my mind in short order. I'd already read through my copy of *The Lion, the Witch and the Wardrobe*, and I wandered down to the hotel store to get a snack and look for another book. They didn't have any books in English, or at least nothing *good.*

But then I saw that they had *Daredevil.*

I don't remember the issue, but Daredevil was taking on Tatterdemalion, and it was, for a seven-year-old, an extremely dark, creepy, and rather scary story. I was so young, I'd never seen the word "damn" in print until I read that issue.

It was amazing.

I went back to the hotel store. I bought them out of all, I dunno, eight or nine titles they carried. *The Hulk, Spider-Man, Doctor Strange,* and *Thor. Batman, Teen Titans,* and *Superman*. Since they were all the reading I had, I made the most of it. I read them all, several times. I studied the art. I tried drawing a few of the pictures myself (making the discovery that I had almost zero natural talent for such work). And it was all downhill from there.

I read comics for the rest of my childhood, and when I started writing my own stories, they were all strongly influenced by the characters and scenes and situations I found there. Harry Dresden, in my head, has always been a comic book hero. The biggest scenes and confrontations in The Dresden Files almost always crystallize into a single image in my imagination, and that image becomes the basis for the scene around it. I don't have the skill to share those images with other people by creating them myself. I've always had to do it with words, instead.

But then the Dabel Brothers came along with a good idea and a guy named Ardian Syaf.

Ardian is amazing. I mean, it's one thing to turn out a single good piece that you focus enormous thought and effort in. It's another thing entirely to turn in one solid piece after another, on a deadline, day after day. And it's still *another* thing to do that with someone else at your elbow going, "Hey, no, you need to fix this detail. Hey, his nose is too long. Hey, why is this shadow laying over that detail? Can't you make all the shadows fall different ways so we can see better?"

If you'd asked me before we got started, I never would have thought that an artist would have the patience to keep working to make me happy with the characters he's giving a face and form to. I have frequently sent him pictures of two people who look nothing alike and said things like, "He looks like both of these guys, make him look like that." I have asked him to convey aspects of a character that, frankly, simply cannot be displayed visually. Week after week, poor Ard has put out one page after another, all of them solidly professional, many of them truly outstanding, while getting the kind of feedback and requests that would try the patience of a saint's guardian angel.

Here are some of the results. It's my story, adapted almost *too* faithfully from the book by Mark Powers. Ardian has given the characters faces and bodies, and breathed life into the action. Sometimes looking at the pages is positively eerie for me—because I'm seeing, in the real world, things that I'd only previously seen in my imagination. Sometimes, actually seeing those images has been downright shocking. I'll stare and blink for a minute and then say, "Did I write that?" And I'll look and read it from the book, which brings up all the associated images that have been back in the dusty vaults of my head, and **THERE THEY ARE**, on my computer monitor.

It was, is, and continues to be *amazing.*

I hope you enjoy reading this work as much as I enjoyed both creating the story and seeing it come together on the page. It's even more fun than Acapulco.

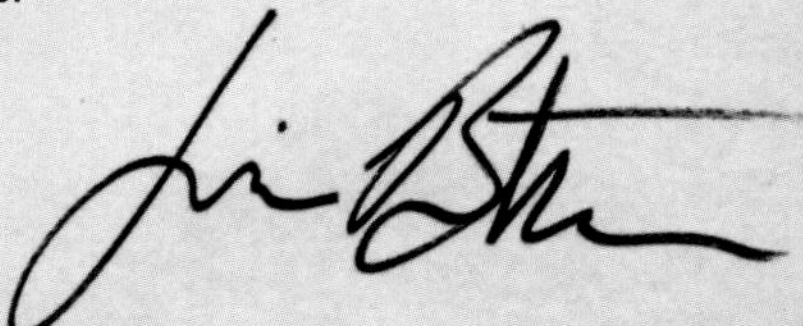

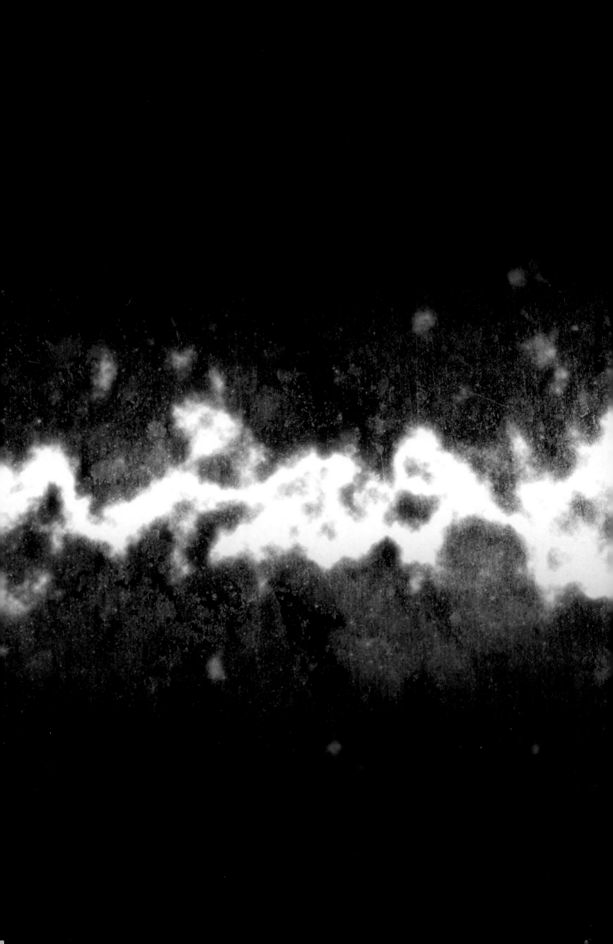

CHAPTER ONE

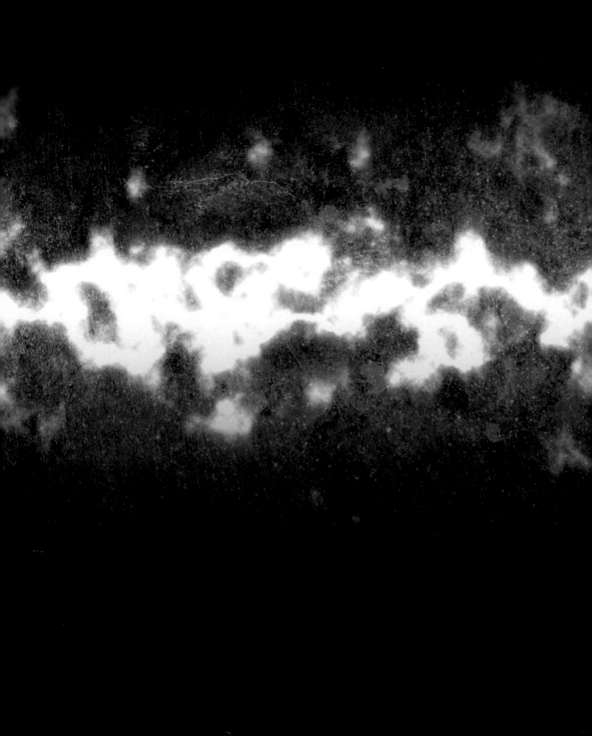

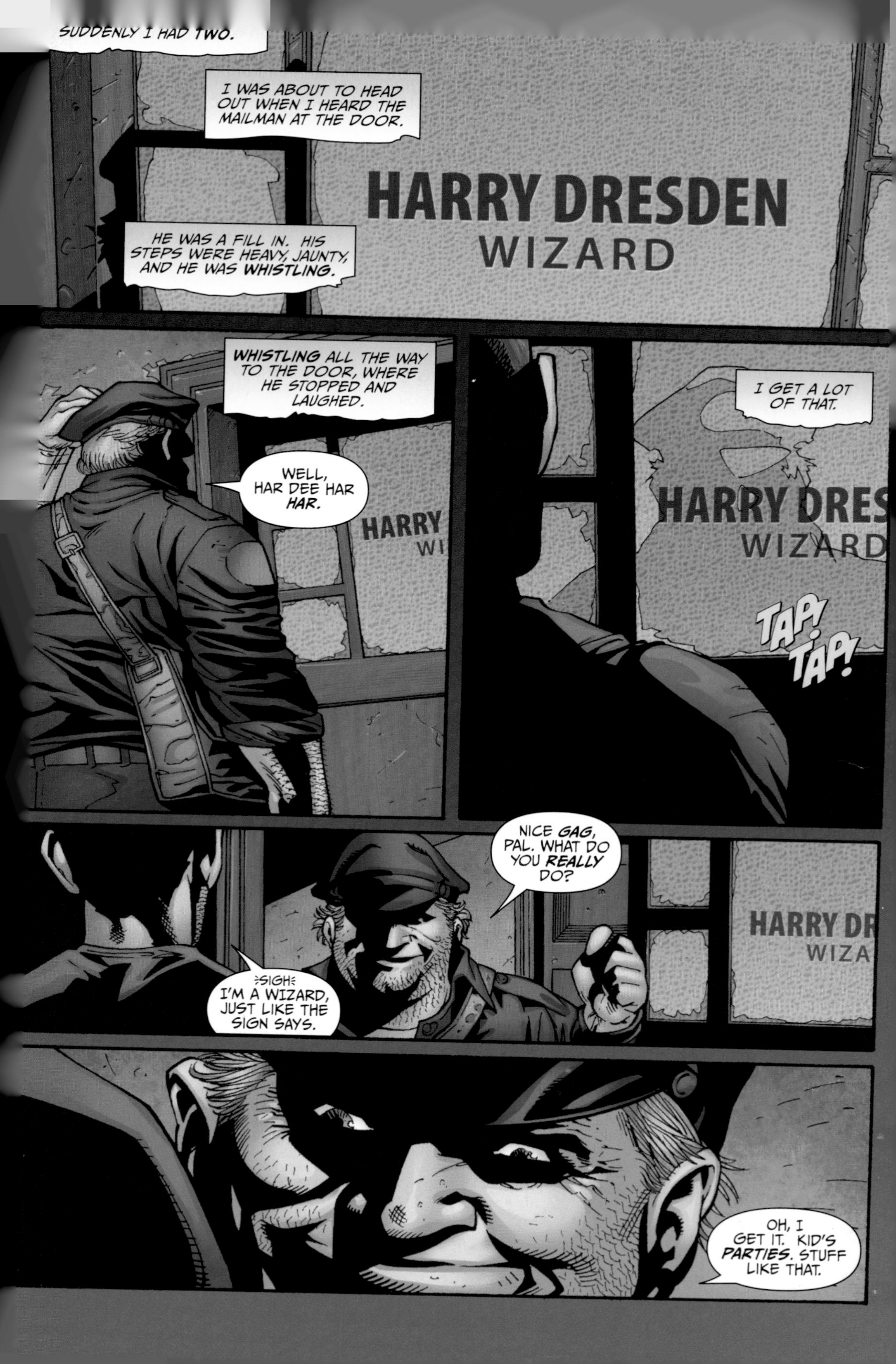
SUDDENLY I HAD TWO.
I WAS ABOUT TO HEAD OUT WHEN I HEARD THE MAILMAN AT THE DOOR.
HARRY DRESDEN
WIZARD
HE WAS A FILL IN. HIS STEPS WERE HEAVY, JAUNTY, AND HE WAS WHISTLING.
WHISTLING ALL THE WAY TO THE DOOR, WHERE HE STOPPED AND LAUGHED.
WELL, HAR DEE HAR HAR.
I GET A LOT OF THAT.
TAP! TAP!
NICE GAG, PAL. WHAT DO YOU REALLY DO?
SIGH
I'M A WIZARD, JUST LIKE THE SIGN SAYS.
OH, I GET IT. KID'S PARTIES. STUFF LIKE THAT.

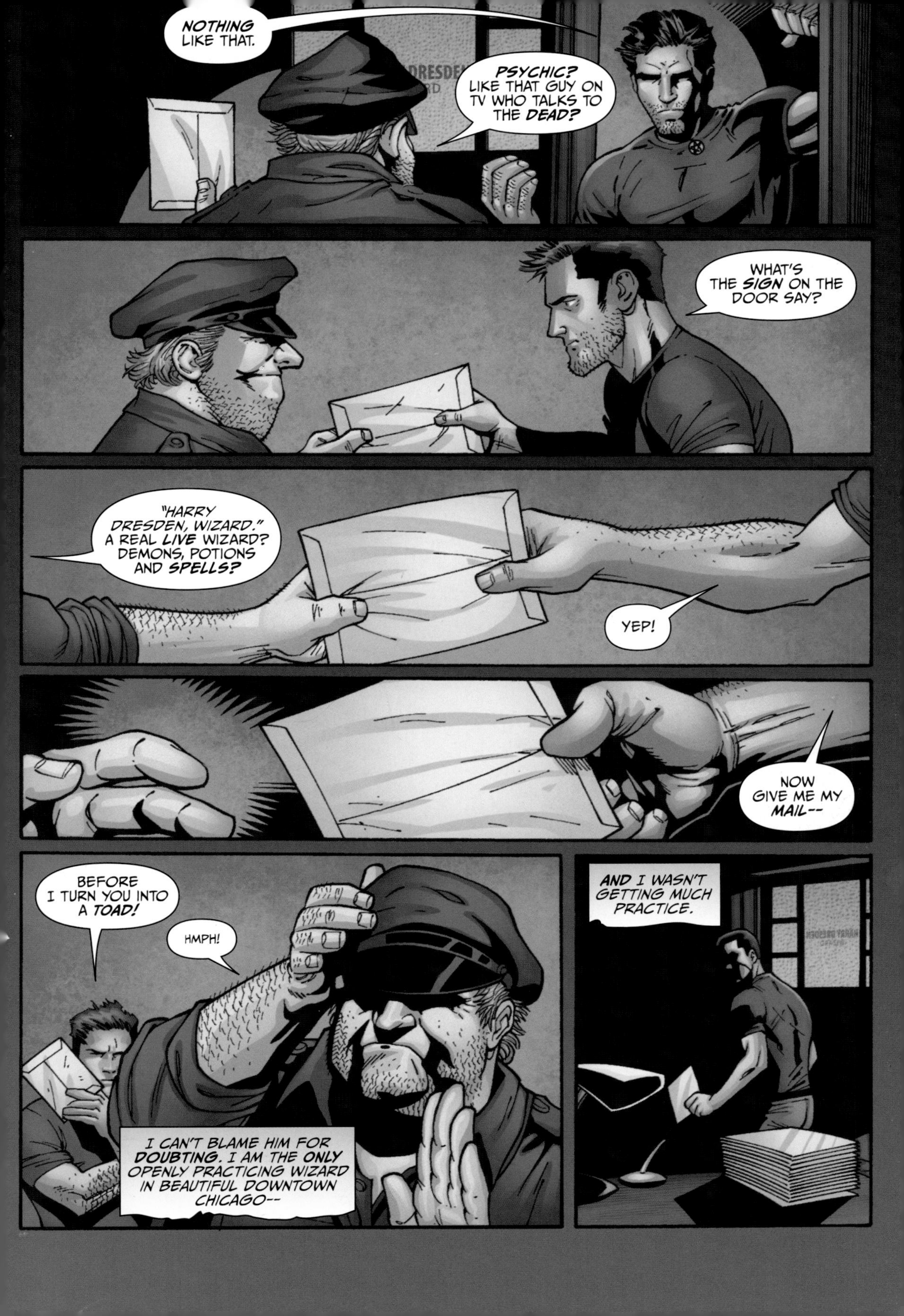
NOTHING LIKE THAT.
PSYCHIC? LIKE THAT GUY ON TV WHO TALKS TO THE DEAD?
WHAT'S THE SIGN ON THE DOOR SAY?
"HARRY DRESDEN, WIZARD." A REAL LIVE WIZARD? DEMONS, POTIONS AND SPELLS?
YEP!
NOW GIVE ME MY MAIL--
BEFORE I TURN YOU INTO A TOAD!
HMPH!
I CAN'T BLAME HIM FOR DOUBTING. I AM THE ONLY OPENLY PRACTICING WIZARD IN BEAUTIFUL DOWNTOWN CHICAGO--
AND I WASN'T GETTING MUCH PRACTICE.

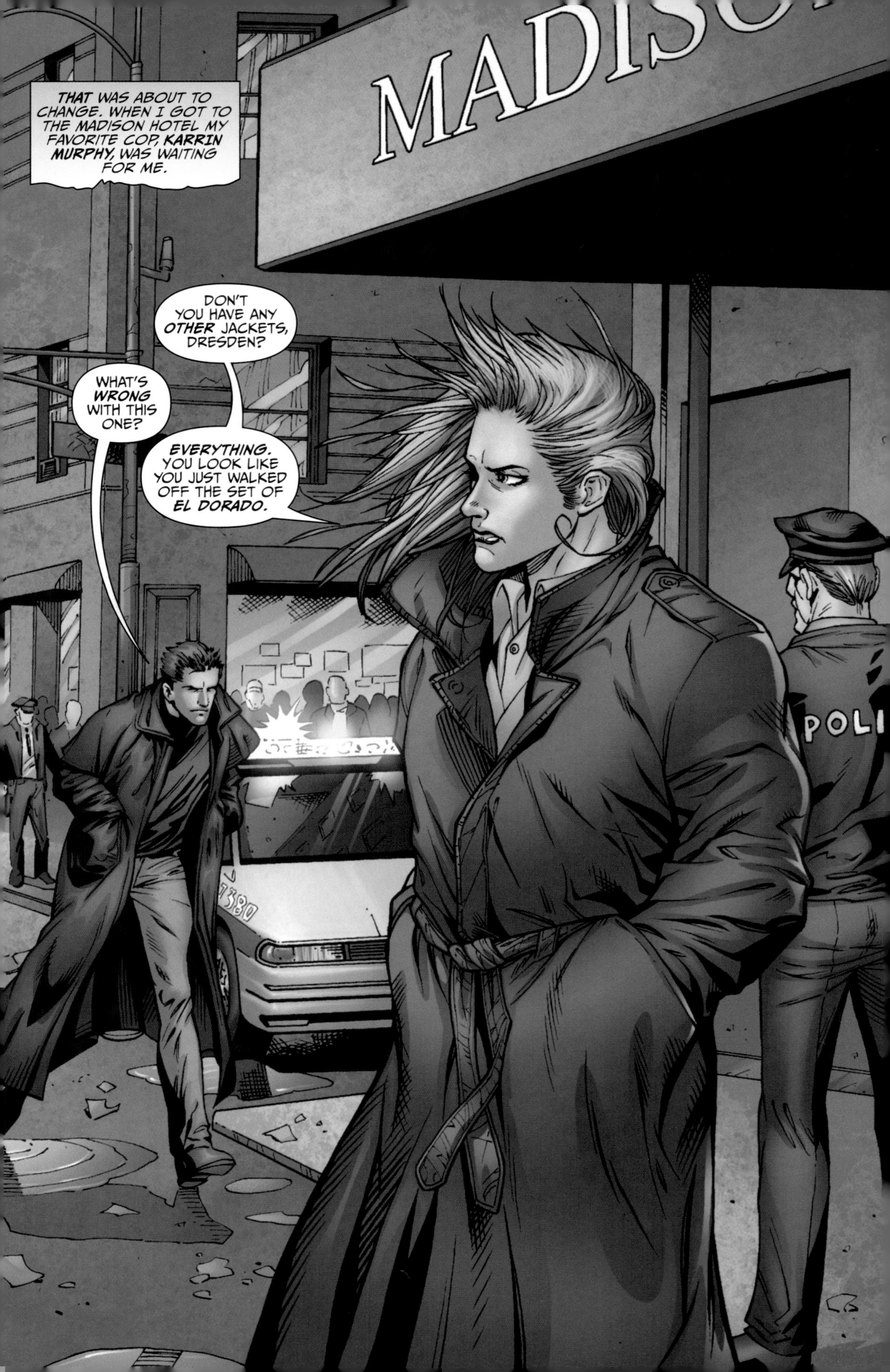
MADISO
THAT WAS ABOUT TO CHANGE. WHEN I GOT TO THE MADISON HOTEL MY FAVORITE COP, KARRIN MURPHY, WAS WAITING FOR ME.
DON'T YOU HAVE ANY OTHER JACKETS, DRESDEN?
WHAT'S WRONG WITH THIS ONE?
EVERYTHING. YOU LOOK LIKE YOU JUST WALKED OFF THE SET OF EL DORADO.
POLI

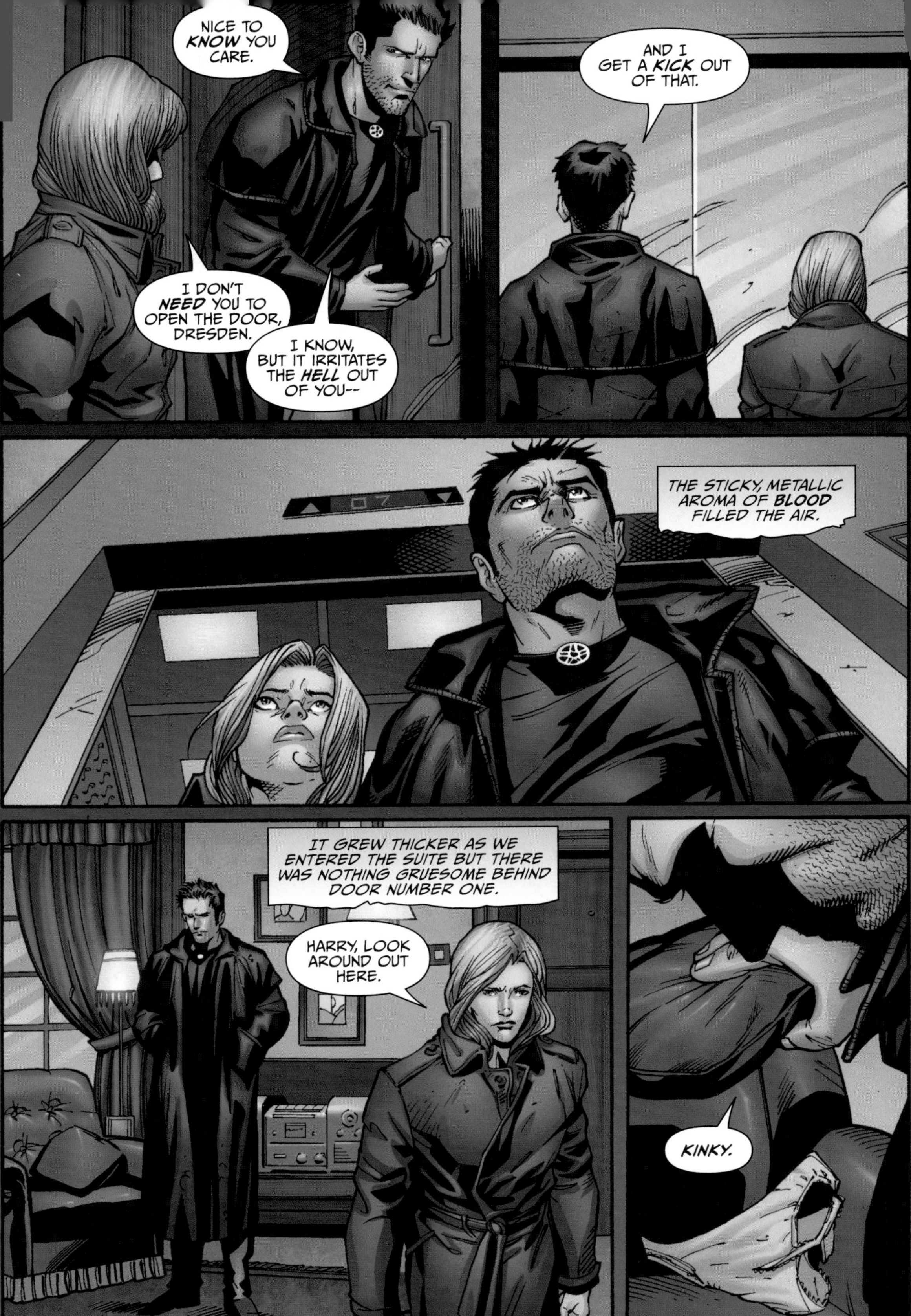
NICE TO KNOW YOU CARE.
I DON'T NEED YOU TO OPEN THE DOOR, DRESDEN.
I KNOW, BUT IT IRRITATES THE HELL OUT OF YOU--
AND I GET A KICK OUT OF THAT.
07
THE STICKY, METALLIC AROMA OF BLOOD FILLED THE AIR.
IT GREW THICKER AS WE ENTERED THE SUITE BUT THERE WAS NOTHING GRUESOME BEHIND DOOR NUMBER ONE.
HARRY, LOOK AROUND OUT HERE.
KINKY.

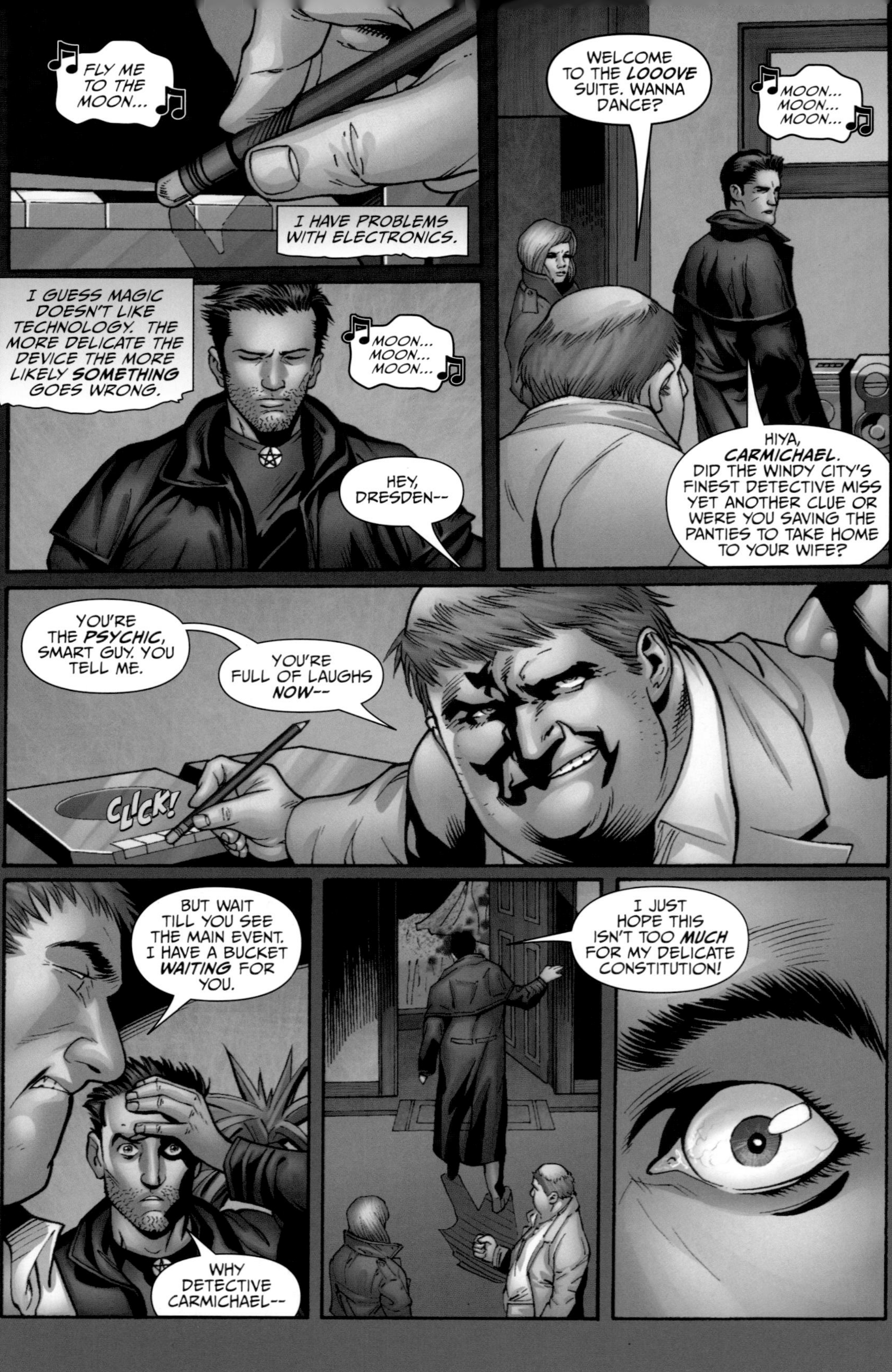

FLY ME TO THE MOON...
I HAVE PROBLEMS WITH ELECTRONICS.
WELCOME TO THE LOOOVE SUITE. WANNA DANCE?
MOON... MOON... MOON...
I GUESS MAGIC DOESN'T LIKE TECHNOLOGY. THE MORE DELICATE THE DEVICE THE MORE LIKELY SOMETHING GOES WRONG.
MOON... MOON... MOON...
HEY, DRESDEN--
HIYA, CARMICHAEL. DID THE WINDY CITY'S FINEST DETECTIVE MISS YET ANOTHER CLUE OR WERE YOU SAVING THE PANTIES TO TAKE HOME TO YOUR WIFE?
YOU'RE THE PSYCHIC, SMART GUY. YOU TELL ME.
YOU'RE FULL OF LAUGHS NOW--
CLICK!
BUT WAIT TILL YOU SEE THE MAIN EVENT. I HAVE A BUCKET WAITING FOR YOU.
WHY DETECTIVE CARMICHAEL--
I JUST HOPE THIS ISN'T TOO MUCH FOR MY DELICATE CONSTITUTION!

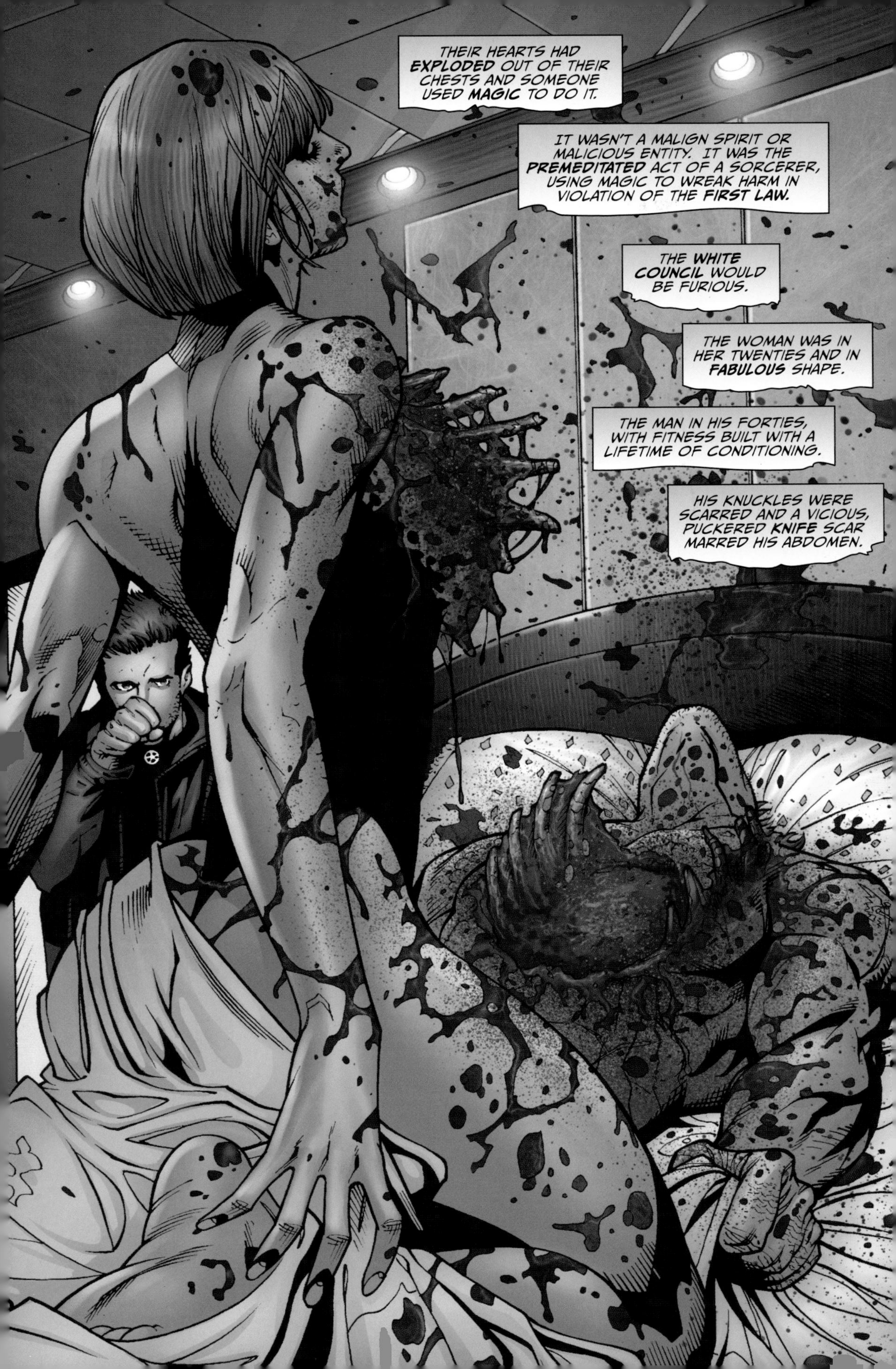
THEIR HEARTS HAD EXPLODED OUT OF THEIR CHESTS AND SOMEONE USED MAGIC TO DO IT.
IT WASN'T A MALIGN SPIRIT OR MALICIOUS ENTITY. IT WAS THE PREMEDITATED ACT OF A SORCERER, USING MAGIC TO WREAK HARM IN VIOLATION OF THE FIRST LAW.
THE WHITE COUNCIL WOULD BE FURIOUS.
THE WOMAN WAS IN HER TWENTIES AND IN FABULOUS SHAPE.
THE MAN IN HIS FORTIES, WITH FITNESS BUILT WITH A LIFETIME OF CONDITIONING.
HIS KNUCKLES WERE SCARRED AND A VICIOUS, PUCKERED KNIFE SCAR MARRED HIS ABDOMEN.

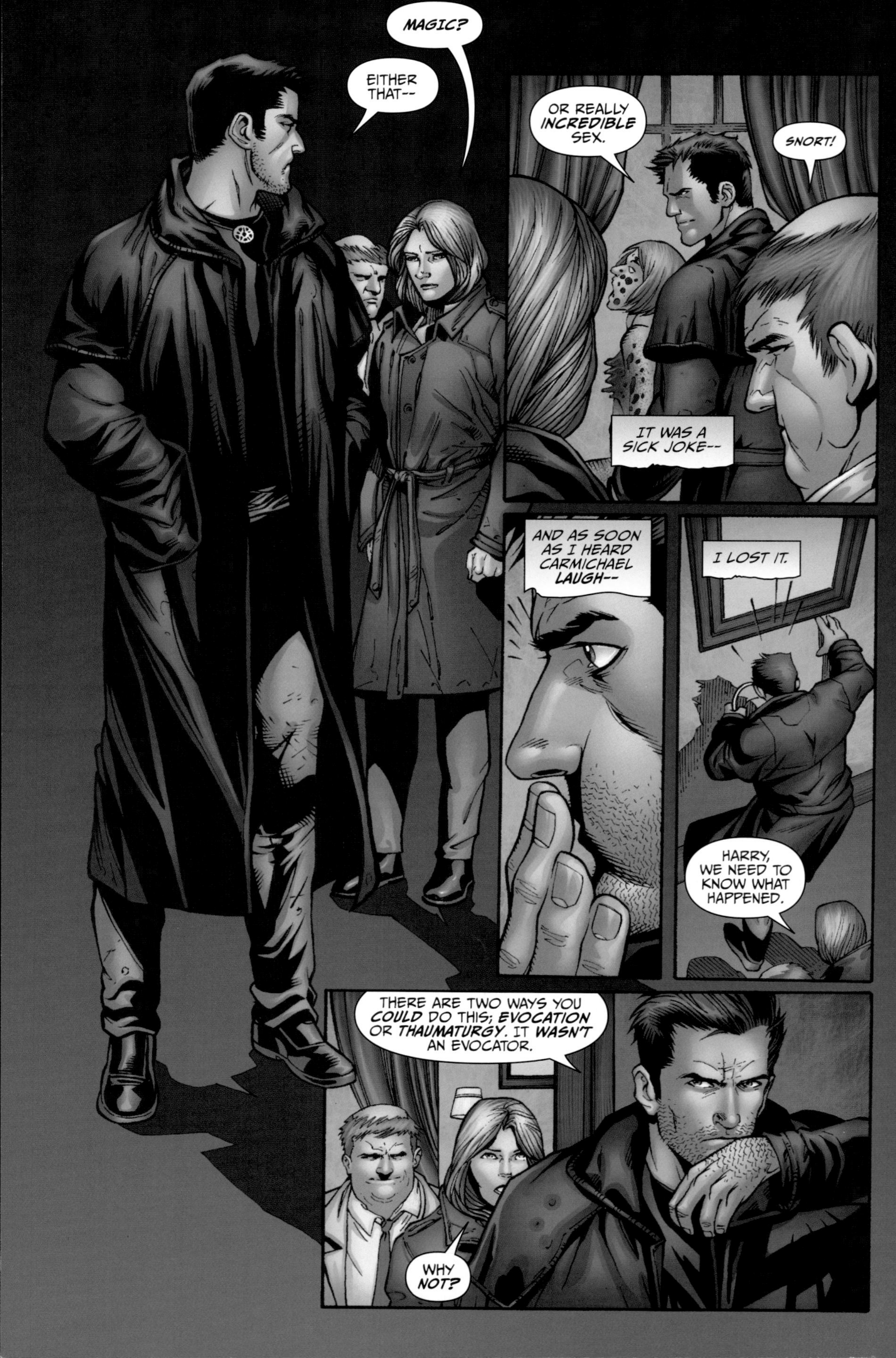
MAGIC?
EITHER THAT--
OR REALLY INCREDIBLE SEX.
SNORT!
IT WAS A SICK JOKE--
AND AS SOON AS I HEARD CARMICHAEL LAUGH--
I LOST IT.
HARRY, WE NEED TO KNOW WHAT HAPPENED.
THERE ARE TWO WAYS YOU COULD DO THIS; EVOCATION OR THAUMATURGY. IT WASN'T AN EVOCATOR.
WHY NOT?

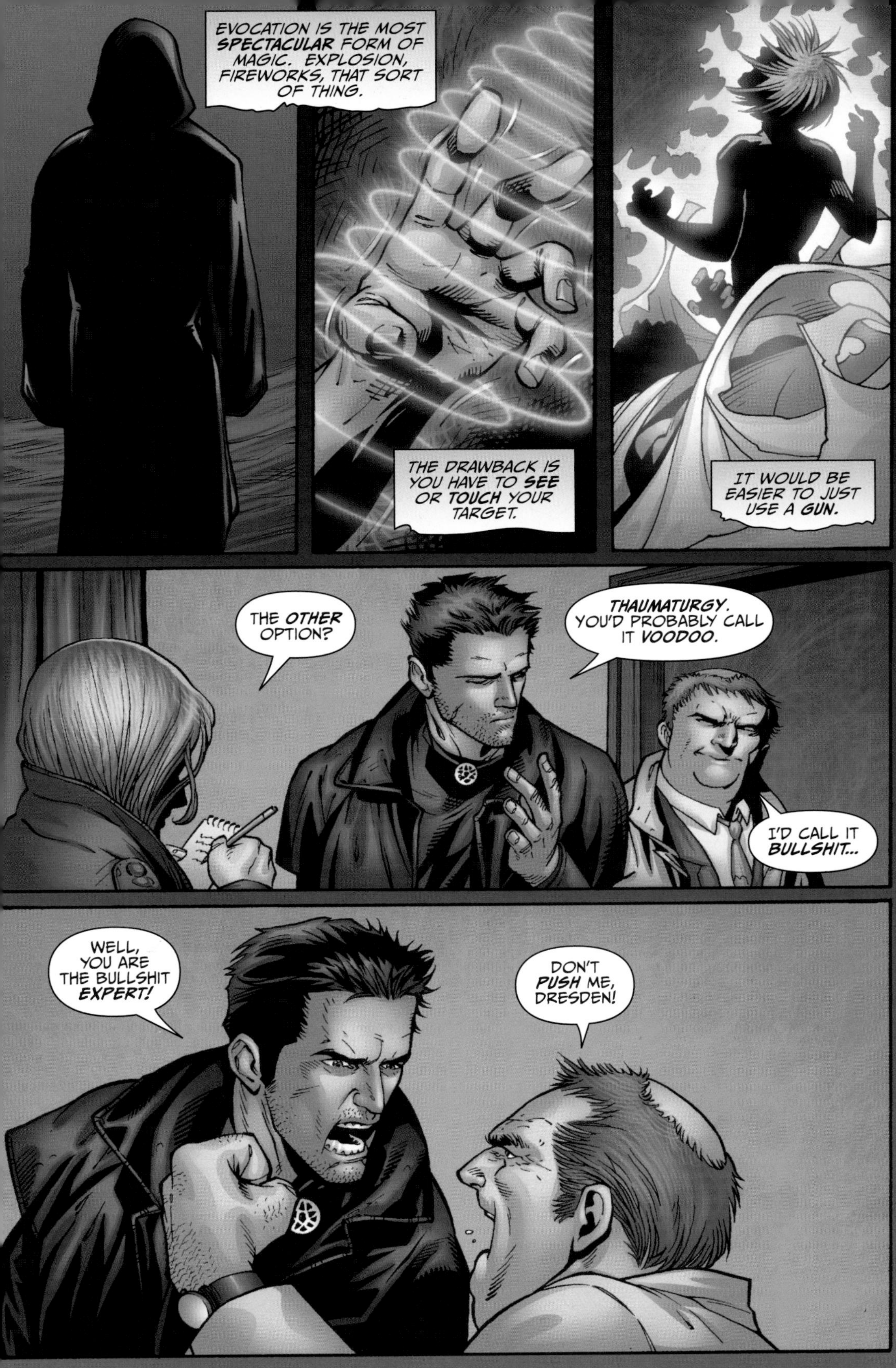
EVOCATION IS THE MOST SPECTACULAR FORM OF MAGIC. EXPLOSION, FIREWORKS, THAT SORT OF THING.
THE DRAWBACK IS YOU HAVE TO SEE OR TOUCH YOUR TARGET.
IT WOULD BE EASIER TO JUST USE A GUN.
THE OTHER OPTION?
THAUMATURGY. YOU'D PROBABLY CALL IT VOODOO.
I'D CALL IT BULLSHIT...
WELL, YOU ARE THE BULLSHIT EXPERT!
DON'T PUSH ME, DRESDEN!

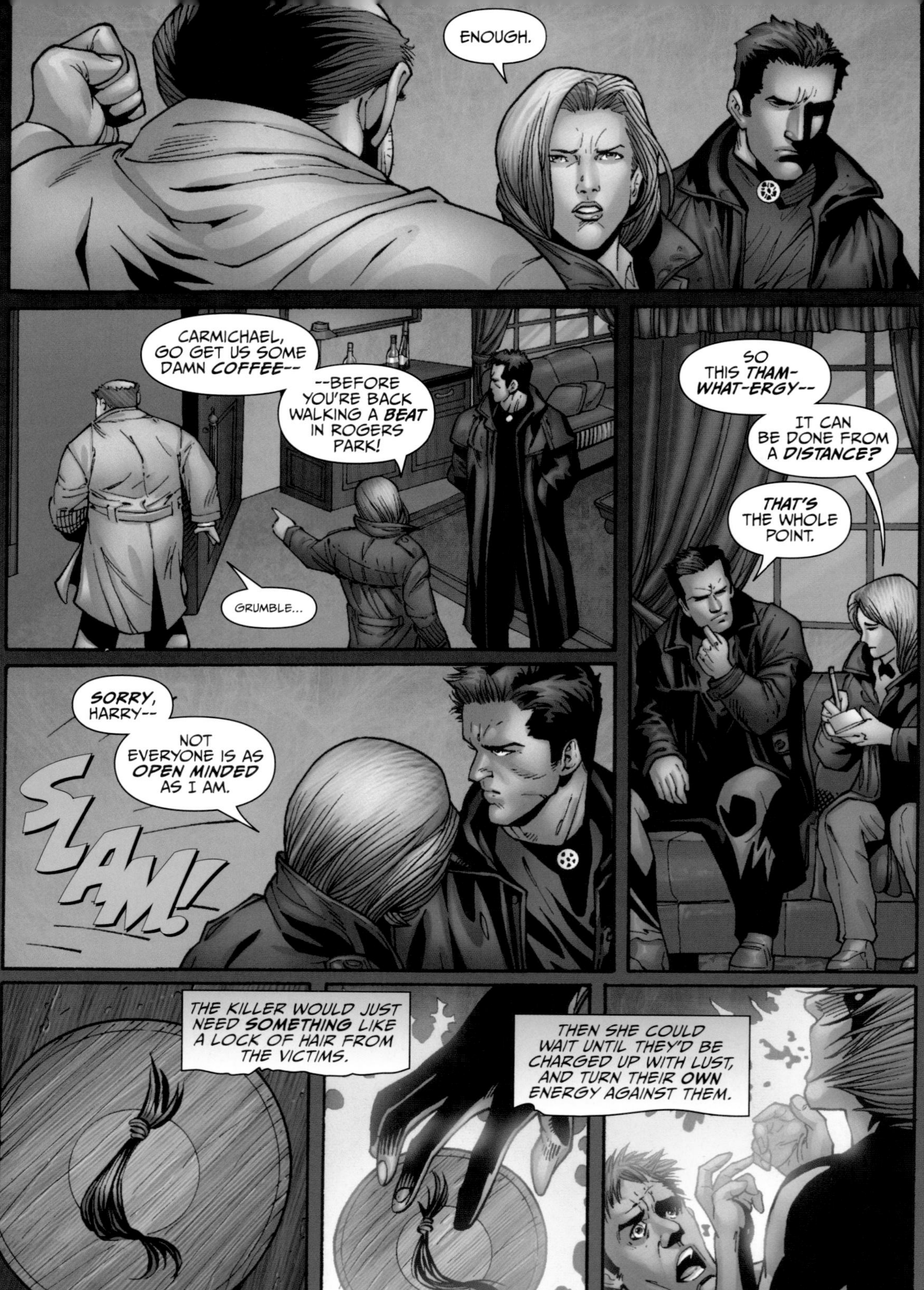
ENOUGH.
CARMICHAEL, GO GET US SOME DAMN COFFEE--
--BEFORE YOU'RE BACK WALKING A BEAT IN ROGERS PARK!
GRUMBLE...
SORRY, HARRY--
NOT EVERYONE IS AS OPEN MINDED AS I AM.
SLAM!
SO THIS THAM-WHAT-ERGY--
IT CAN BE DONE FROM A DISTANCE?
THAT'S THE WHOLE POINT.
THE KILLER WOULD JUST NEED SOMETHING LIKE A LOCK OF HAIR FROM THE VICTIMS.
THEN SHE COULD WAIT UNTIL THEY'D BE CHARGED UP WITH LUST, AND TURN THEIR OWN ENERGY AGAINST THEM.

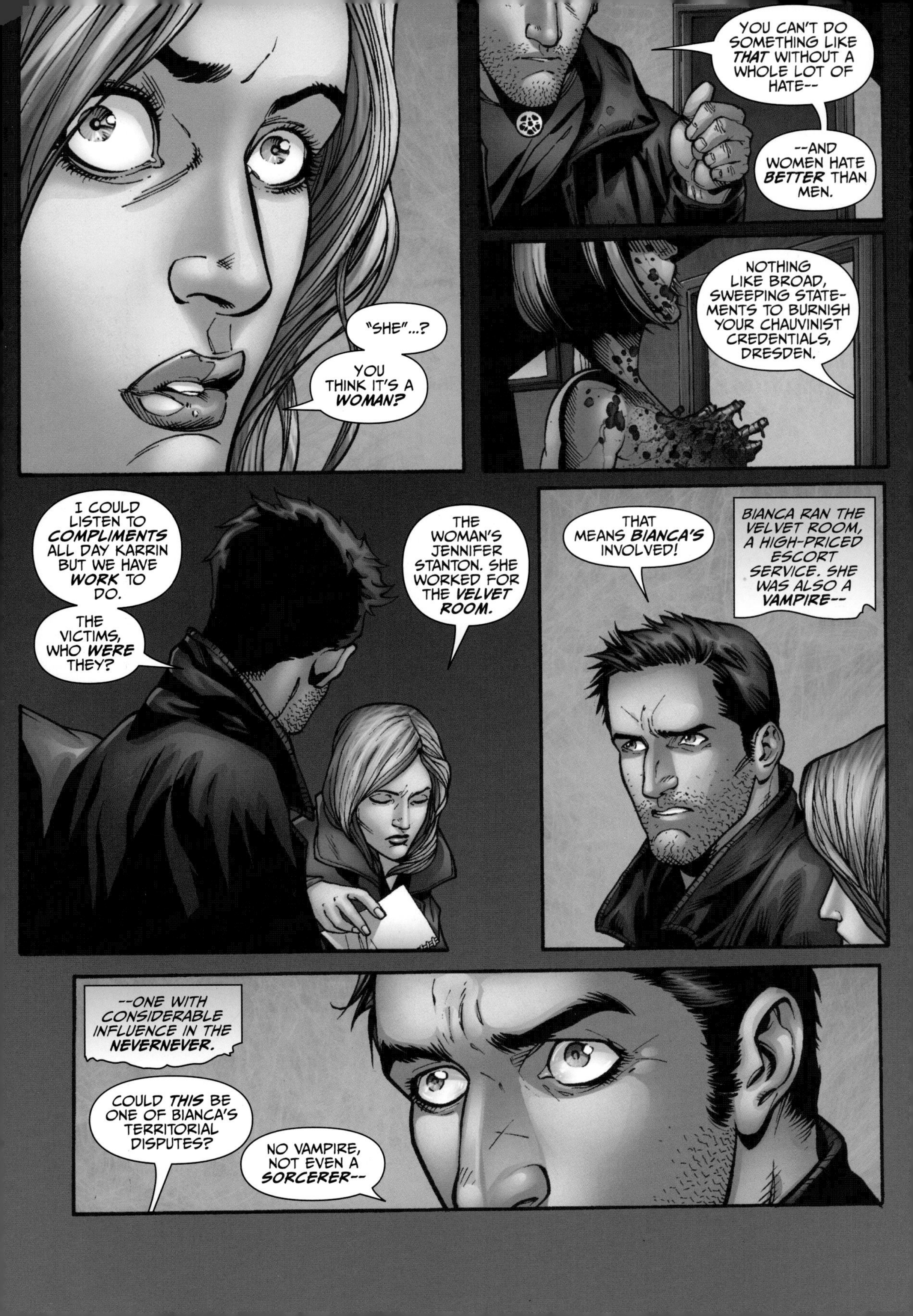
"SHE"...?
YOU THINK IT'S A WOMAN?
YOU CAN'T DO SOMETHING LIKE THAT WITHOUT A WHOLE LOT OF HATE--
--AND WOMEN HATE BETTER THAN MEN.
NOTHING LIKE BROAD, SWEEPING STATEMENTS TO BURNISH YOUR CHAUVINIST CREDENTIALS, DRESDEN.
I COULD LISTEN TO COMPLIMENTS ALL DAY KARRIN BUT WE HAVE WORK TO DO.
THE VICTIMS, WHO WERE THEY?
THE WOMAN'S JENNIFER STANTON. SHE WORKED FOR THE VELVET ROOM.
THAT MEANS BIANCA'S INVOLVED!
BIANCA RAN THE VELVET ROOM, A HIGH-PRICED ESCORT SERVICE. SHE WAS ALSO A VAMPIRE--
--ONE WITH CONSIDERABLE INFLUENCE IN THE NEVERNEVER.
COULD THIS BE ONE OF BIANCA'S TERRITORIAL DISPUTES?
NO VAMPIRE, NOT EVEN A SORCERER--

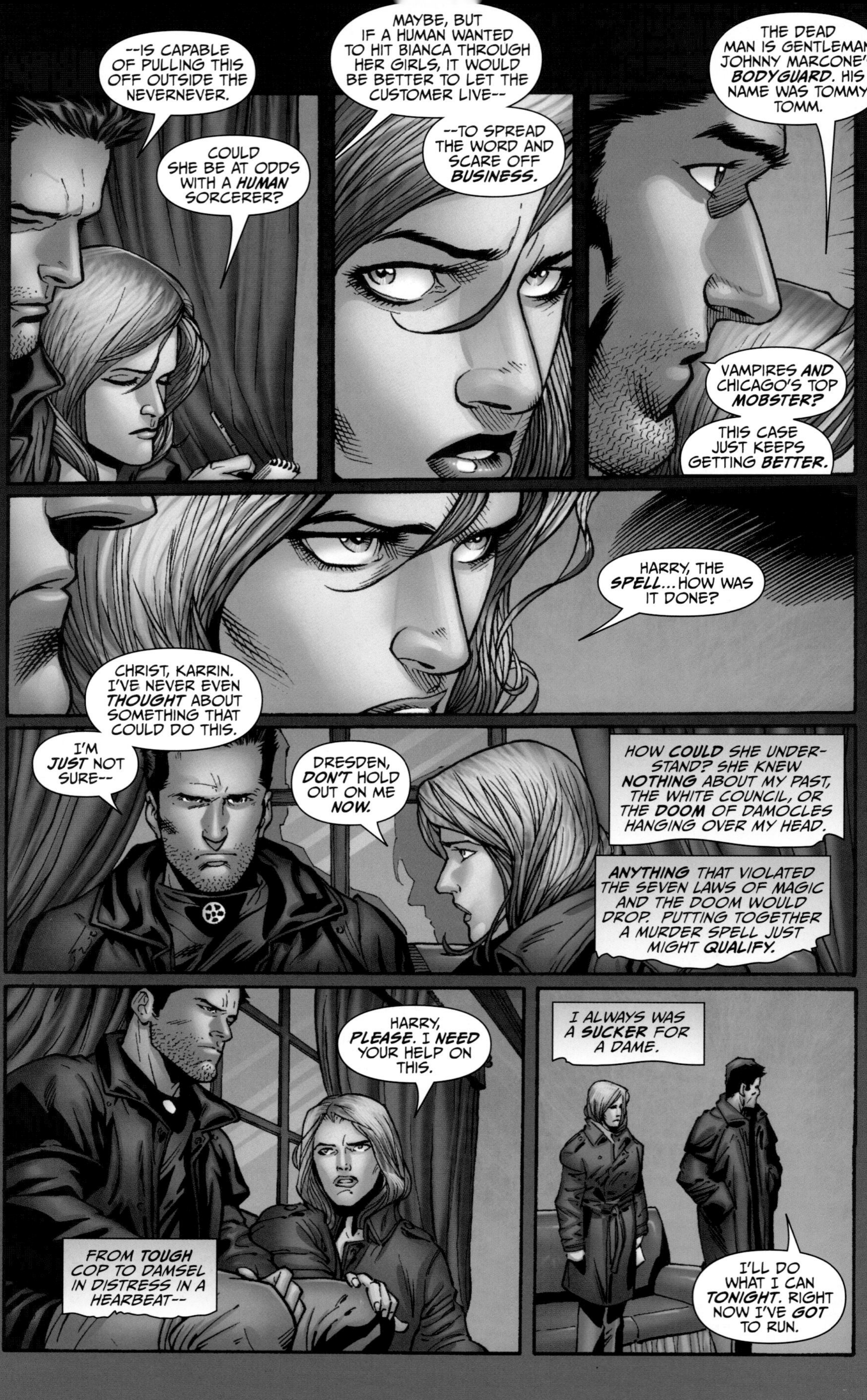
--IS CAPABLE OF PULLING THIS OFF OUTSIDE THE NEVERNEVER.
COULD SHE BE AT ODDS WITH A *HUMAN* SORCERER?
MAYBE, BUT IF A HUMAN WANTED TO HIT BIANCA THROUGH HER GIRLS, IT WOULD BE BETTER TO LET THE CUSTOMER LIVE--
--TO SPREAD THE WORD AND SCARE OFF *BUSINESS.*
THE DEAD MAN IS GENTLEMAN JOHNNY MARCONE'S *BODYGUARD*. HIS NAME WAS TOMMY TOMM.
VAMPIRES *AND* CHICAGO'S TOP *MOBSTER?*
THIS CASE JUST KEEPS GETTING *BETTER.*
HARRY, THE *SPELL*...HOW WAS IT DONE?
CHRIST, KARRIN. I'VE NEVER EVEN *THOUGHT* ABOUT SOMETHING THAT COULD DO THIS.
I'M *JUST* NOT SURE--
DRESDEN, *DON'T* HOLD OUT ON ME *NOW.*
HOW ***COULD*** *SHE UNDER-STAND? SHE KNEW* ***NOTHING*** *ABOUT MY PAST, THE WHITE COUNCIL, OR THE* ***DOOM*** *OF DAMOCLES HANGING OVER MY HEAD.*
ANYTHING *THAT VIOLATED THE SEVEN LAWS OF MAGIC AND THE DOOM WOULD DROP. PUTTING TOGETHER A MURDER SPELL JUST MIGHT* ***QUALIFY.***
HARRY, *PLEASE*. I *NEED* YOUR HELP ON THIS.
FROM ***TOUGH*** *COP TO DAMSEL IN DISTRESS IN A HEARBEAT--*
I ALWAYS WAS A ***SUCKER*** *FOR A DAME.*
I'LL DO WHAT I CAN *TONIGHT*. RIGHT NOW I'VE *GOT* TO RUN.

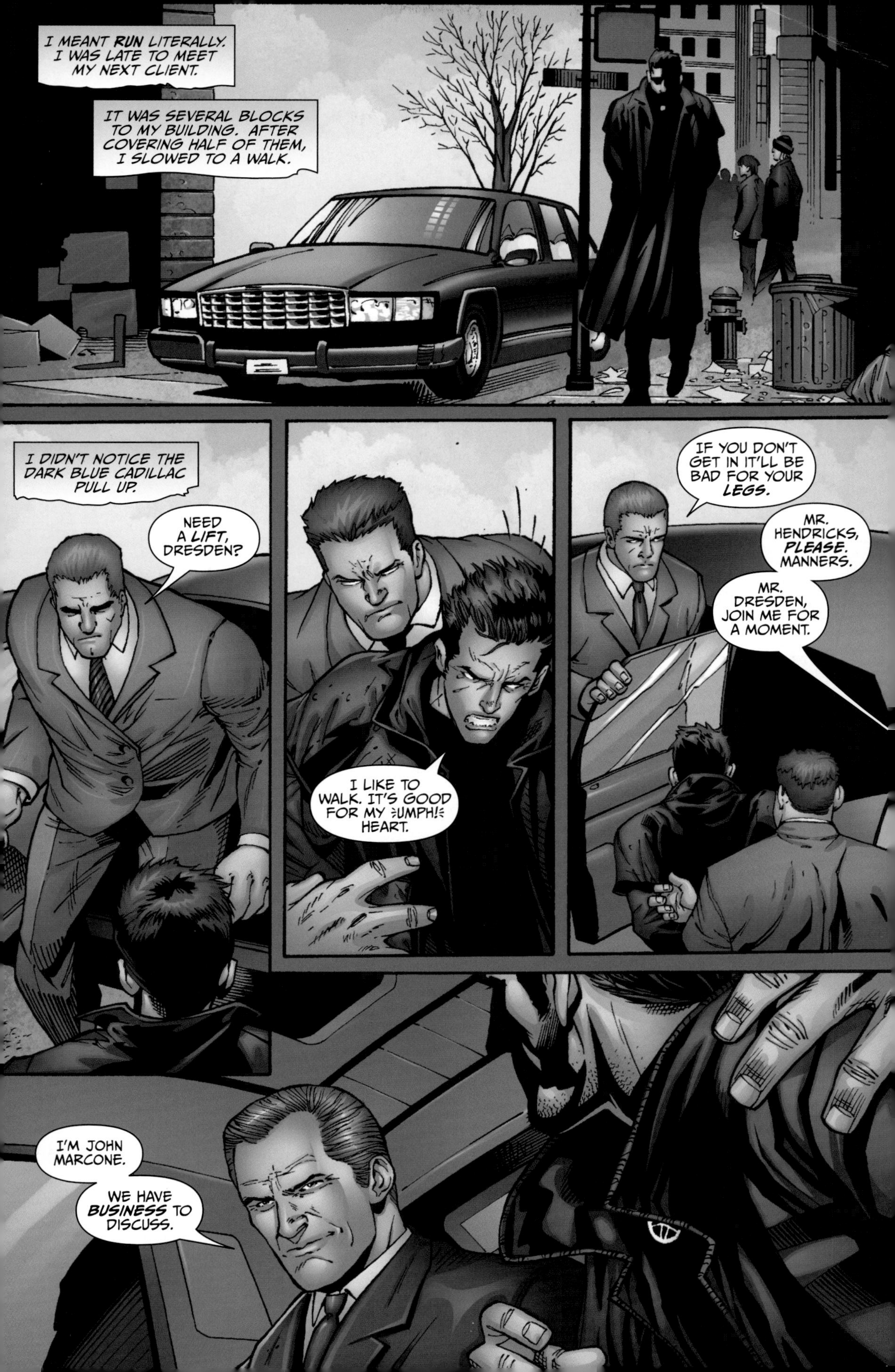
I MEANT RUN LITERALLY. I WAS LATE TO MEET MY NEXT CLIENT.
IT WAS SEVERAL BLOCKS TO MY BUILDING. AFTER COVERING HALF OF THEM, I SLOWED TO A WALK.
I DIDN'T NOTICE THE DARK BLUE CADILLAC PULL UP.
NEED A LIFT, DRESDEN?
I LIKE TO WALK. IT'S GOOD FOR MY UMPH! HEART.
IF YOU DON'T GET IN IT'LL BE BAD FOR YOUR LEGS.
MR. HENDRICKS, PLEASE. MANNERS.
MR. DRESDEN, JOIN ME FOR A MOMENT.
I'M JOHN MARCONE.
WE HAVE BUSINESS TO DISCUSS.

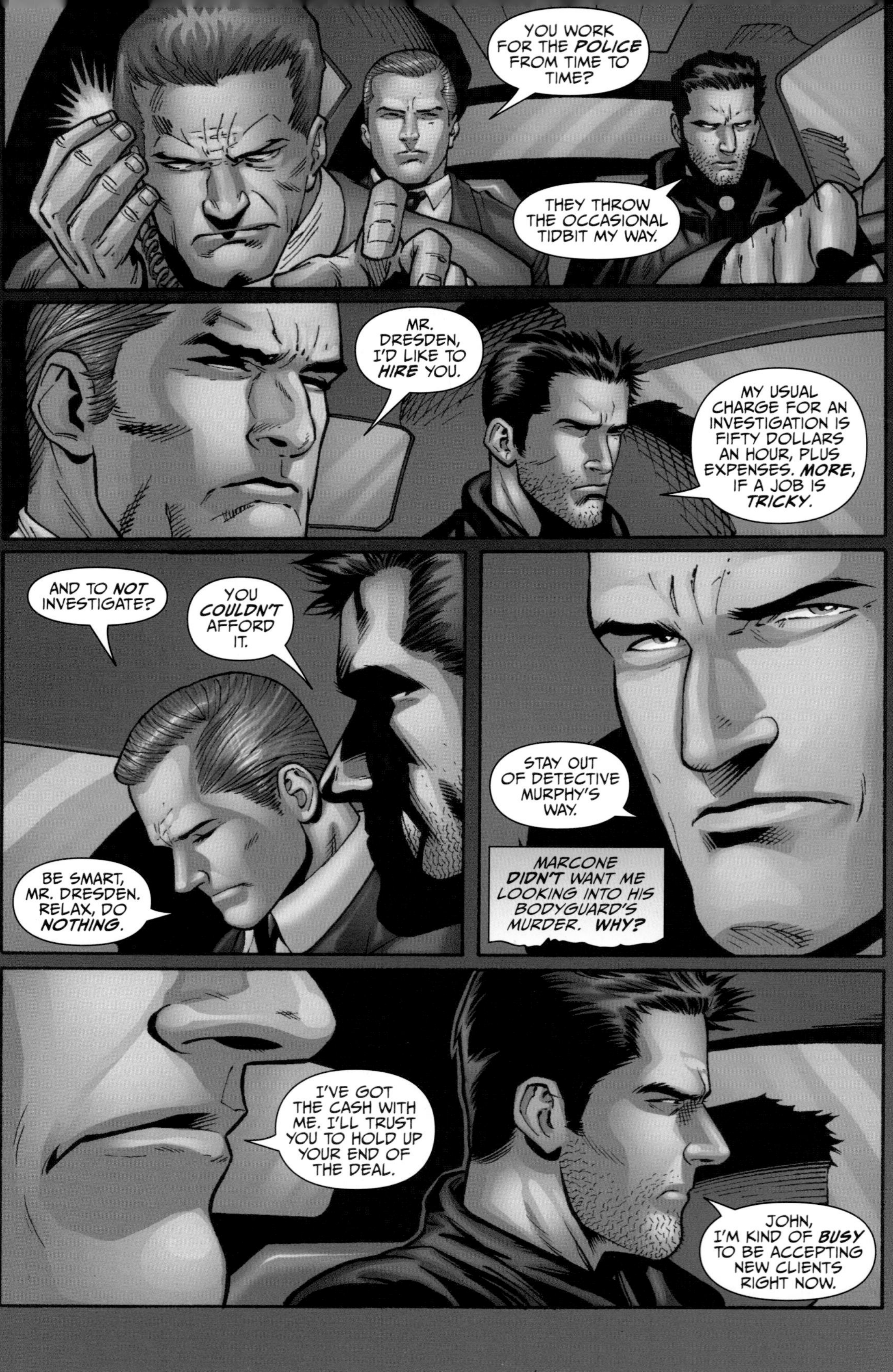
YOU WORK FOR THE *POLICE* FROM TIME TO TIME?
THEY THROW THE OCCASIONAL TIDBIT MY WAY.
MR. DRESDEN, I'D LIKE TO *HIRE* YOU.
MY USUAL CHARGE FOR AN INVESTIGATION IS FIFTY DOLLARS AN HOUR, PLUS EXPENSES. *MORE,* IF A JOB IS *TRICKY.*
AND TO *NOT* INVESTIGATE?
YOU *COULDN'T* AFFORD IT.
BE SMART, MR. DRESDEN. RELAX, DO *NOTHING.*
STAY OUT OF DETECTIVE MURPHY'S WAY.
MARCONE ***DIDN'T*** *WANT ME LOOKING INTO HIS BODYGUARD'S MURDER.* ***WHY?***
I'VE GOT THE CASH WITH ME. I'LL TRUST YOU TO HOLD UP YOUR END OF THE DEAL.
JOHN, I'M KIND OF *BUSY* TO BE ACCEPTING NEW CLIENTS RIGHT NOW.

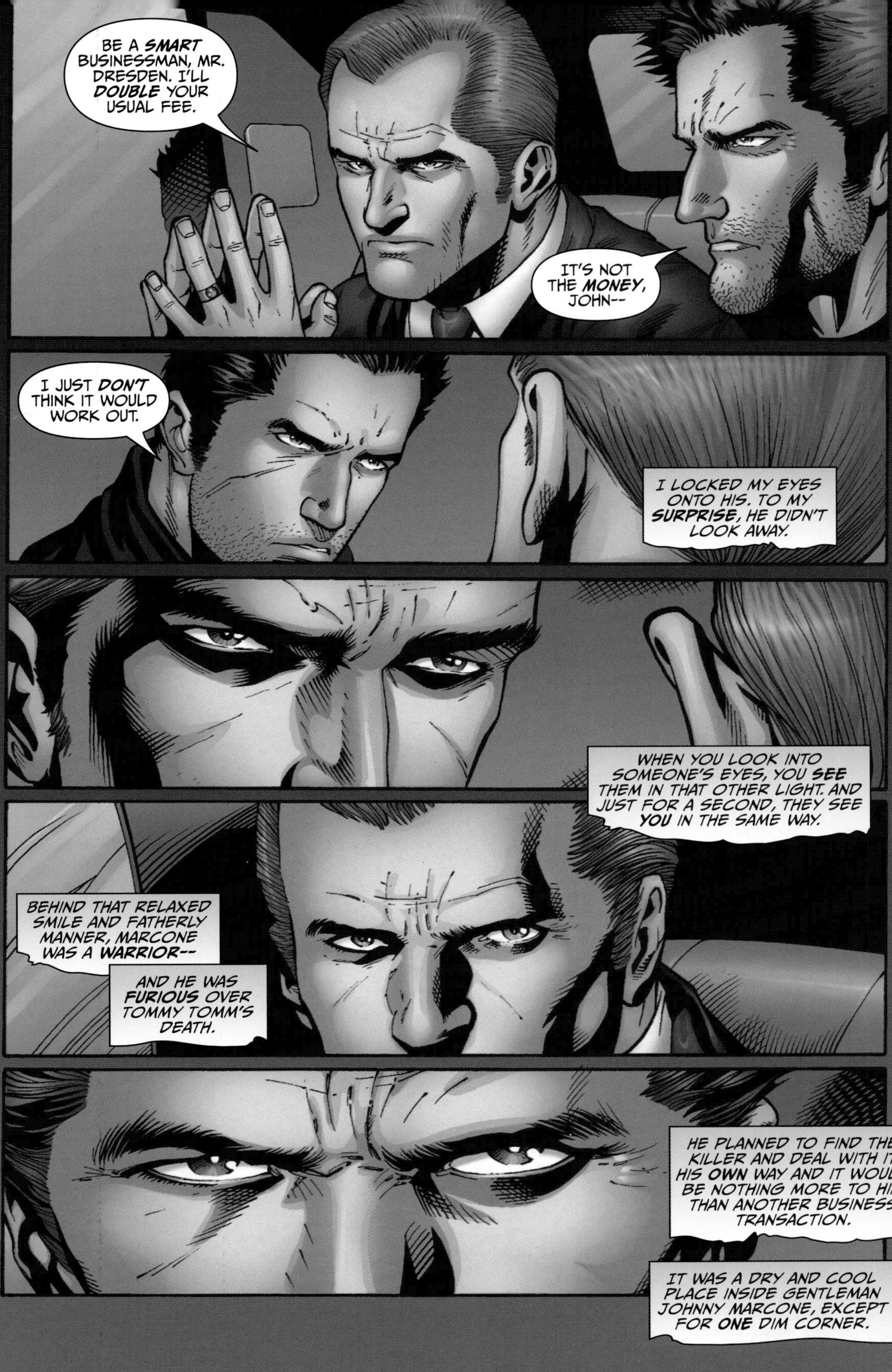
BE A SMART BUSINESSMAN, MR. DRESDEN. I'LL DOUBLE YOUR USUAL FEE.
IT'S NOT THE MONEY, JOHN--
I JUST DON'T THINK IT WOULD WORK OUT.
I LOCKED MY EYES ONTO HIS. TO MY SURPRISE, HE DIDN'T LOOK AWAY.
WHEN YOU LOOK INTO SOMEONE'S EYES, YOU SEE THEM IN THAT OTHER LIGHT. AND JUST FOR A SECOND, THEY SEE YOU IN THE SAME WAY.
BEHIND THAT RELAXED SMILE AND FATHERLY MANNER, MARCONE WAS A WARRIOR--
AND HE WAS FURIOUS OVER TOMMY TOMM'S DEATH.
HE PLANNED TO FIND THE KILLER AND DEAL WITH IT HIS OWN WAY AND IT WOULD BE NOTHING MORE TO HIM THAN ANOTHER BUSINESS TRANSACTION.
IT WAS A DRY AND COOL PLACE INSIDE GENTLEMAN JOHNNY MARCONE, EXCEPT FOR ONE DIM CORNER.

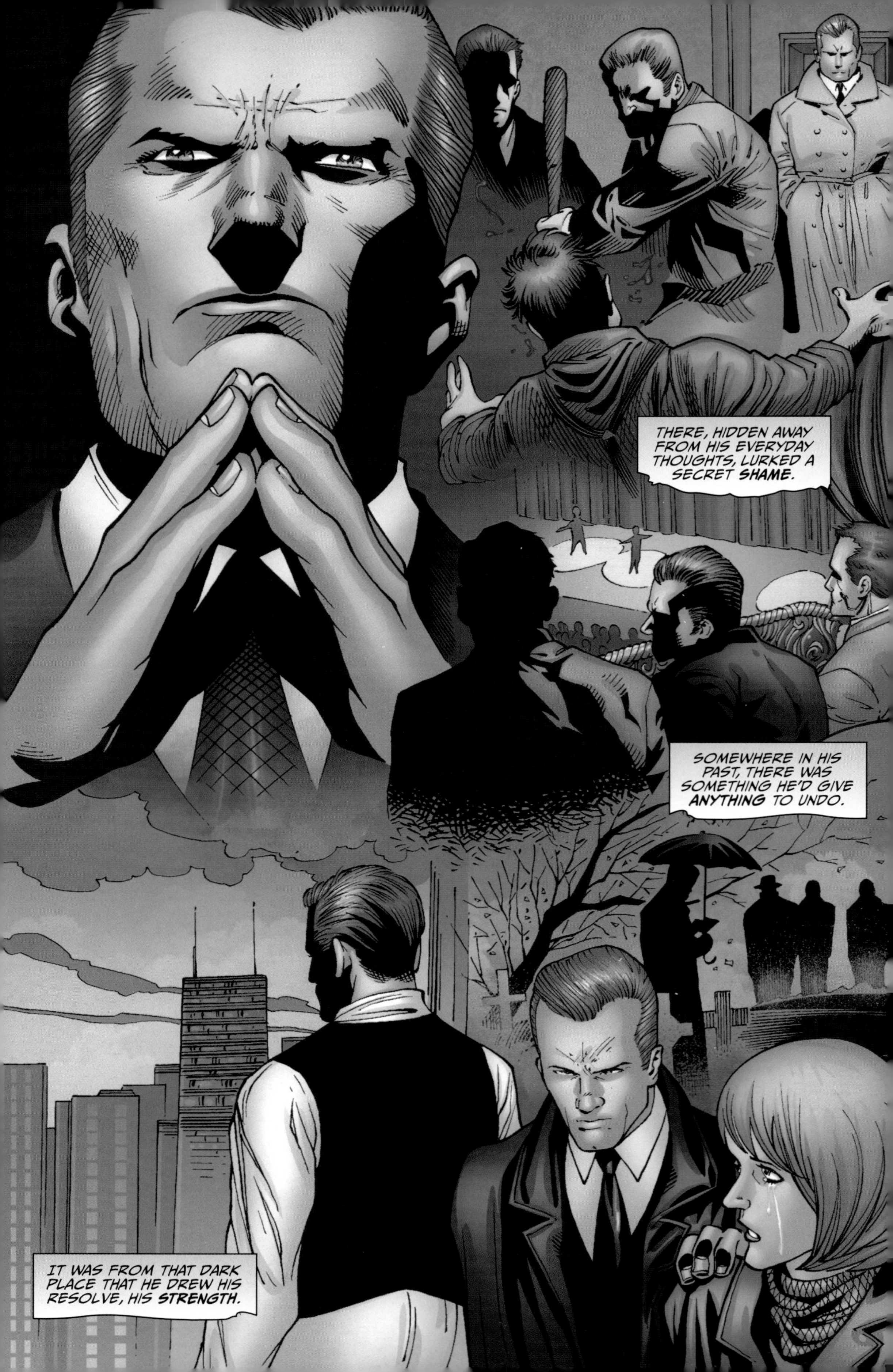
THERE, HIDDEN AWAY FROM HIS EVERYDAY THOUGHTS, LURKED A SECRET SHAME.
SOMEWHERE IN HIS PAST, THERE WAS SOMETHING HE'D GIVE ANYTHING TO UNDO.
IT WAS FROM THAT DARK PLACE THAT HE DREW HIS RESOLVE, HIS STRENGTH.

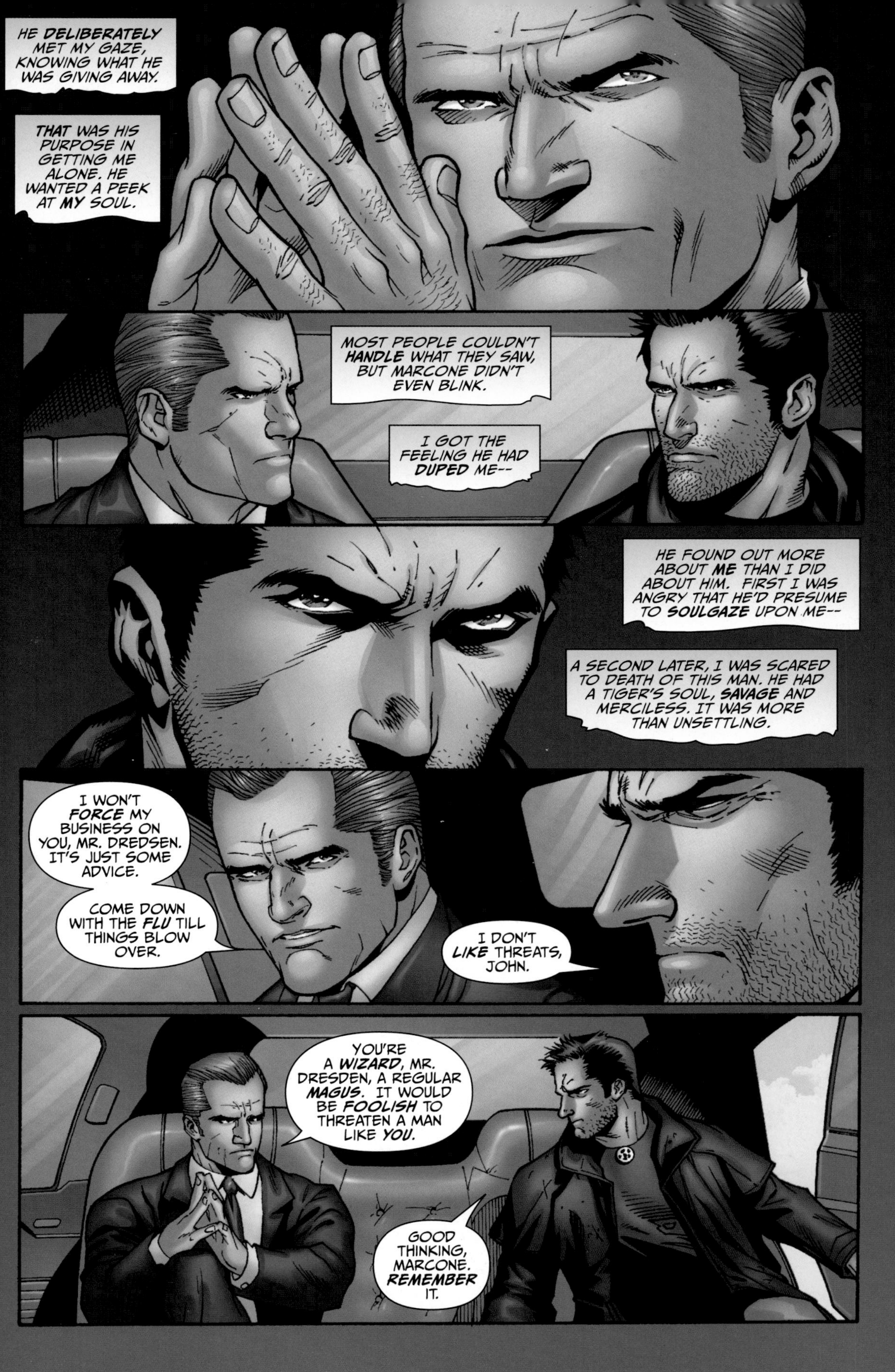
HE DELIBERATELY MET MY GAZE, KNOWING WHAT HE WAS GIVING AWAY.
THAT WAS HIS PURPOSE IN GETTING ME ALONE. HE WANTED A PEEK AT MY SOUL.
MOST PEOPLE COULDN'T HANDLE WHAT THEY SAW, BUT MARCONE DIDN'T EVEN BLINK.
I GOT THE FEELING HE HAD DUPED ME--
HE FOUND OUT MORE ABOUT ME THAN I DID ABOUT HIM. FIRST I WAS ANGRY THAT HE'D PRESUME TO SOULGAZE UPON ME--
A SECOND LATER, I WAS SCARED TO DEATH OF THIS MAN. HE HAD A TIGER'S SOUL, SAVAGE AND MERCILESS. IT WAS MORE THAN UNSETTLING.
I WON'T FORCE MY BUSINESS ON YOU, MR. DREDSEN. IT'S JUST SOME ADVICE.
COME DOWN WITH THE FLU TILL THINGS BLOW OVER.
I DON'T LIKE THREATS, JOHN.
YOU'RE A WIZARD, MR. DRESDEN, A REGULAR MAGUS. IT WOULD BE FOOLISH TO THREATEN A MAN LIKE YOU.
GOOD THINKING, MARCONE. REMEMBER IT.

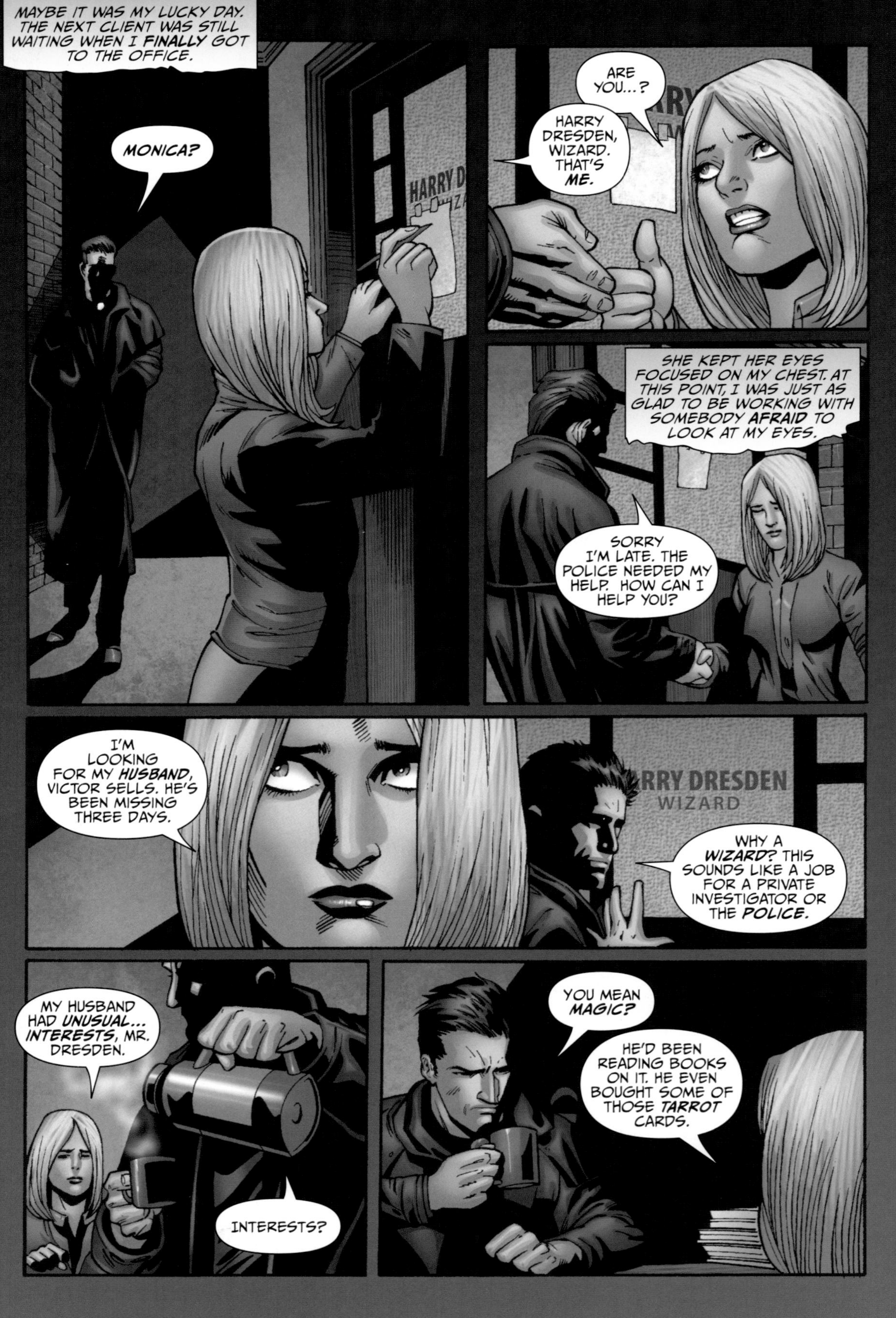
MAYBE IT WAS MY LUCKY DAY. THE NEXT CLIENT WAS STILL WAITING WHEN I FINALLY GOT TO THE OFFICE.
MONICA?
HARRY D
WIZA
ARE YOU...?
HARRY DRESDEN, WIZARD. THAT'S ME.
SHE KEPT HER EYES FOCUSED ON MY CHEST. AT THIS POINT, I WAS JUST AS GLAD TO BE WORKING WITH SOMEBODY AFRAID TO LOOK AT MY EYES.
SORRY I'M LATE. THE POLICE NEEDED MY HELP. HOW CAN I HELP YOU?
I'M LOOKING FOR MY HUSBAND, VICTOR SELLS. HE'S BEEN MISSING THREE DAYS.
RRY DRESDEN
WIZARD
WHY A WIZARD? THIS SOUNDS LIKE A JOB FOR A PRIVATE INVESTIGATOR OR THE POLICE.
MY HUSBAND HAD UNUSUAL... INTERESTS, MR. DRESDEN.
INTERESTS?
YOU MEAN MAGIC?
HE'D BEEN READING BOOKS ON IT. HE EVEN BOUGHT SOME OF THOSE TARROT CARDS.

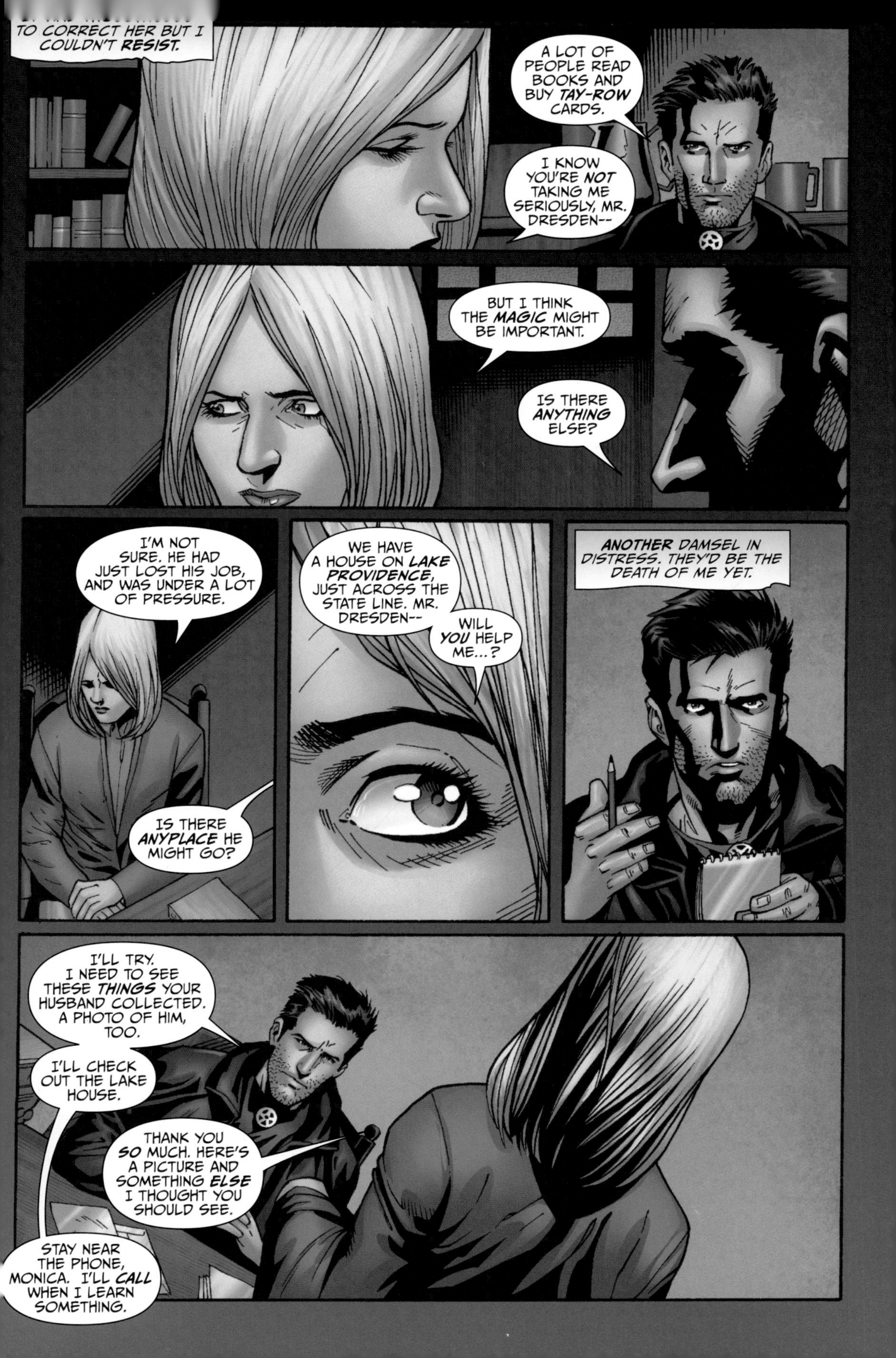
TO CORRECT HER BUT I COULDN'T RESIST.
A LOT OF PEOPLE READ BOOKS AND BUY TAY-ROW CARDS.
I KNOW YOU'RE NOT TAKING ME SERIOUSLY, MR. DRESDEN--
BUT I THINK THE MAGIC MIGHT BE IMPORTANT.
IS THERE ANYTHING ELSE?
I'M NOT SURE. HE HAD JUST LOST HIS JOB, AND WAS UNDER A LOT OF PRESSURE.
IS THERE ANYPLACE HE MIGHT GO?
WE HAVE A HOUSE ON LAKE PROVIDENCE, JUST ACROSS THE STATE LINE. MR. DRESDEN--
WILL YOU HELP ME...?
ANOTHER DAMSEL IN DISTRESS. THEY'D BE THE DEATH OF ME YET.
I'LL TRY. I NEED TO SEE THESE THINGS YOUR HUSBAND COLLECTED. A PHOTO OF HIM, TOO.
I'LL CHECK OUT THE LAKE HOUSE.
THANK YOU SO MUCH. HERE'S A PICTURE AND SOMETHING ELSE I THOUGHT YOU SHOULD SEE.
STAY NEAR THE PHONE, MONICA. I'LL CALL WHEN I LEARN SOMETHING.

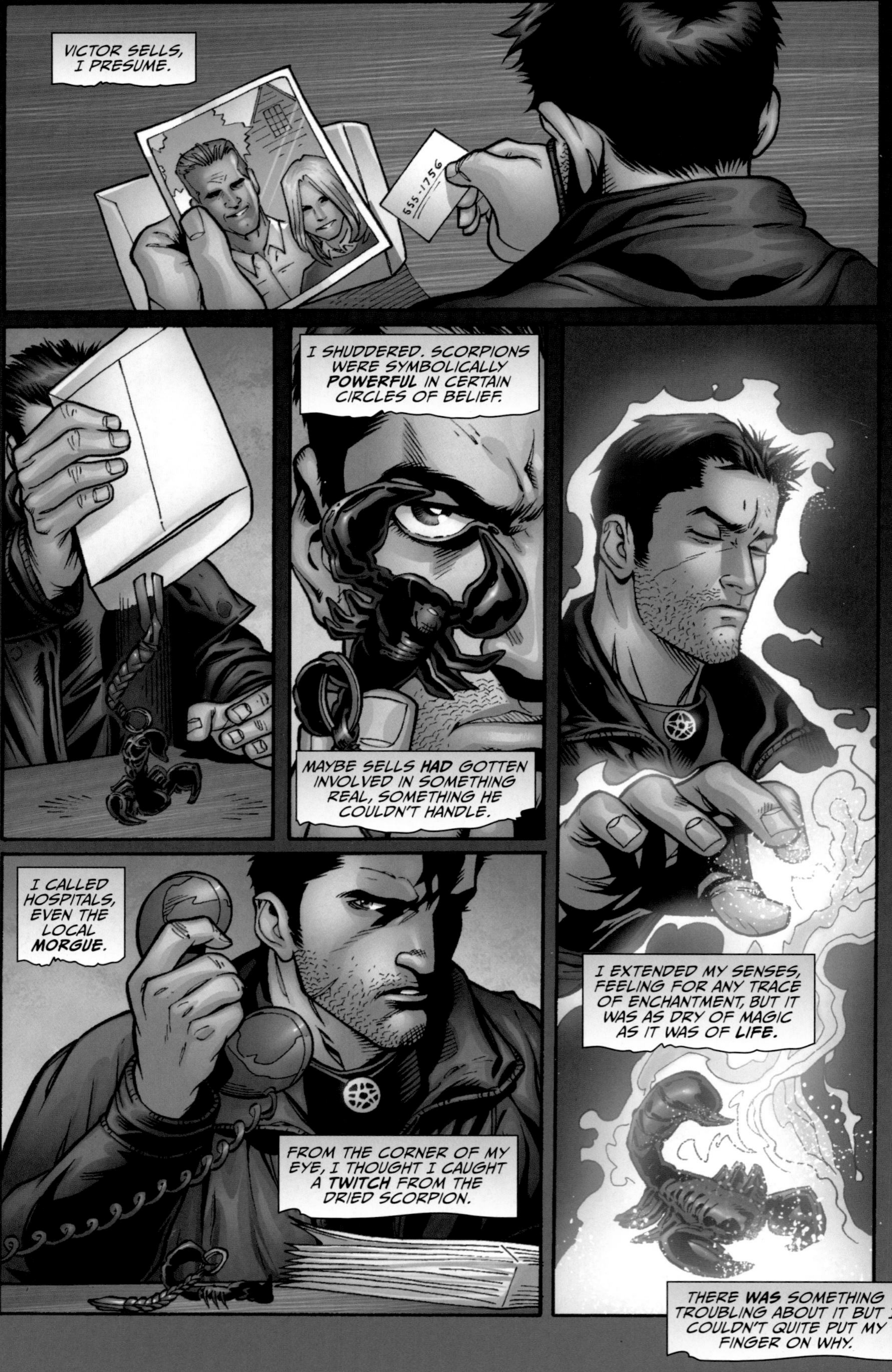
VICTOR SELLS, I PRESUME.
555-1756
I SHUDDERED. SCORPIONS WERE SYMBOLICALLY POWERFUL IN CERTAIN CIRCLES OF BELIEF.
MAYBE SELLS HAD GOTTEN INVOLVED IN SOMETHING REAL, SOMETHING HE COULDN'T HANDLE.
I EXTENDED MY SENSES, FEELING FOR ANY TRACE OF ENCHANTMENT, BUT IT WAS AS DRY OF MAGIC AS IT WAS OF LIFE.
I CALLED HOSPITALS, EVEN THE LOCAL MORGUE.
FROM THE CORNER OF MY EYE, I THOUGHT I CAUGHT A TWITCH FROM THE DRIED SCORPION.
THERE WAS SOMETHING TROUBLING ABOUT IT BUT I COULDN'T QUITE PUT MY FINGER ON WHY.

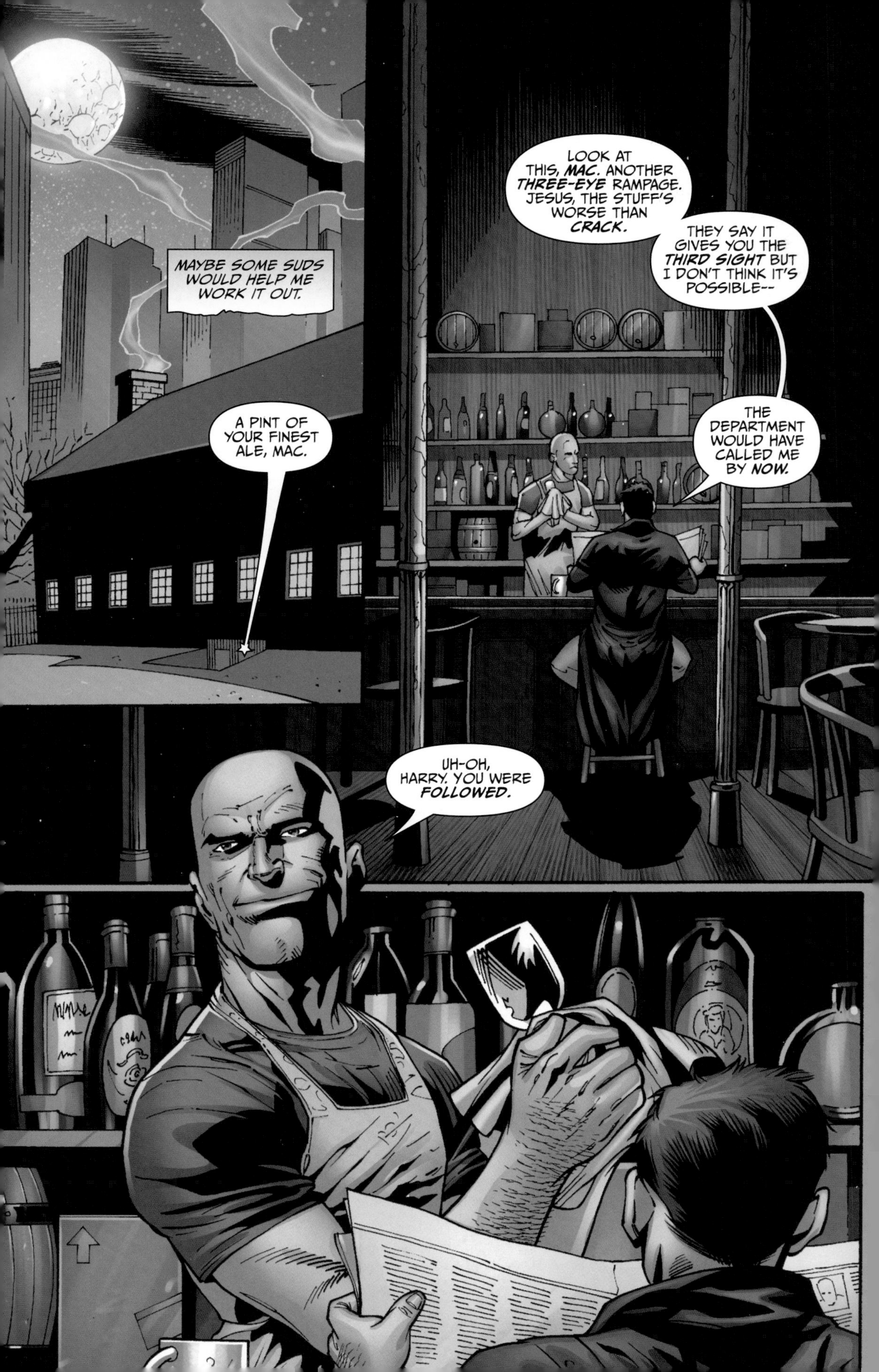
MAYBE SOME SUDS WOULD HELP ME WORK IT OUT.
A PINT OF YOUR FINEST ALE, MAC.
LOOK AT THIS, MAC. ANOTHER THREE-EYE RAMPAGE. JESUS, THE STUFF'S WORSE THAN CRACK.
THEY SAY IT GIVES YOU THE THIRD SIGHT BUT I DON'T THINK IT'S POSSIBLE--
THE DEPARTMENT WOULD HAVE CALLED ME BY NOW.
UH-OH, HARRY. YOU WERE FOLLOWED.

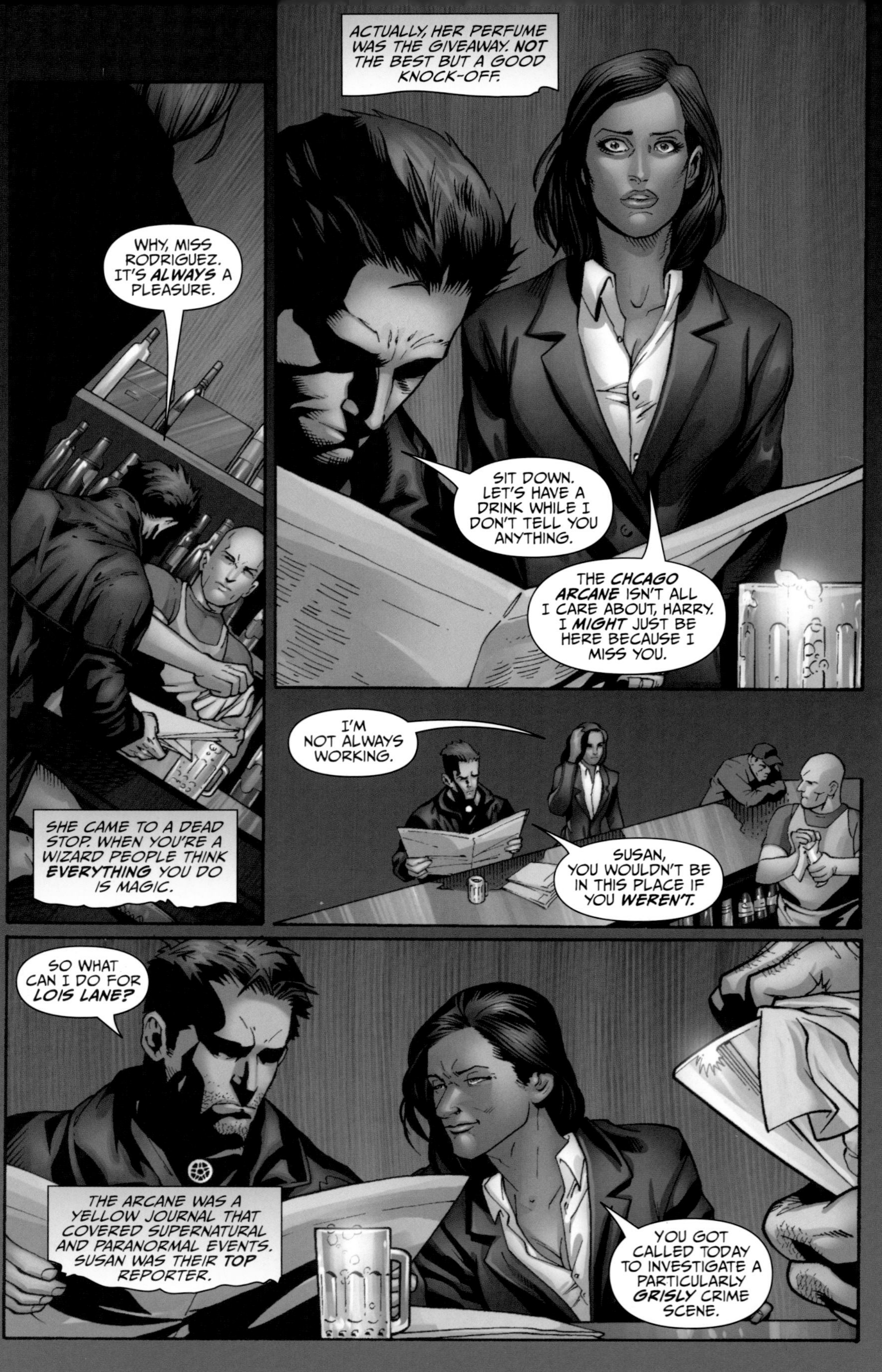
ACTUALLY, HER PERFUME WAS THE GIVEAWAY. NOT THE BEST BUT A GOOD KNOCK-OFF.
WHY, MISS RODRIGUEZ. IT'S ALWAYS A PLEASURE.
SIT DOWN. LET'S HAVE A DRINK WHILE I DON'T TELL YOU ANYTHING.
THE CHCAGO ARCANE ISN'T ALL I CARE ABOUT, HARRY. I MIGHT JUST BE HERE BECAUSE I MISS YOU.
SHE CAME TO A DEAD STOP. WHEN YOU'RE A WIZARD PEOPLE THINK EVERYTHING YOU DO IS MAGIC.
I'M NOT ALWAYS WORKING.
SUSAN, YOU WOULDN'T BE IN THIS PLACE IF YOU WEREN'T.
SO WHAT CAN I DO FOR LOIS LANE?
THE ARCANE WAS A YELLOW JOURNAL THAT COVERED SUPERNATURAL AND PARANORMAL EVENTS. SUSAN WAS THEIR TOP REPORTER.
YOU GOT CALLED TODAY TO INVESTIGATE A PARTICULARLY GRISLY CRIME SCENE.

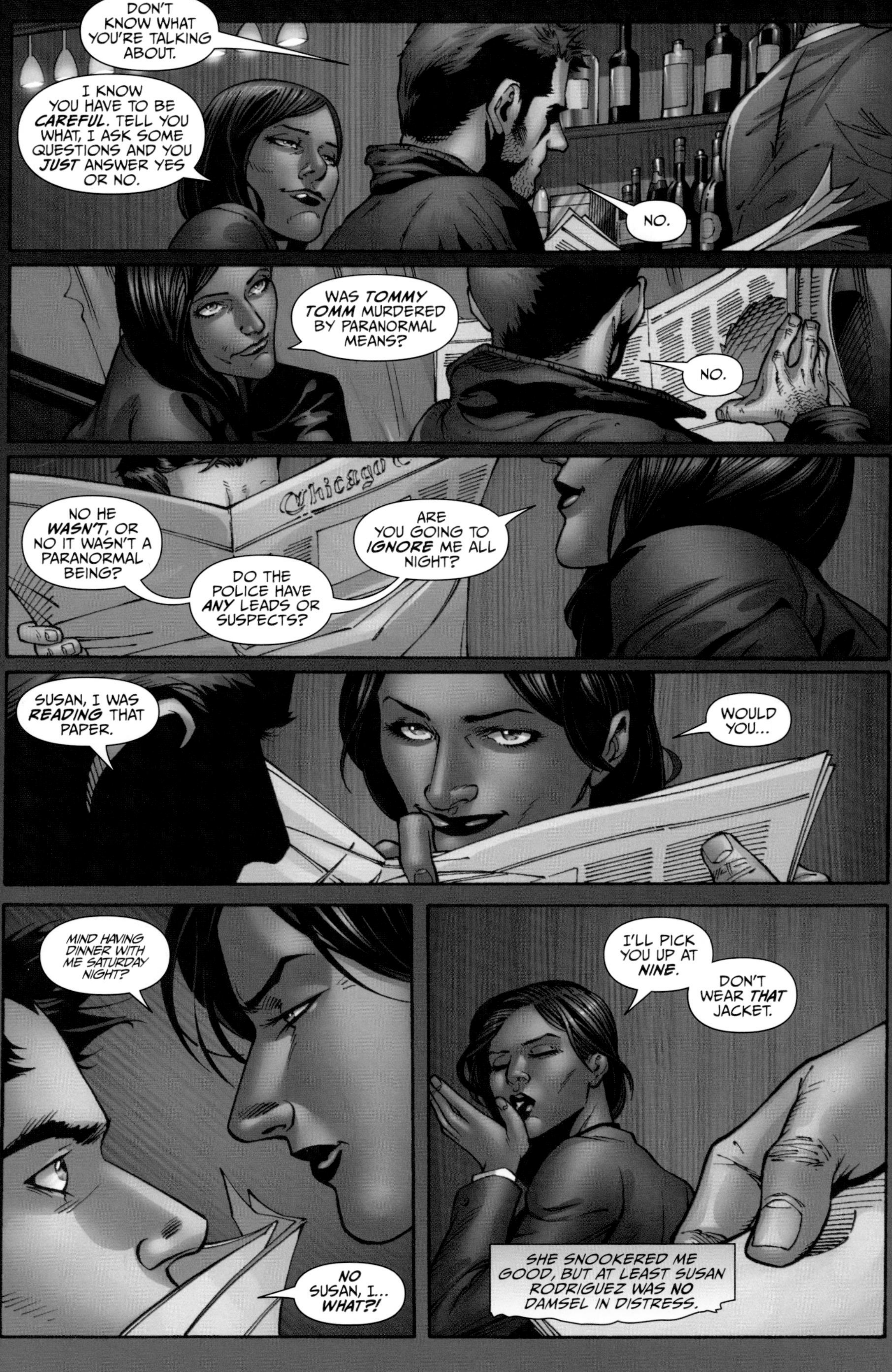
DON'T KNOW WHAT YOU'RE TALKING ABOUT.
I KNOW YOU HAVE TO BE CAREFUL. TELL YOU WHAT, I ASK SOME QUESTIONS AND YOU JUST ANSWER YES OR NO.
NO.
WAS TOMMY TOMM MURDERED BY PARANORMAL MEANS?
NO.
NO HE WASN'T, OR NO IT WASN'T A PARANORMAL BEING?
DO THE POLICE HAVE ANY LEADS OR SUSPECTS?
ARE YOU GOING TO IGNORE ME ALL NIGHT?
SUSAN, I WAS READING THAT PAPER.
WOULD YOU...
MIND HAVING DINNER WITH ME SATURDAY NIGHT?
NO SUSAN, I... WHAT?!
I'LL PICK YOU UP AT NINE.
DON'T WEAR THAT JACKET.
SHE SNOOKERED ME GOOD, BUT AT LEAST SUSAN RODRIGUEZ WAS NO DAMSEL IN DISTRESS.

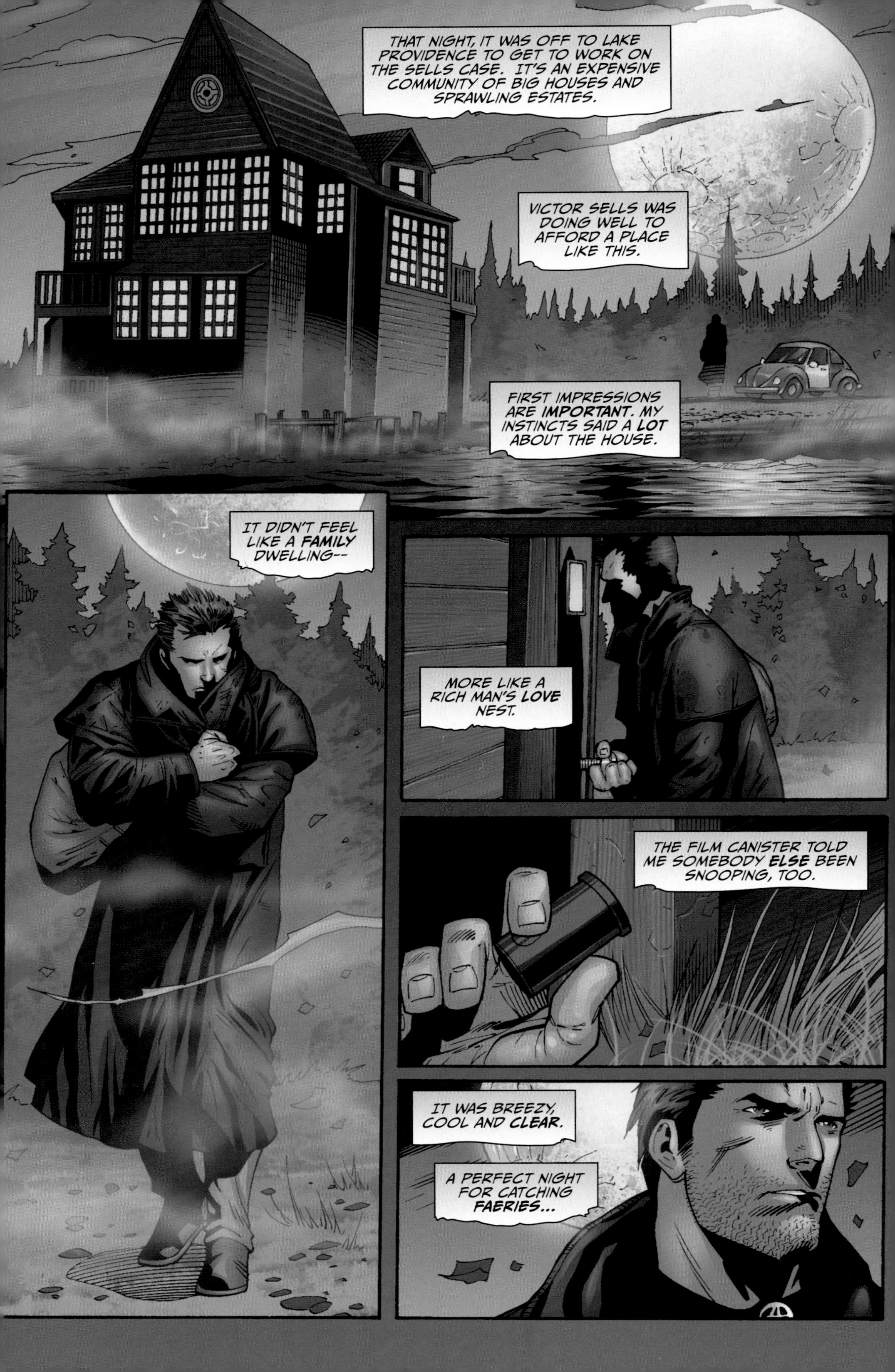
THAT NIGHT, IT WAS OFF TO LAKE PROVIDENCE TO GET TO WORK ON THE SELLS CASE. IT'S AN EXPENSIVE COMMUNITY OF BIG HOUSES AND SPRAWLING ESTATES.
VICTOR SELLS WAS DOING WELL TO AFFORD A PLACE LIKE THIS.
FIRST IMPRESSIONS ARE **IMPORTANT**. MY INSTINCTS SAID A **LOT** ABOUT THE HOUSE.
IT DIDN'T FEEL LIKE A **FAMILY** DWELLING--
MORE LIKE A RICH MAN'S **LOVE** NEST.
THE FILM CANISTER TOLD ME SOMEBODY **ELSE** BEEN SNOOPING, TOO.
IT WAS BREEZY, COOL AND **CLEAR**.
A PERFECT NIGHT FOR CATCHING **FAERIES**...

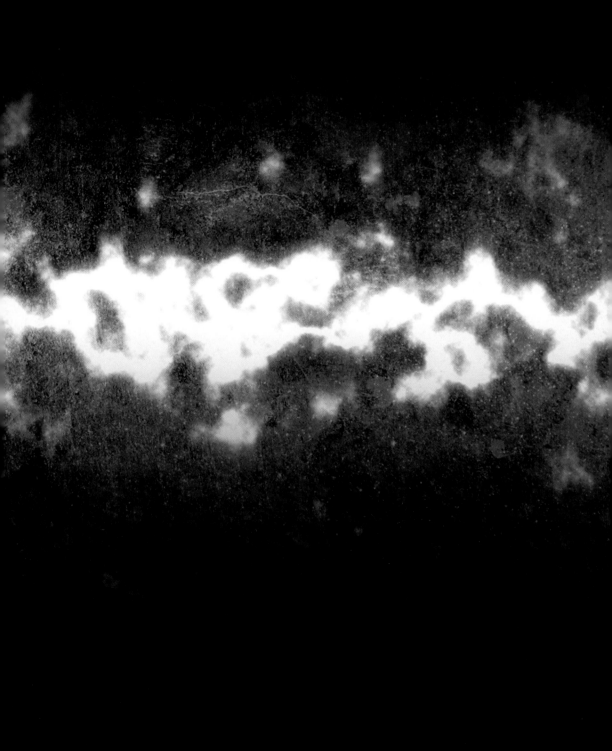

CHAPTER TWO

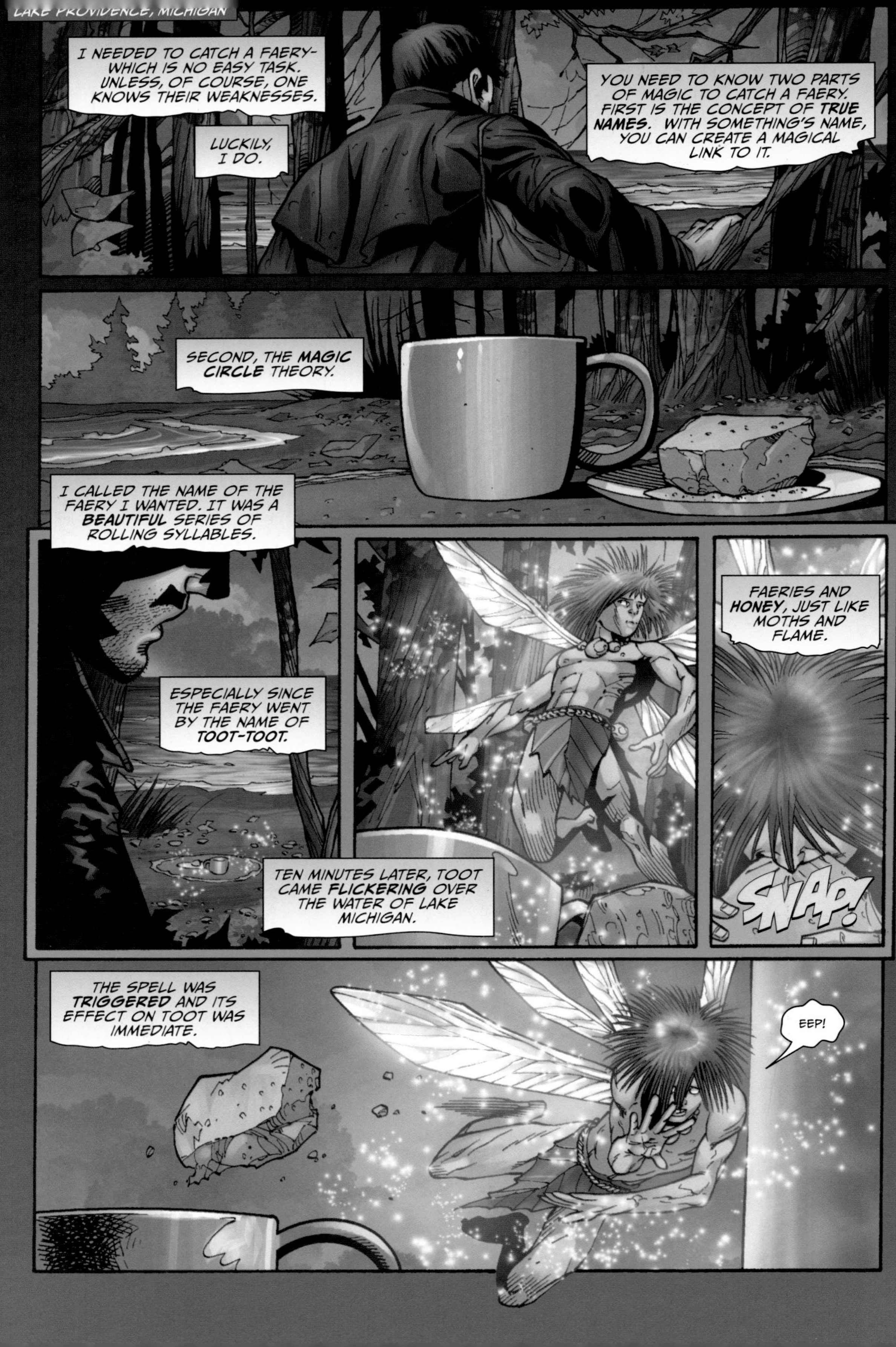

LAKE PROVIDENCE, MICHIGAN
I NEEDED TO CATCH A FAERY-WHICH IS NO EASY TASK. UNLESS, OF COURSE, ONE KNOWS THEIR WEAKNESSES.
LUCKILY, I DO.
YOU NEED TO KNOW TWO PARTS OF MAGIC TO CATCH A FAERY. FIRST IS THE CONCEPT OF TRUE NAMES. WITH SOMETHING'S NAME, YOU CAN CREATE A MAGICAL LINK TO IT.
SECOND, THE MAGIC CIRCLE THEORY.
I CALLED THE NAME OF THE FAERY I WANTED. IT WAS A BEAUTIFUL SERIES OF ROLLING SYLLABLES.
ESPECIALLY SINCE THE FAERY WENT BY THE NAME OF TOOT-TOOT.
TEN MINUTES LATER, TOOT CAME FLICKERING OVER THE WATER OF LAKE MICHIGAN.
FAERIES AND HONEY, JUST LIKE MOTHS AND FLAME.
SNAP!
THE SPELL WAS TRIGGERED AND ITS EFFECT ON TOOT WAS IMMEDIATE.
EEP!

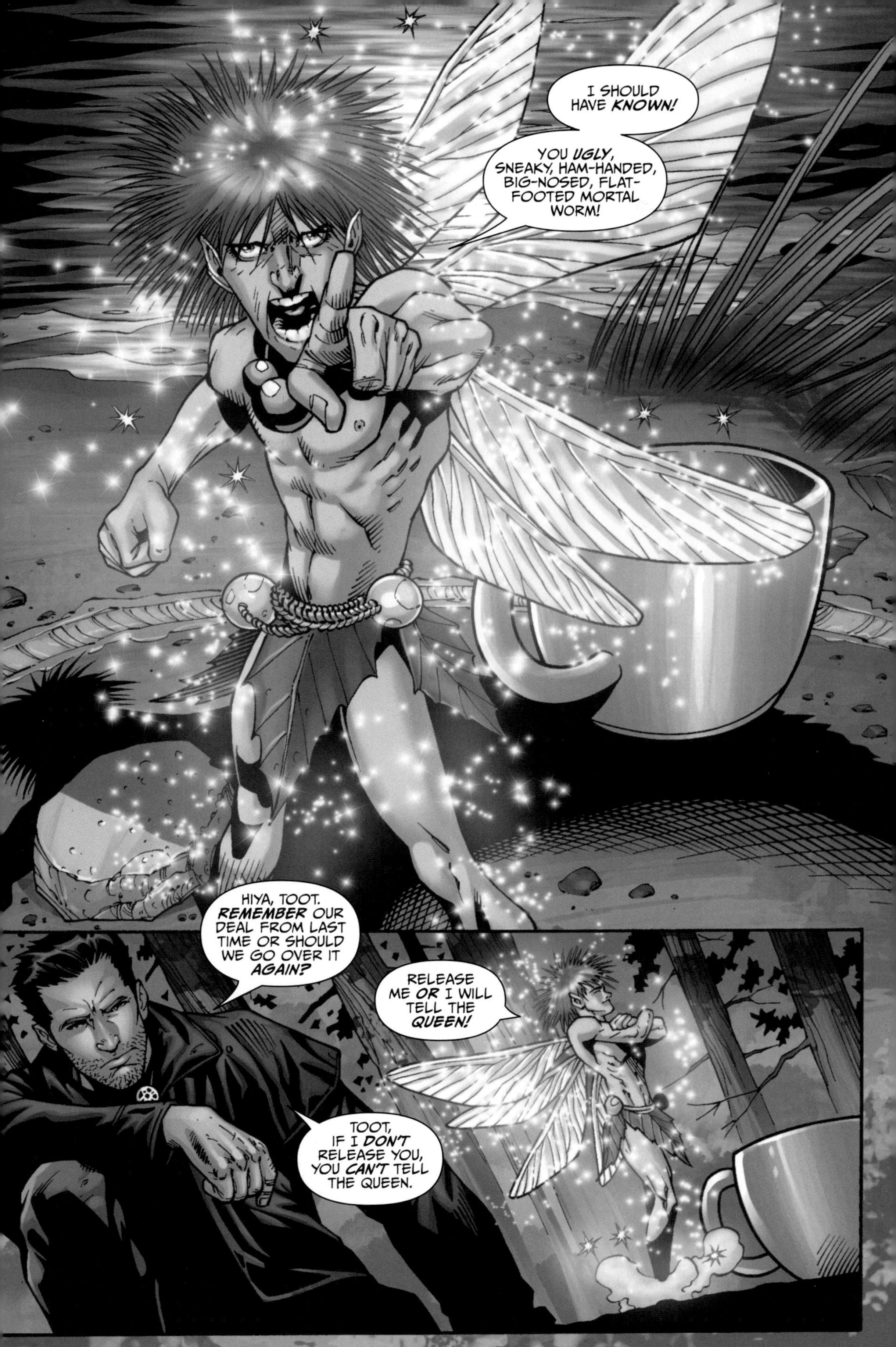

I SHOULD HAVE KNOWN!
YOU UGLY, SNEAKY, HAM-HANDED, BIG-NOSED, FLAT-FOOTED MORTAL WORM!
HIYA, TOOT. REMEMBER OUR DEAL FROM LAST TIME OR SHOULD WE GO OVER IT AGAIN?
RELEASE ME OR I WILL TELL THE QUEEN!
TOOT, IF I DON'T RELEASE YOU, YOU CAN'T TELL THE QUEEN.

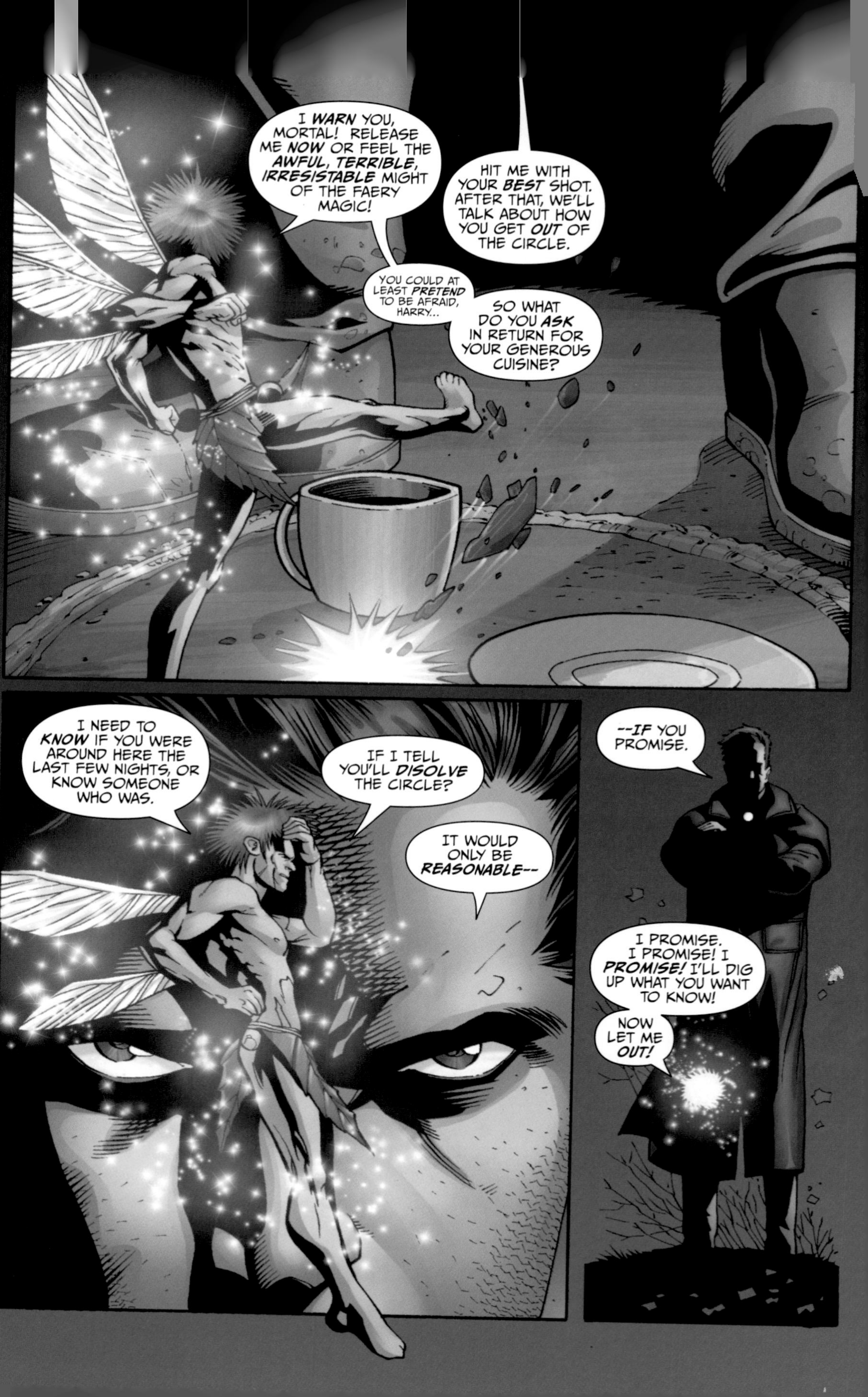
I WARN YOU, MORTAL! RELEASE ME NOW OR FEEL THE AWFUL, TERRIBLE, IRRESISTABLE MIGHT OF THE FAERY MAGIC!
HIT ME WITH YOUR BEST SHOT. AFTER THAT, WE'LL TALK ABOUT HOW YOU GET OUT OF THE CIRCLE.
YOU COULD AT LEAST PRETEND TO BE AFRAID, HARRY...
SO WHAT DO YOU ASK IN RETURN FOR YOUR GENEROUS CUISINE?
I NEED TO KNOW IF YOU WERE AROUND HERE THE LAST FEW NIGHTS, OR KNOW SOMEONE WHO WAS.
IF I TELL YOU'LL DISOLVE THE CIRCLE?
IT WOULD ONLY BE REASONABLE--
--IF YOU PROMISE.
I PROMISE. I PROMISE! I PROMISE! I'LL DIG UP WHAT YOU WANT TO KNOW!
NOW LET ME OUT!

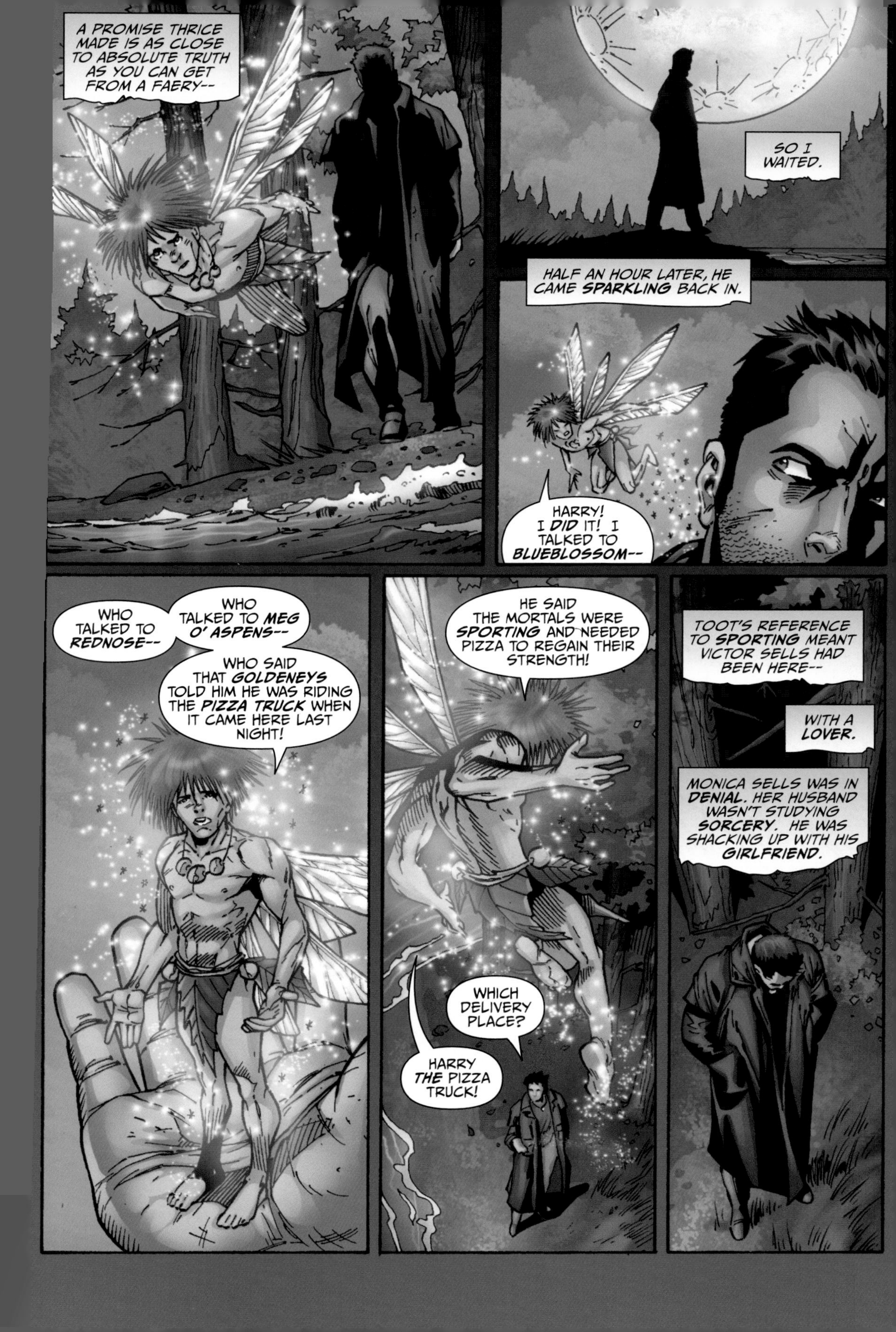

A PROMISE THRICE MADE IS AS CLOSE TO ABSOLUTE TRUTH AS YOU CAN GET FROM A FAERY--
SO I WAITED.
HALF AN HOUR LATER, HE CAME SPARKLING BACK IN.
HARRY! I DID IT! I TALKED TO BLUEBLOSSOM--
WHO TALKED TO REDNOSE--
WHO TALKED TO MEG O' ASPENS--
WHO SAID THAT GOLDENEYS TOLD HIM HE WAS RIDING THE PIZZA TRUCK WHEN IT CAME HERE LAST NIGHT!
HE SAID THE MORTALS WERE SPORTING AND NEEDED PIZZA TO REGAIN THEIR STRENGTH!
WHICH DELIVERY PLACE?
HARRY THE PIZZA TRUCK!
TOOT'S REFERENCE TO SPORTING MEANT VICTOR SELLS HAD BEEN HERE--
WITH A LOVER.
MONICA SELLS WAS IN DENIAL. HER HUSBAND WASN'T STUDYING SORCERY. HE WAS SHACKING UP WITH HIS GIRLFRIEND.

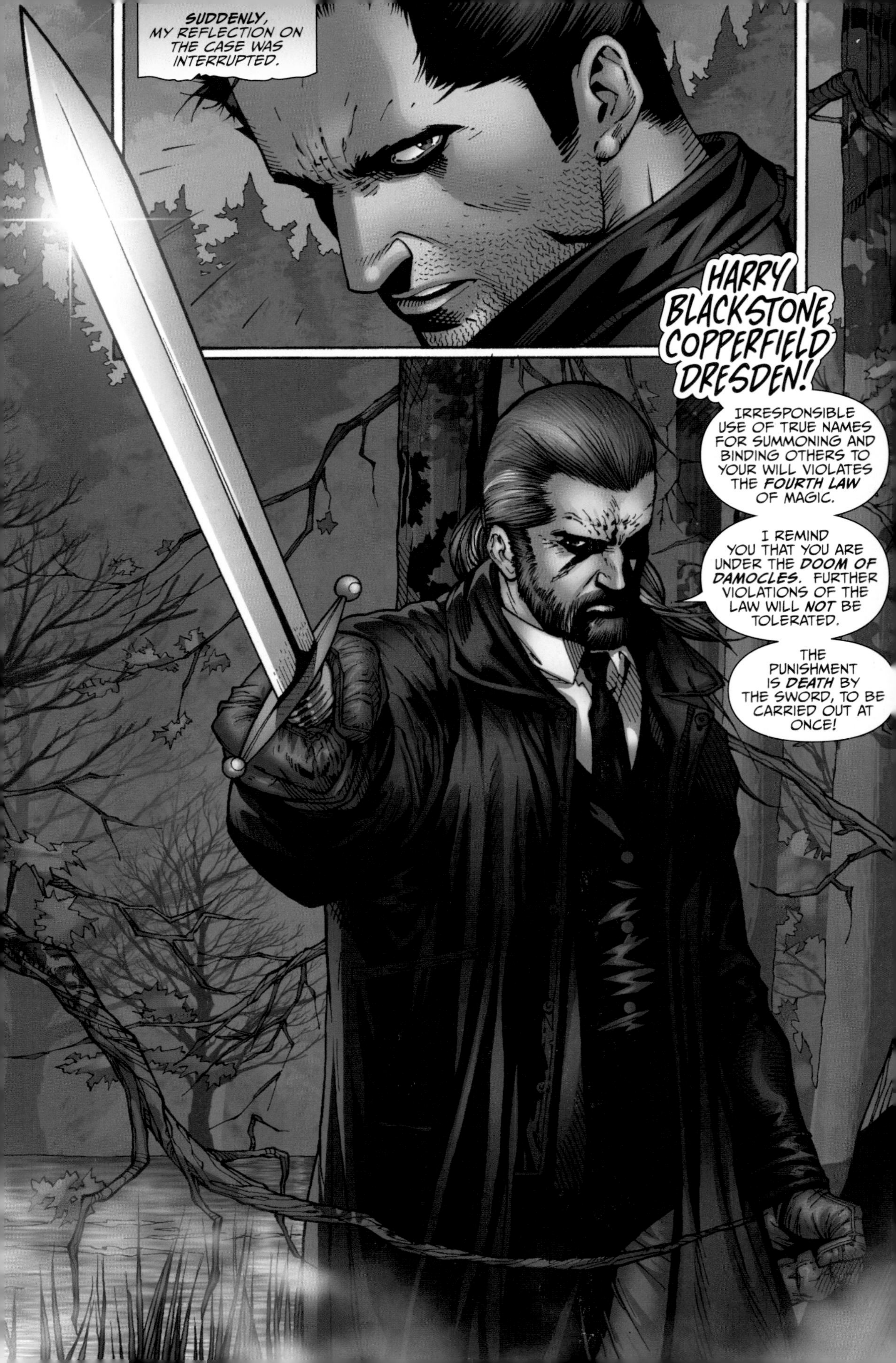
SUDDENLY, MY REFLECTION ON THE CASE WAS INTERRUPTED.
HARRY BLACKSTONE COPPERFIELD DRESDEN!
IRRESPONSIBLE USE OF TRUE NAMES FOR SUMMONING AND BINDING OTHERS TO YOUR WILL VIOLATES THE FOURTH LAW OF MAGIC.
I REMIND YOU THAT YOU ARE UNDER THE DOOM OF DAMOCLES. FURTHER VIOLATIONS OF THE LAW WILL NOT BE TOLERATED.
THE PUNISHMENT IS DEATH BY THE SWORD, TO BE CARRIED OUT AT ONCE!

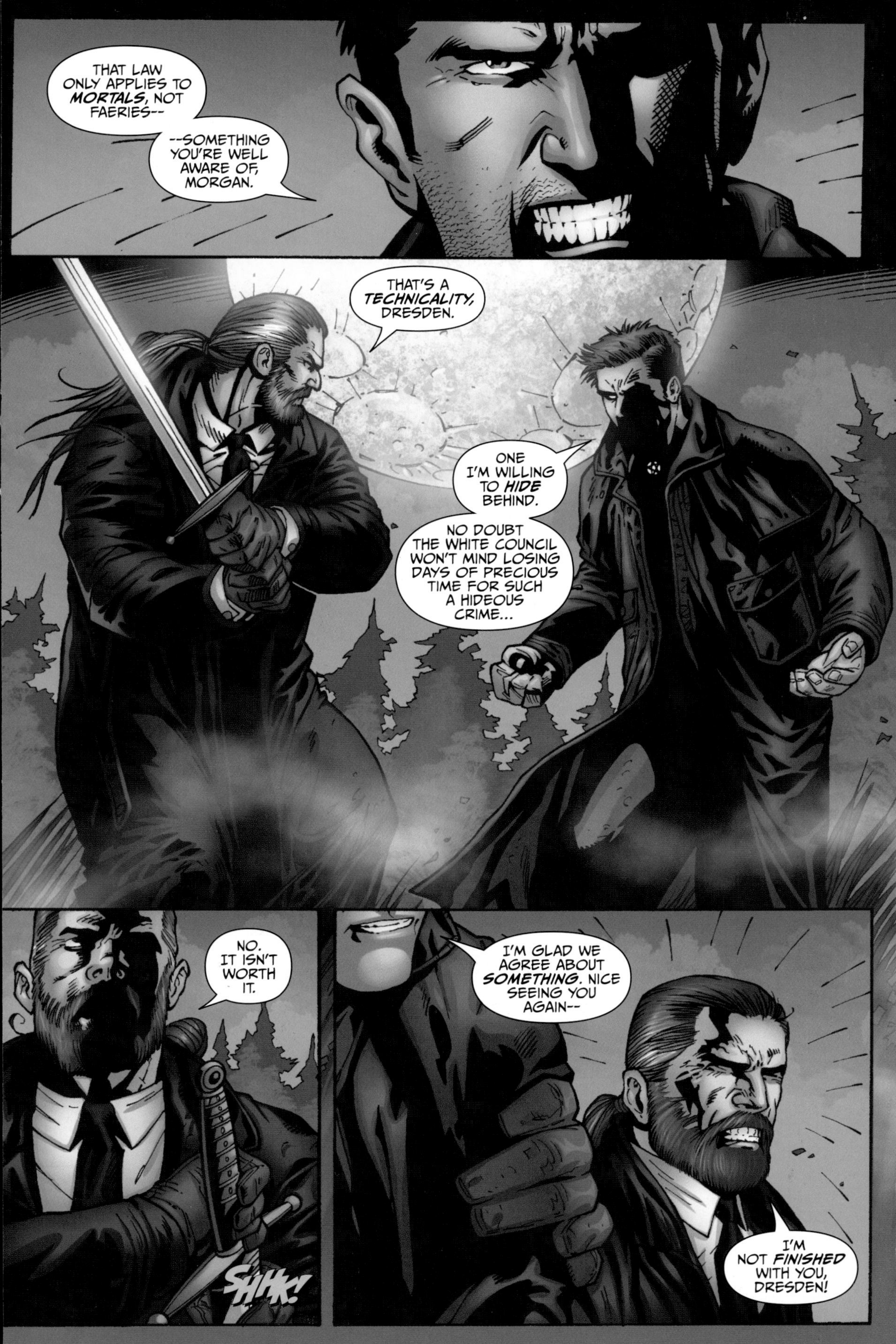
THAT LAW ONLY APPLIES TO MORTALS, NOT FAERIES--
--SOMETHING YOU'RE WELL AWARE OF, MORGAN.
THAT'S A TECHNICALITY, DRESDEN.
ONE I'M WILLING TO HIDE BEHIND.
NO DOUBT THE WHITE COUNCIL WON'T MIND LOSING DAYS OF PRECIOUS TIME FOR SUCH A HIDEOUS CRIME...
NO. IT ISN'T WORTH IT.
SHHK!
I'M GLAD WE AGREE ABOUT SOMETHING. NICE SEEING YOU AGAIN--
I'M NOT FINISHED WITH YOU, DRESDEN!

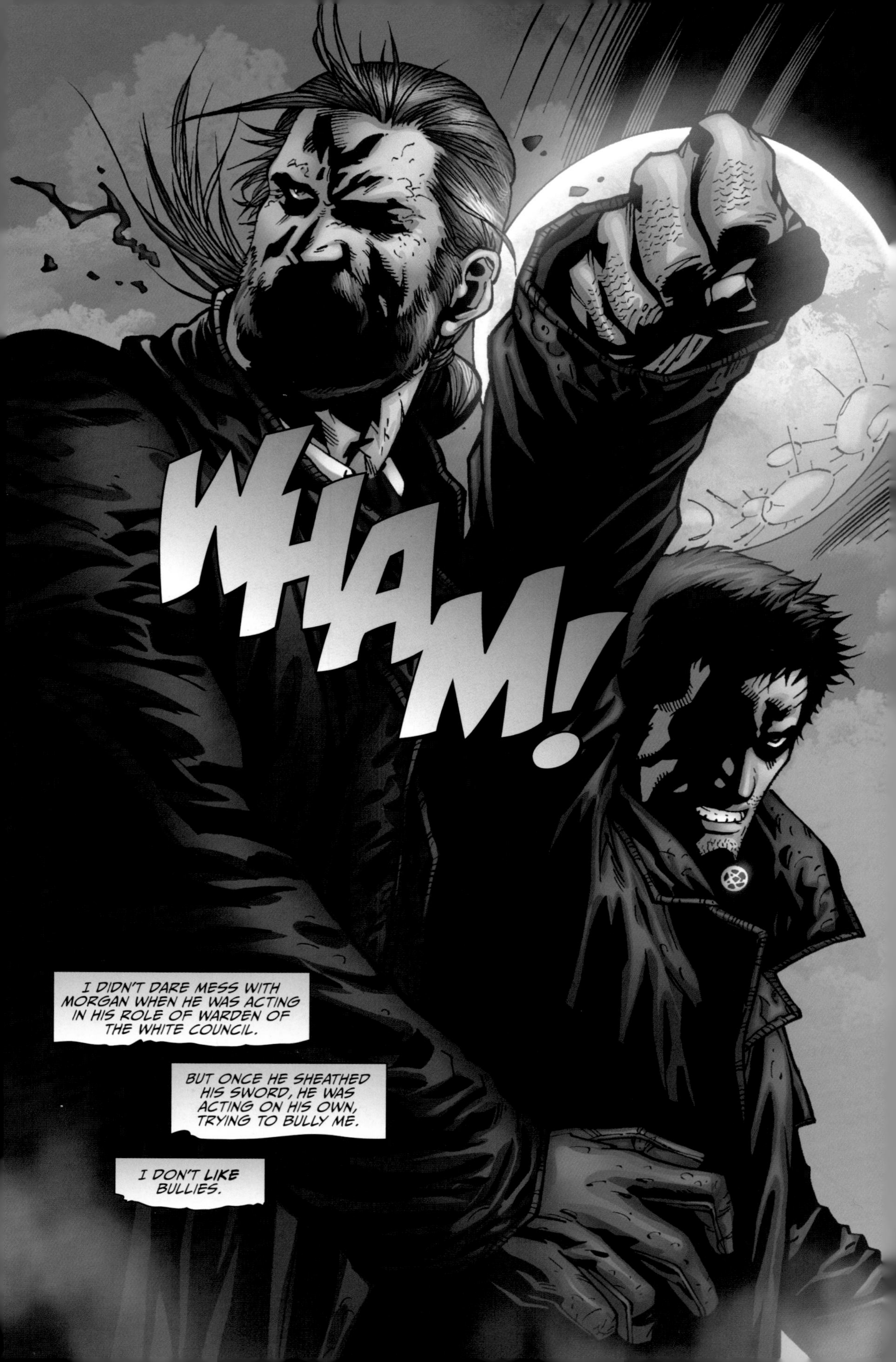
WHAM!
I DIDN'T DARE MESS WITH MORGAN WHEN HE WAS ACTING IN HIS ROLE OF WARDEN OF THE WHITE COUNCIL.
BUT ONCE HE SHEATHED HIS SWORD, HE WAS ACTING ON HIS OWN, TRYING TO BULLY ME.
I DON'T LIKE BULLIES.

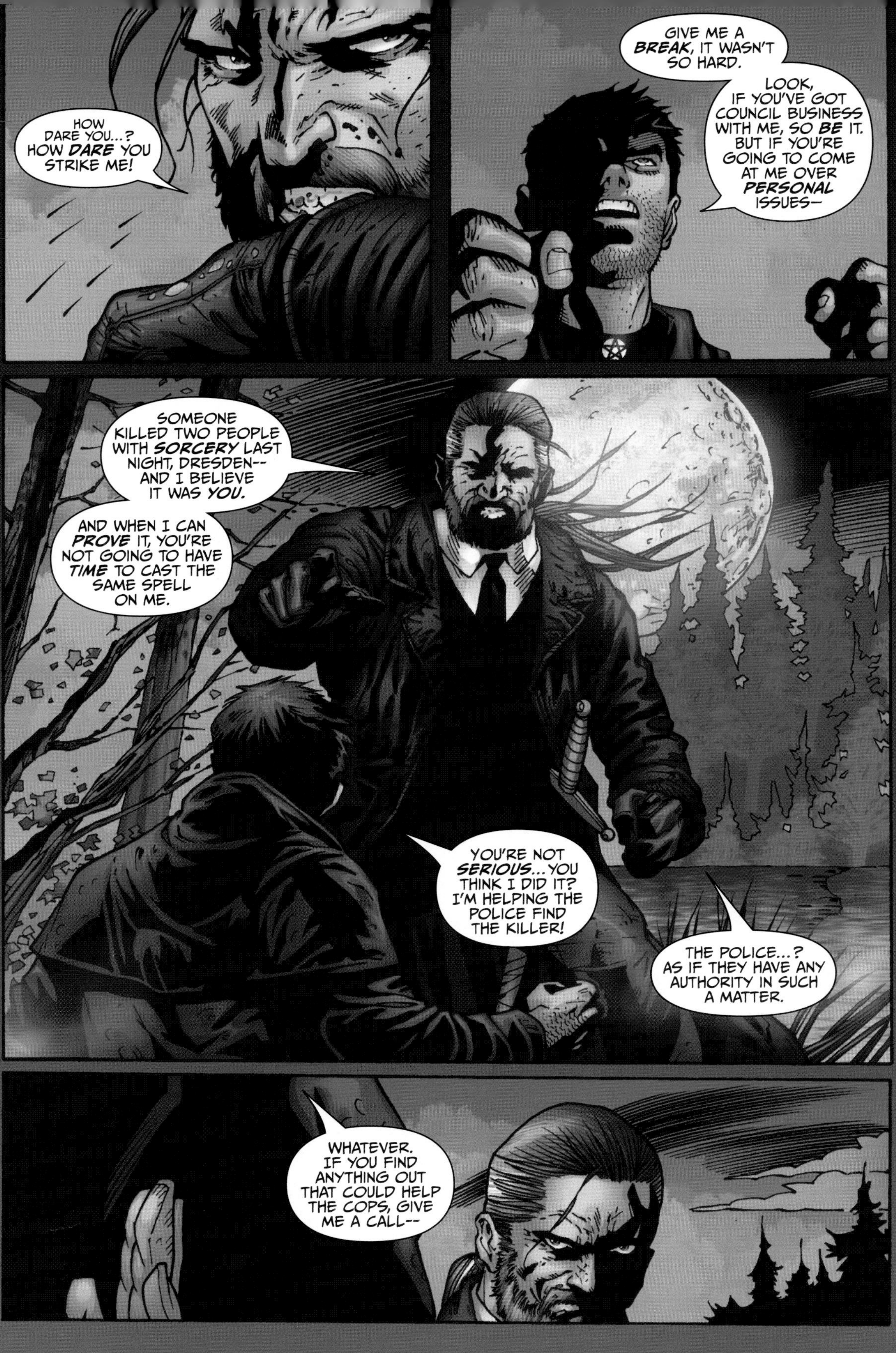
HOW DARE YOU...? HOW DARE YOU STRIKE ME!
GIVE ME A BREAK, IT WASN'T SO HARD.
LOOK, IF YOU'VE GOT COUNCIL BUSINESS WITH ME, SO BE IT. BUT IF YOU'RE GOING TO COME AT ME OVER PERSONAL ISSUES—
SOMEONE KILLED TWO PEOPLE WITH SORCERY LAST NIGHT, DRESDEN-- AND I BELIEVE IT WAS YOU.
AND WHEN I CAN PROVE IT, YOU'RE NOT GOING TO HAVE TIME TO CAST THE SAME SPELL ON ME.
YOU'RE NOT SERIOUS... YOU THINK I DID IT? I'M HELPING THE POLICE FIND THE KILLER!
THE POLICE...? AS IF THEY HAVE ANY AUTHORITY IN SUCH A MATTER.
WHATEVER. IF YOU FIND ANYTHING OUT THAT COULD HELP THE COPS, GIVE ME A CALL--

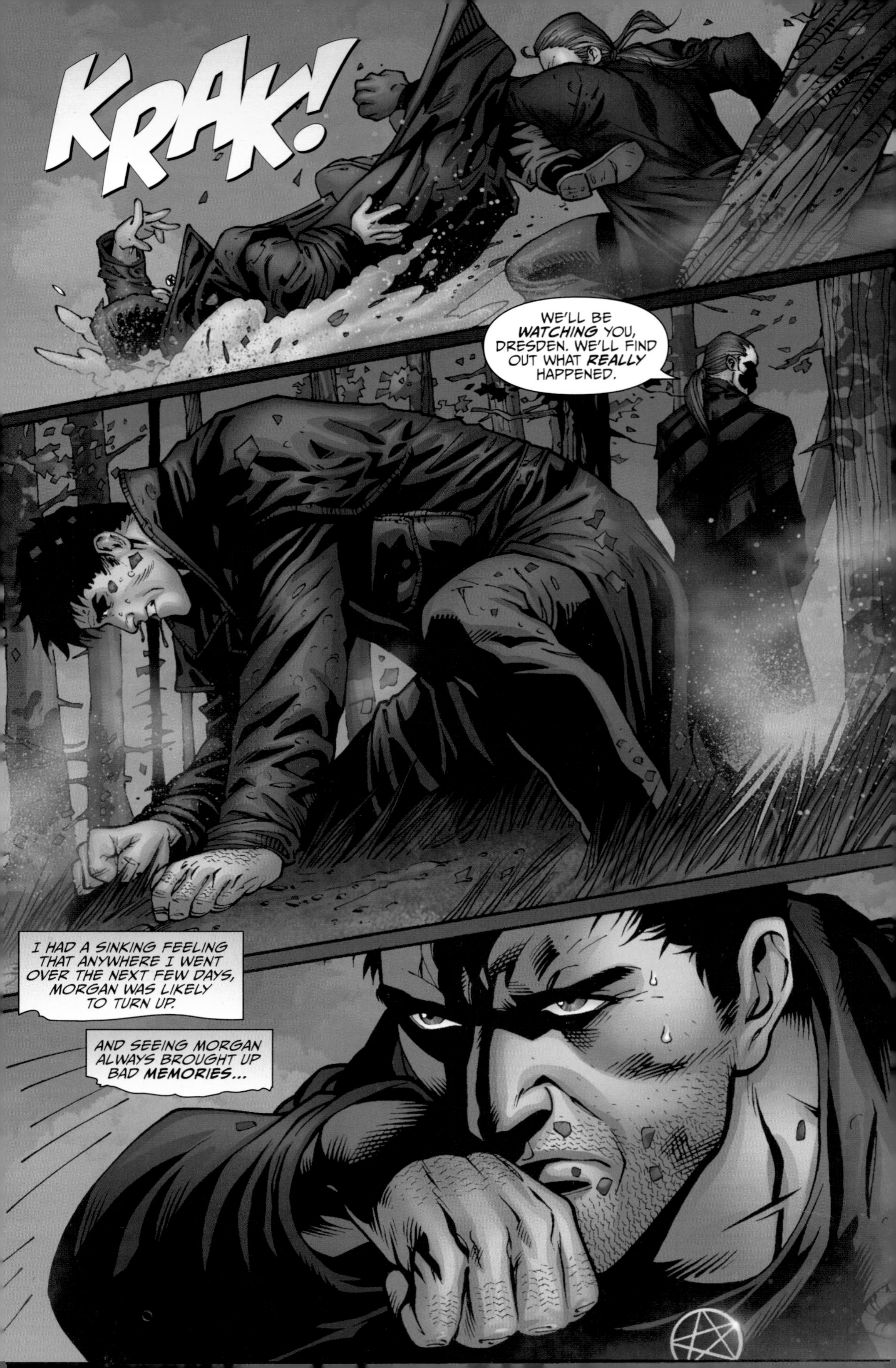
KRAK!
WE'LL BE WATCHING YOU, DRESDEN. WE'LL FIND OUT WHAT REALLY HAPPENED.
I HAD A SINKING FEELING THAT ANYWHERE I WENT OVER THE NEXT FEW DAYS, MORGAN WAS LIKELY TO TURN UP.
AND SEEING MORGAN ALWAYS BROUGHT UP BAD MEMORIES...

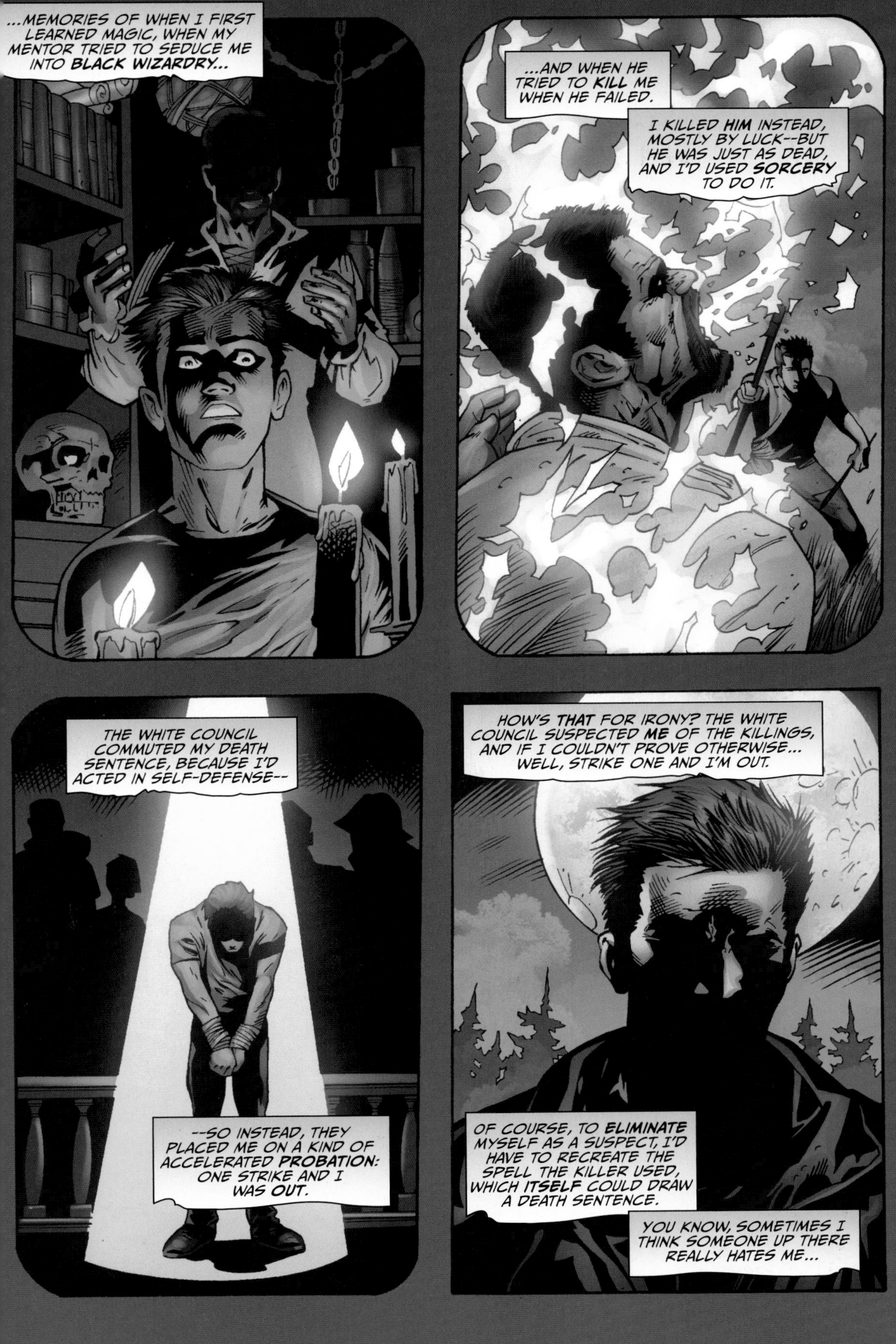
...MEMORIES OF WHEN I FIRST LEARNED MAGIC, WHEN MY MENTOR TRIED TO SEDUCE ME INTO BLACK WIZARDRY...
...AND WHEN HE TRIED TO KILL ME WHEN HE FAILED.
I KILLED HIM INSTEAD, MOSTLY BY LUCK--BUT HE WAS JUST AS DEAD, AND I'D USED SORCERY TO DO IT.
THE WHITE COUNCIL COMMUTED MY DEATH SENTENCE, BECAUSE I'D ACTED IN SELF-DEFENSE--
--SO INSTEAD, THEY PLACED ME ON A KIND OF ACCELERATED PROBATION: ONE STRIKE AND I WAS OUT.
HOW'S THAT FOR IRONY? THE WHITE COUNCIL SUSPECTED ME OF THE KILLINGS, AND IF I COULDN'T PROVE OTHERWISE... WELL, STRIKE ONE AND I'M OUT.
OF COURSE, TO ELIMINATE MYSELF AS A SUSPECT, I'D HAVE TO RECREATE THE SPELL THE KILLER USED, WHICH ITSELF COULD DRAW A DEATH SENTENCE.
YOU KNOW, SOMETIMES I THINK SOMEONE UP THERE REALLY HATES ME...

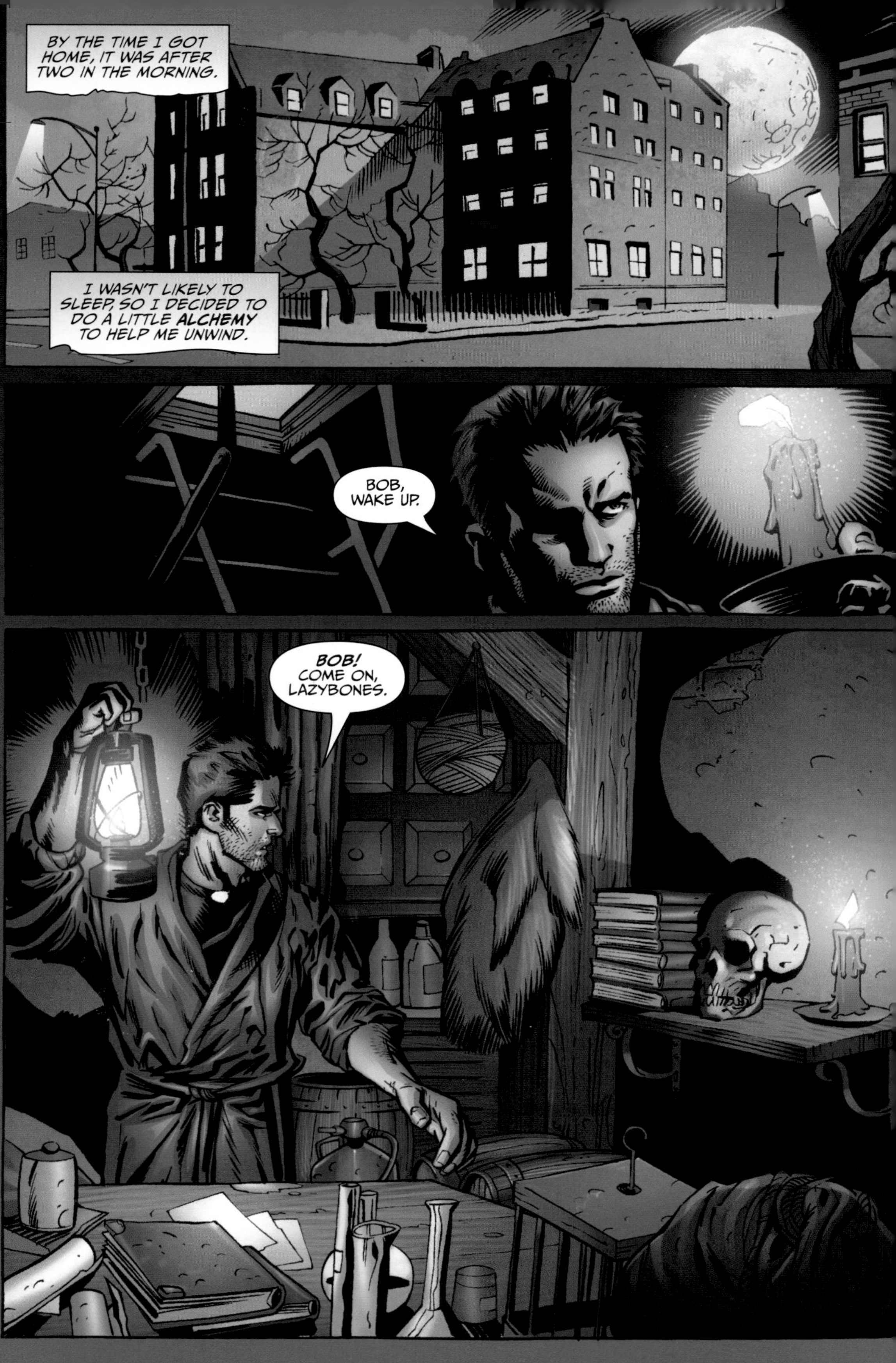
BY THE TIME I GOT HOME, IT WAS AFTER TWO IN THE MORNING.
I WASN'T LIKELY TO SLEEP, SO I DECIDED TO DO A LITTLE **ALCHEMY** TO HELP ME UNWIND.
BOB, WAKE UP.
BOB! COME ON, LAZYBONES.

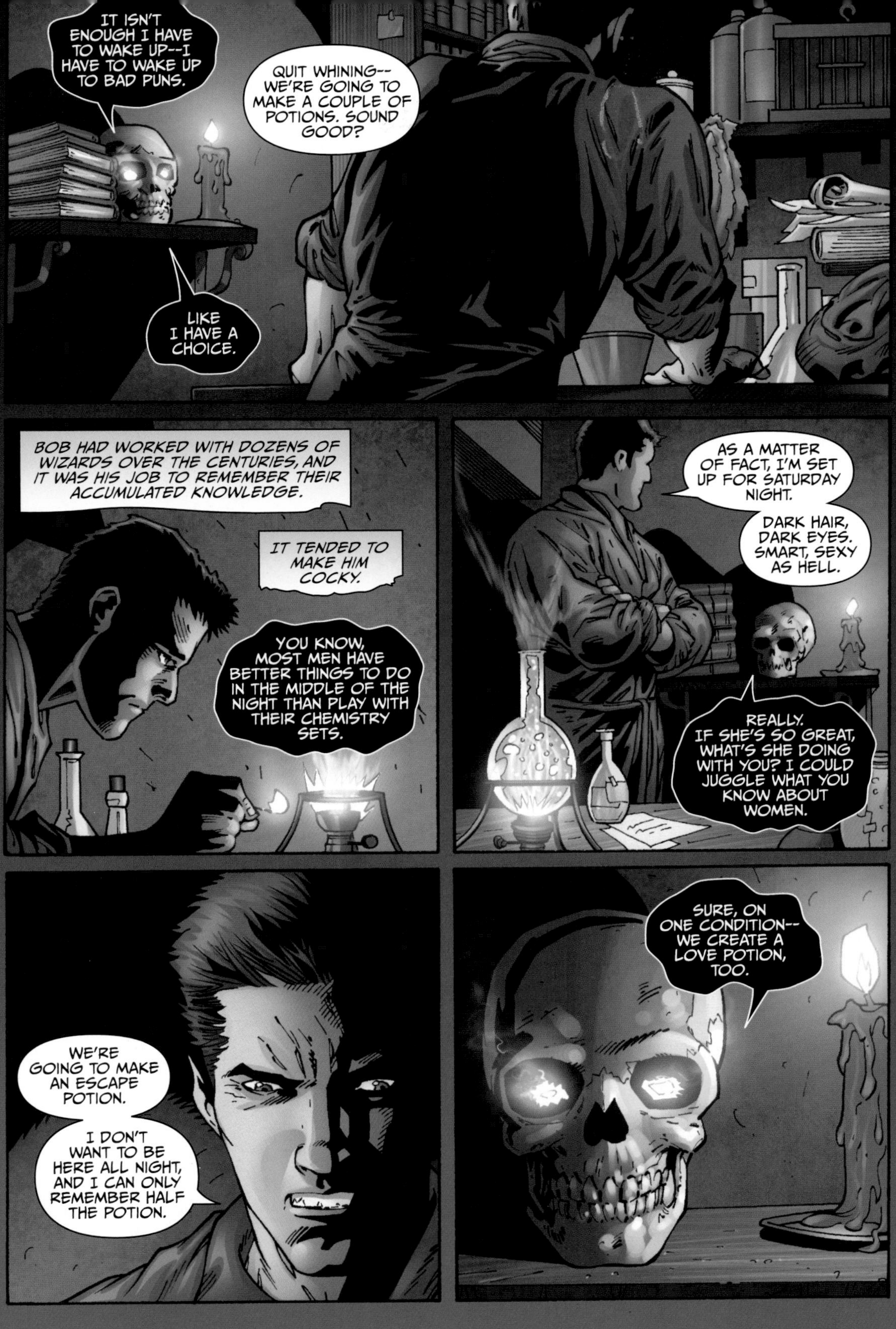
IT ISN'T ENOUGH I HAVE TO WAKE UP--I HAVE TO WAKE UP TO BAD PUNS.
QUIT WHINING--WE'RE GOING TO MAKE A COUPLE OF POTIONS. SOUND GOOD?
LIKE I HAVE A CHOICE.
BOB HAD WORKED WITH DOZENS OF WIZARDS OVER THE CENTURIES, AND IT WAS HIS JOB TO REMEMBER THEIR ACCUMULATED KNOWLEDGE.
IT TENDED TO MAKE HIM COCKY.
YOU KNOW, MOST MEN HAVE BETTER THINGS TO DO IN THE MIDDLE OF THE NIGHT THAN PLAY WITH THEIR CHEMISTRY SETS.
AS A MATTER OF FACT, I'M SET UP FOR SATURDAY NIGHT.
DARK HAIR, DARK EYES. SMART, SEXY AS HELL.
REALLY. IF SHE'S SO GREAT, WHAT'S SHE DOING WITH YOU? I COULD JUGGLE WHAT YOU KNOW ABOUT WOMEN.
WE'RE GOING TO MAKE AN ESCAPE POTION.
I DON'T WANT TO BE HERE ALL NIGHT, AND I CAN ONLY REMEMBER HALF THE POTION.
SURE, ON ONE CONDITION--WE CREATE A LOVE POTION, TOO.

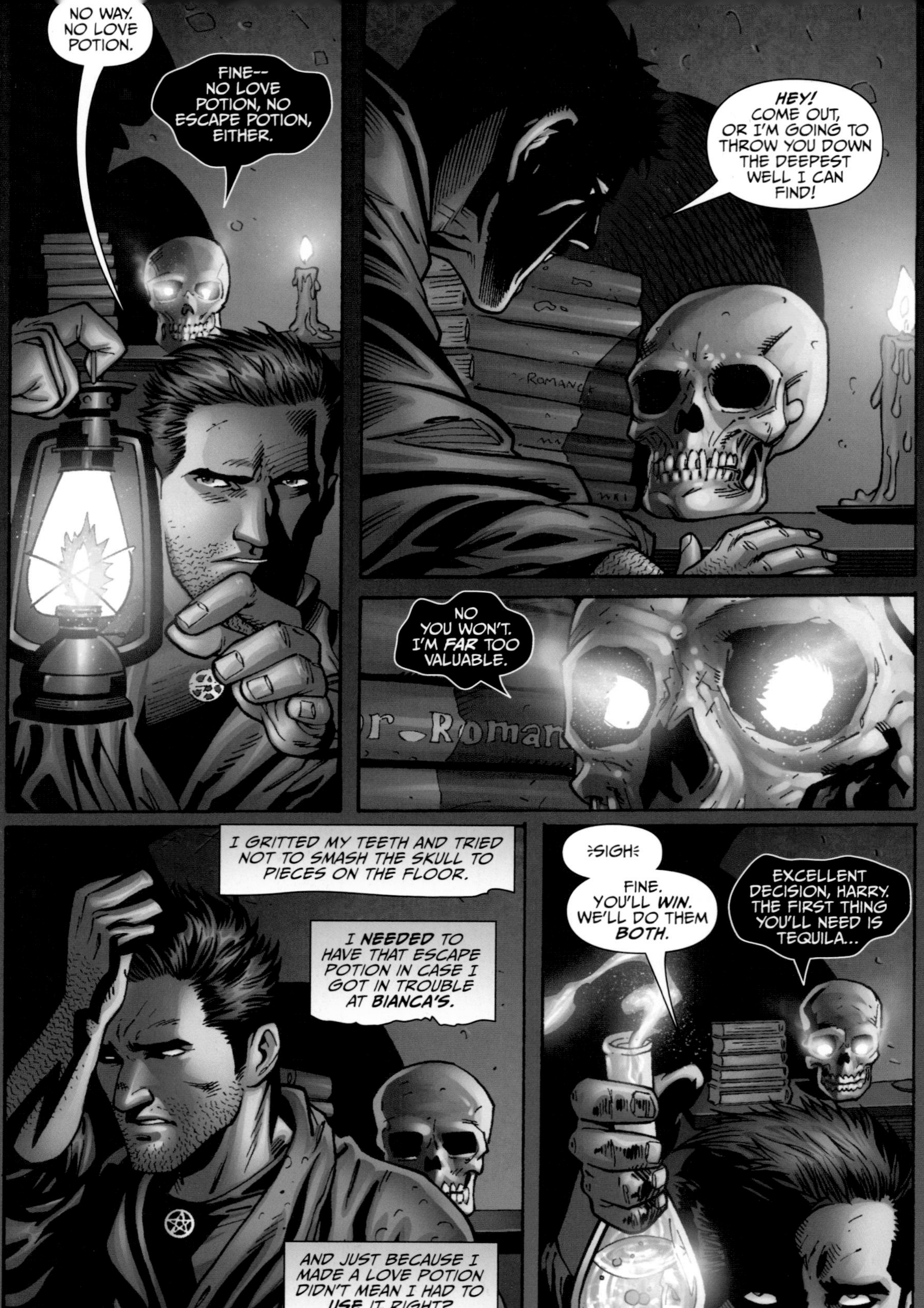
NO WAY. NO LOVE POTION.
FINE-- NO LOVE POTION, NO ESCAPE POTION, EITHER.
HEY! COME OUT, OR I'M GOING TO THROW YOU DOWN THE DEEPEST WELL I CAN FIND!
NO YOU WON'T. I'M FAR TOO VALUABLE.
I GRITTED MY TEETH AND TRIED NOT TO SMASH THE SKULL TO PIECES ON THE FLOOR.
I NEEDED TO HAVE THAT ESCAPE POTION IN CASE I GOT IN TROUBLE AT BIANCA'S.
AND JUST BECAUSE I MADE A LOVE POTION DIDN'T MEAN I HAD TO USE IT, RIGHT?
SIGH
FINE. YOU'LL WIN. WE'LL DO THEM BOTH.
EXCELLENT DECISION, HARRY. THE FIRST THING YOU'LL NEED IS TEQUILA...

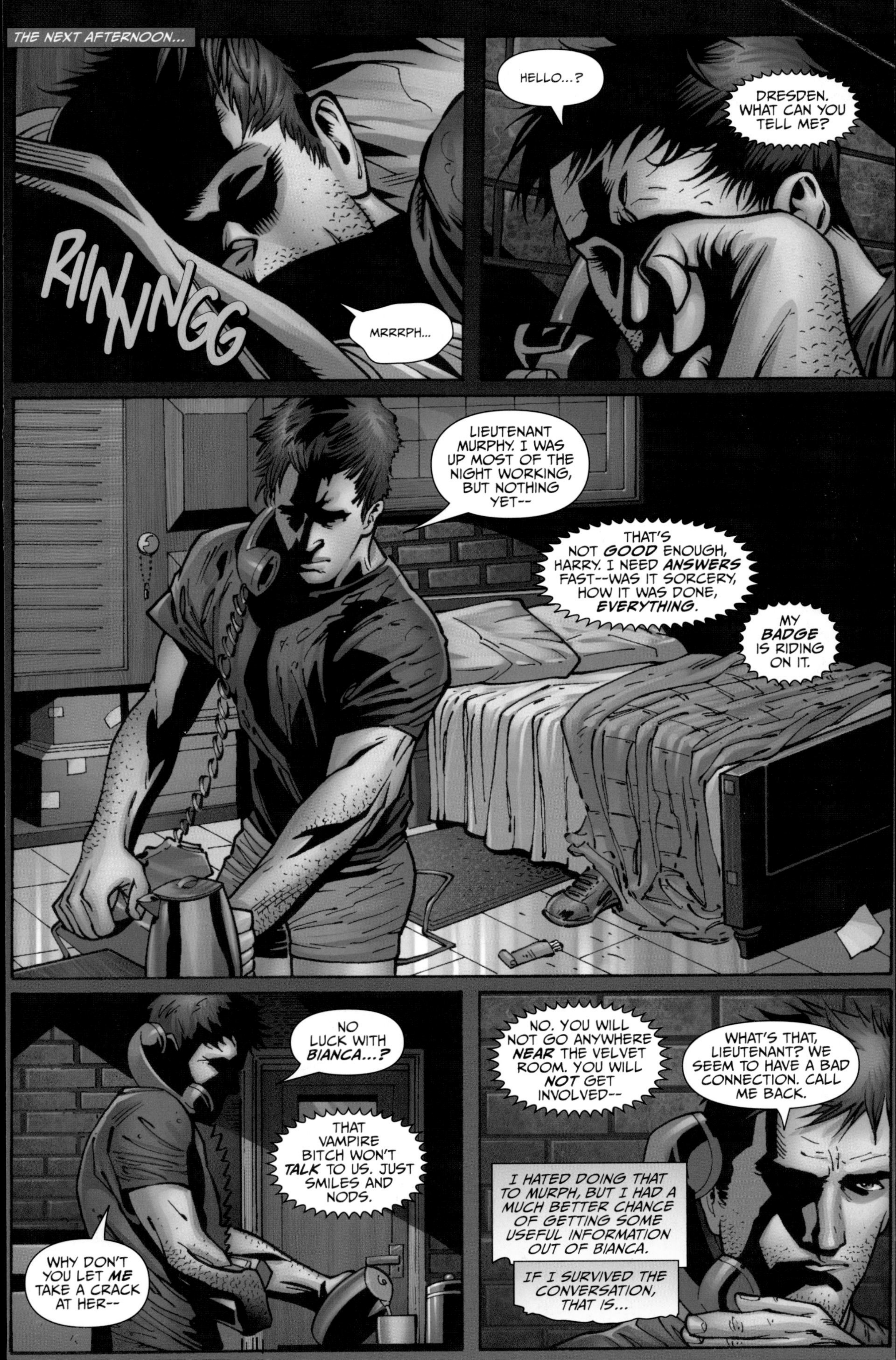
THE NEXT AFTERNOON...
RAINNNGG
MRRRPH...
HELLO...?
DRESDEN. WHAT CAN YOU TELL ME?
LIEUTENANT MURPHY. I WAS UP MOST OF THE NIGHT WORKING, BUT NOTHING YET--
THAT'S NOT GOOD ENOUGH, HARRY. I NEED ANSWERS FAST--WAS IT SORCERY, HOW IT WAS DONE, EVERYTHING.
MY BADGE IS RIDING ON IT.
NO LUCK WITH BIANCA...?
THAT VAMPIRE BITCH WON'T TALK TO US. JUST SMILES AND NODS.
WHY DON'T YOU LET ME TAKE A CRACK AT HER--
NO. YOU WILL NOT GO ANYWHERE NEAR THE VELVET ROOM. YOU WILL NOT GET INVOLVED--
WHAT'S THAT, LIEUTENANT? WE SEEM TO HAVE A BAD CONNECTION. CALL ME BACK.
I HATED DOING THAT TO MURPH, BUT I HAD A MUCH BETTER CHANCE OF GETTING SOME USEFUL INFORMATION OUT OF BIANCA.
IF I SURVIVED THE CONVERSATION, THAT IS...

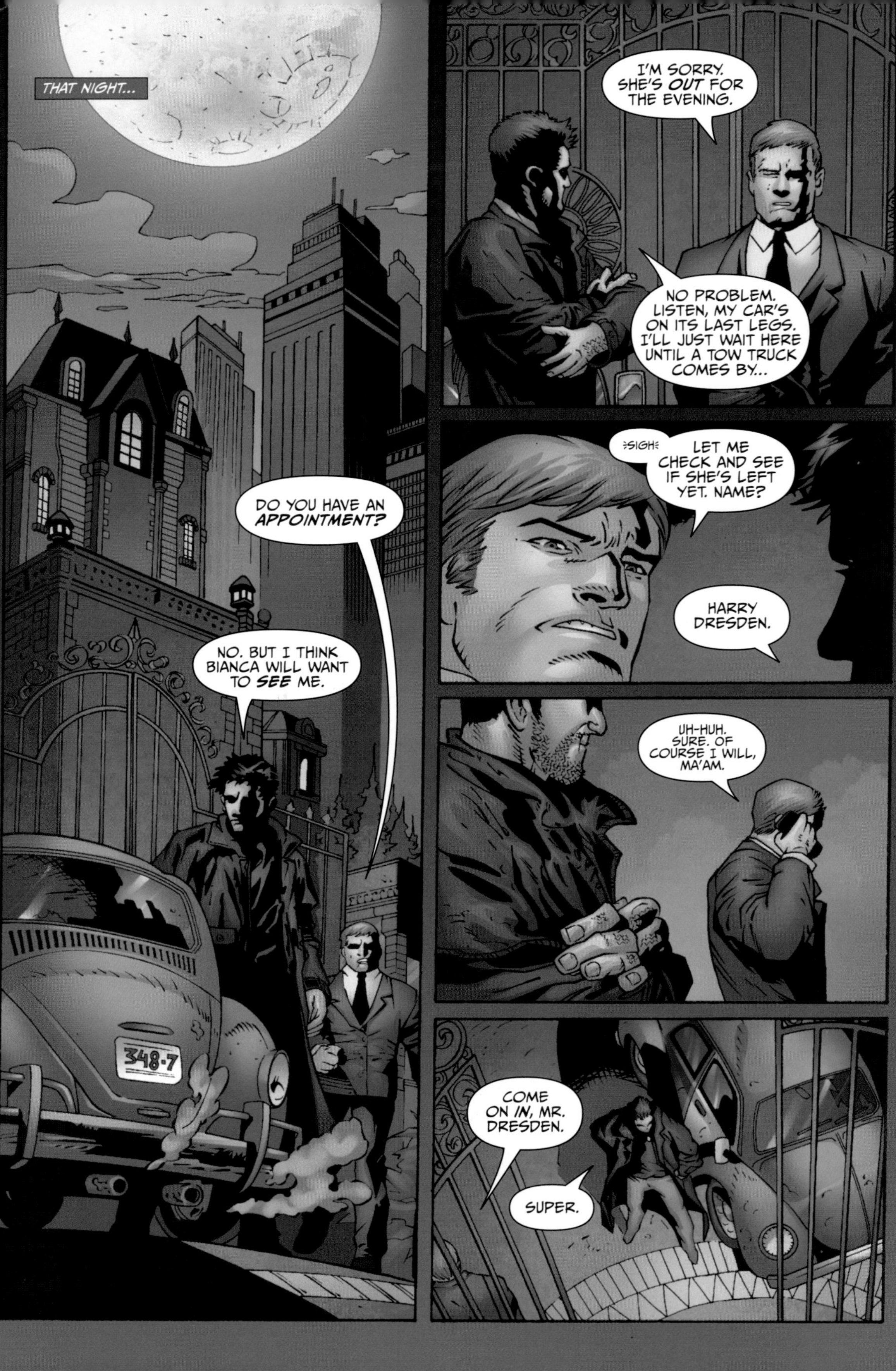
THAT NIGHT...
DO YOU HAVE AN APPOINTMENT?
NO. BUT I THINK BIANCA WILL WANT TO SEE ME.
348-7
I'M SORRY. SHE'S OUT FOR THE EVENING.
NO PROBLEM. LISTEN, MY CAR'S ON ITS LAST LEGS. I'LL JUST WAIT HERE UNTIL A TOW TRUCK COMES BY...
SIGH
LET ME CHECK AND SEE IF SHE'S LEFT YET. NAME?
HARRY DRESDEN.
UH-HUH. SURE. OF COURSE I WILL, MA'AM.
COME ON IN, MR. DRESDEN.
SUPER.

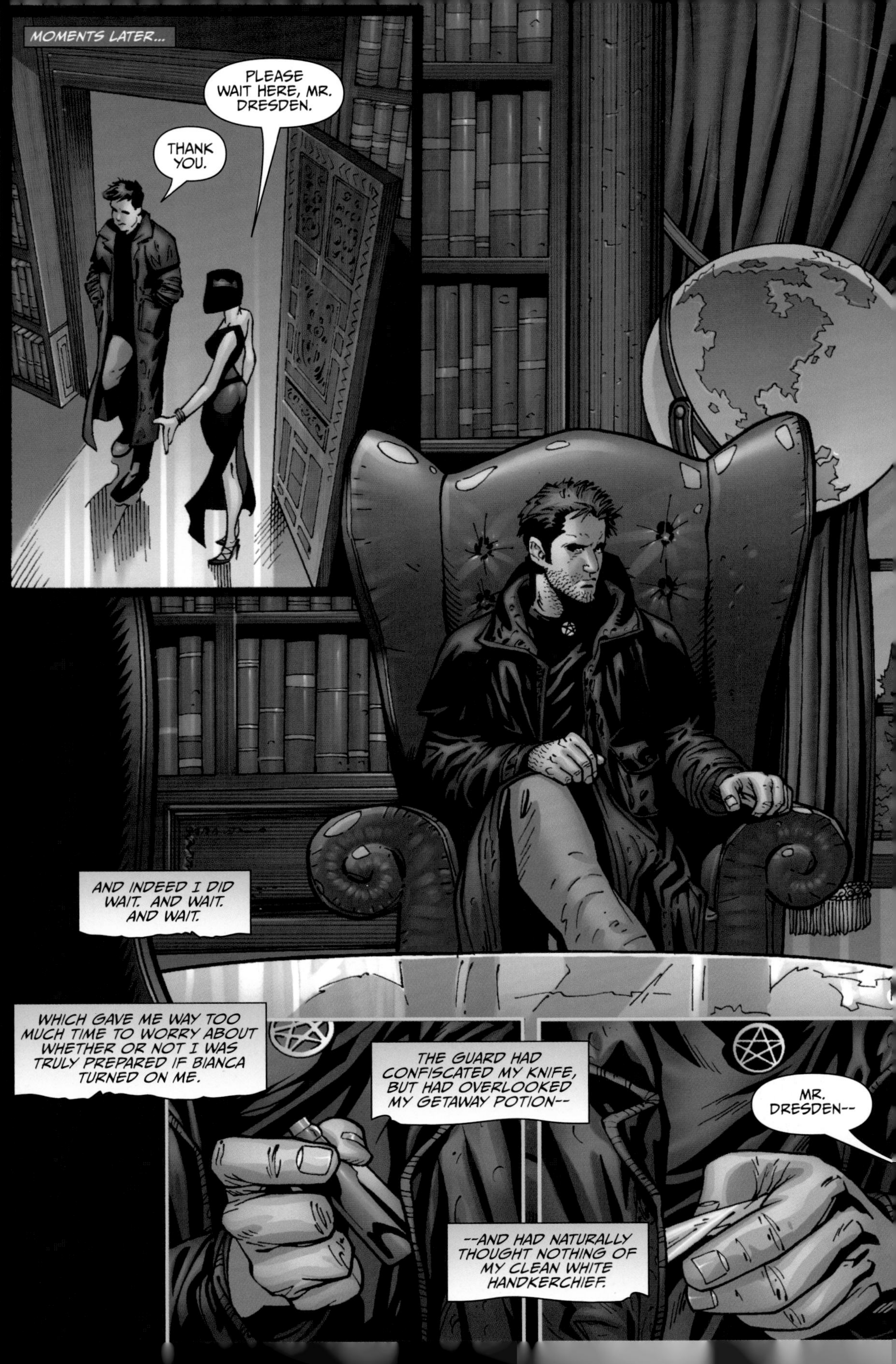
MOMENTS LATER...
PLEASE WAIT HERE, MR. DRESDEN.
THANK YOU.
AND INDEED I DID WAIT. AND WAIT. AND WAIT.
WHICH GAVE ME WAY TOO MUCH TIME TO WORRY ABOUT WHETHER OR NOT I WAS TRULY PREPARED IF BIANCA TURNED ON ME.
THE GUARD HAD CONFISCATED MY KNIFE, BUT HAD OVERLOOKED MY GETAWAY POTION--
--AND HAD NATURALLY THOUGHT NOTHING OF MY CLEAN WHITE HANDKERCHIEF.
MR. DRESDEN--

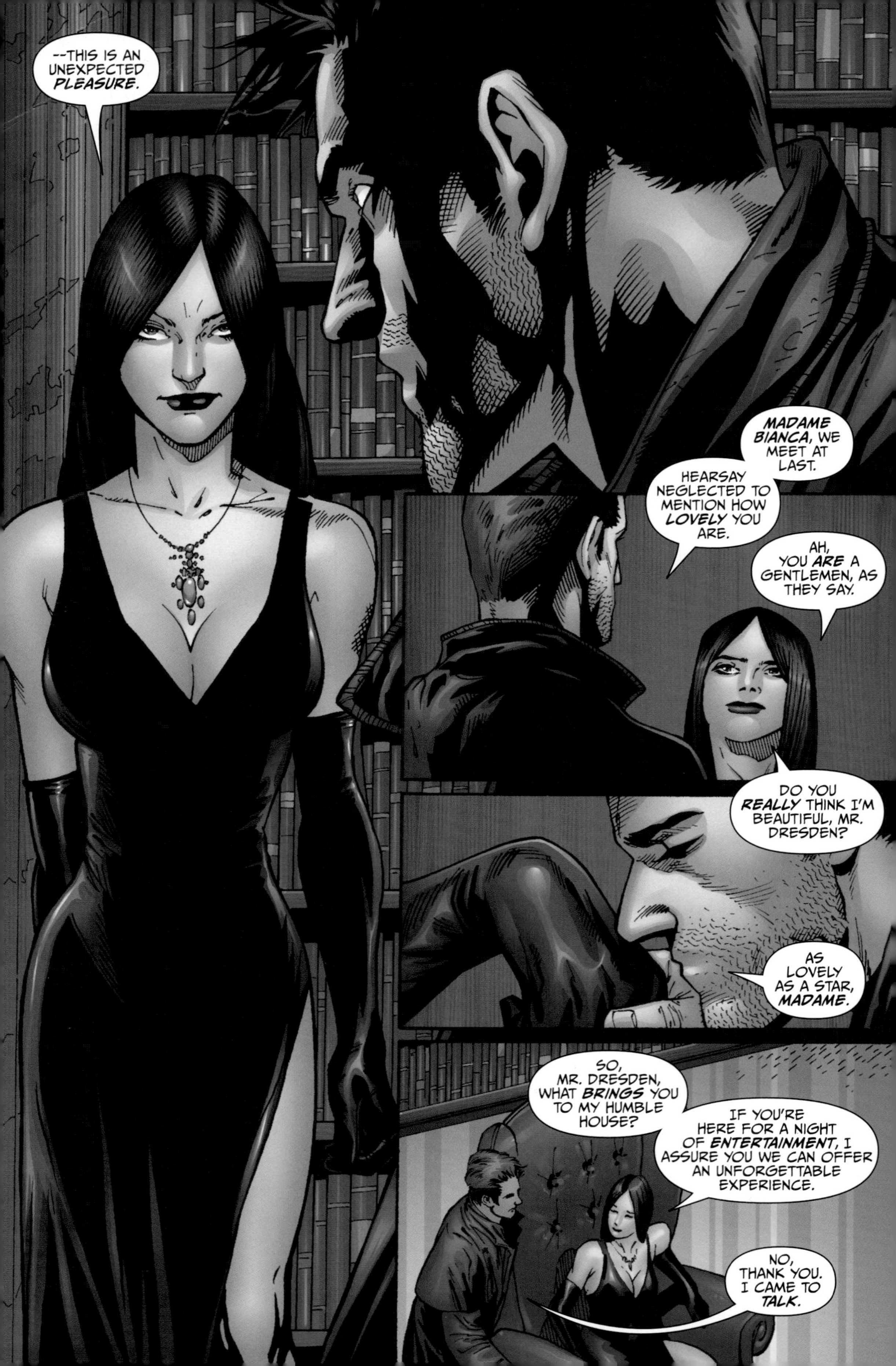
--THIS IS AN UNEXPECTED PLEASURE.
MADAME BIANCA, WE MEET AT LAST.
HEARSAY NEGLECTED TO MENTION HOW LOVELY YOU ARE.
AH, YOU ARE A GENTLEMEN, AS THEY SAY.
DO YOU REALLY THINK I'M BEAUTIFUL, MR. DRESDEN?
AS LOVELY AS A STAR, MADAME.
SO, MR. DRESDEN, WHAT BRINGS YOU TO MY HUMBLE HOUSE?
IF YOU'RE HERE FOR A NIGHT OF ENTERTAINMENT, I ASSURE YOU WE CAN OFFER AN UNFORGETTABLE EXPERIENCE.
NO, THANK YOU. I CAME TO TALK.

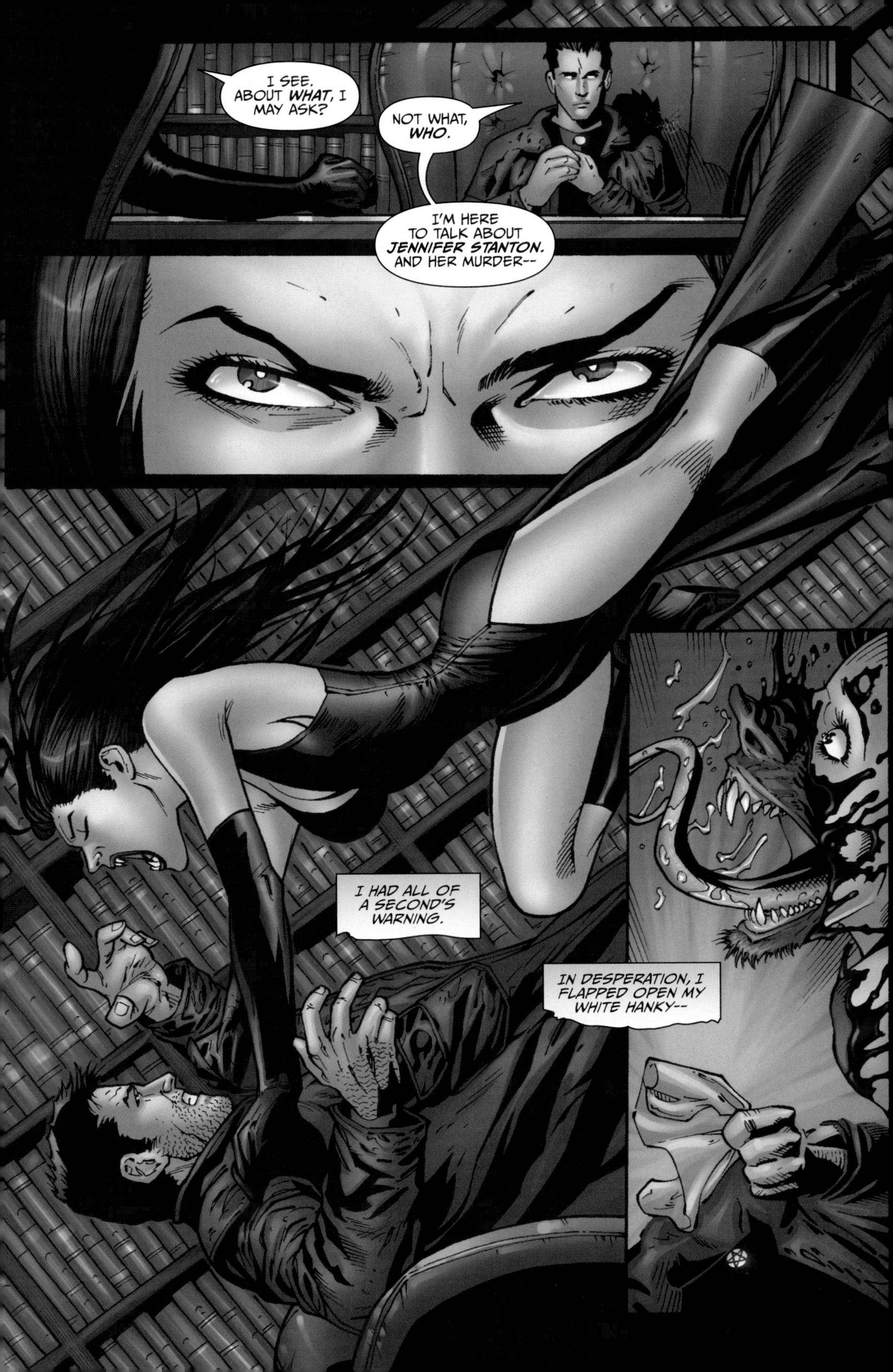

I SEE. ABOUT *WHAT*, I MAY ASK?
NOT WHAT, ***WHO.***
I'M HERE TO TALK ABOUT ***JENNIFER STANTON.*** AND HER MURDER--
I HAD ALL OF A SECOND'S WARNING.
IN DESPERATION, I FLAPPED OPEN MY WHITE HANKY--

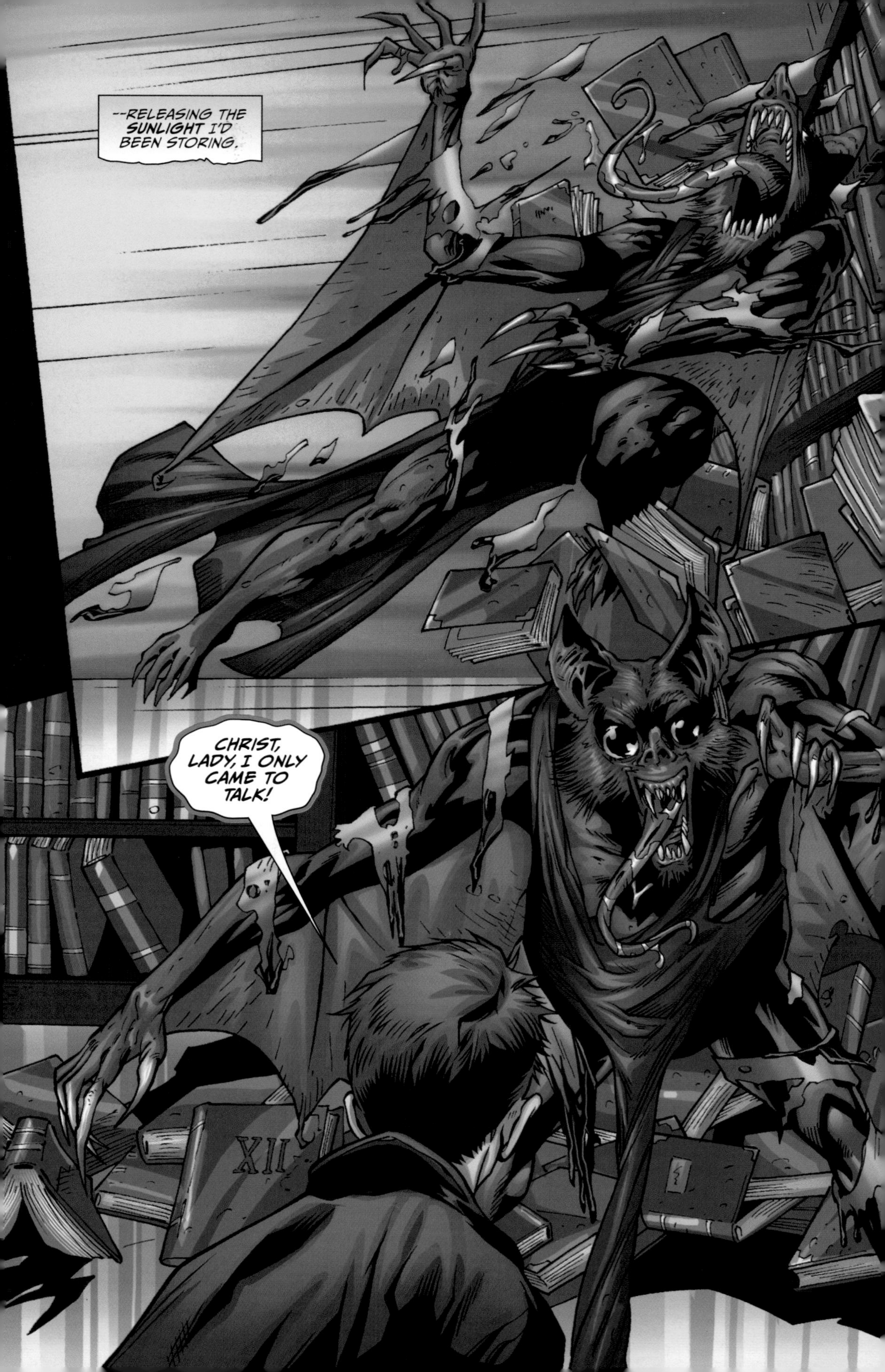
--RELEASING THE SUNLIGHT I'D BEEN STORING.
CHRIST, LADY, I ONLY CAME TO TALK!
XII

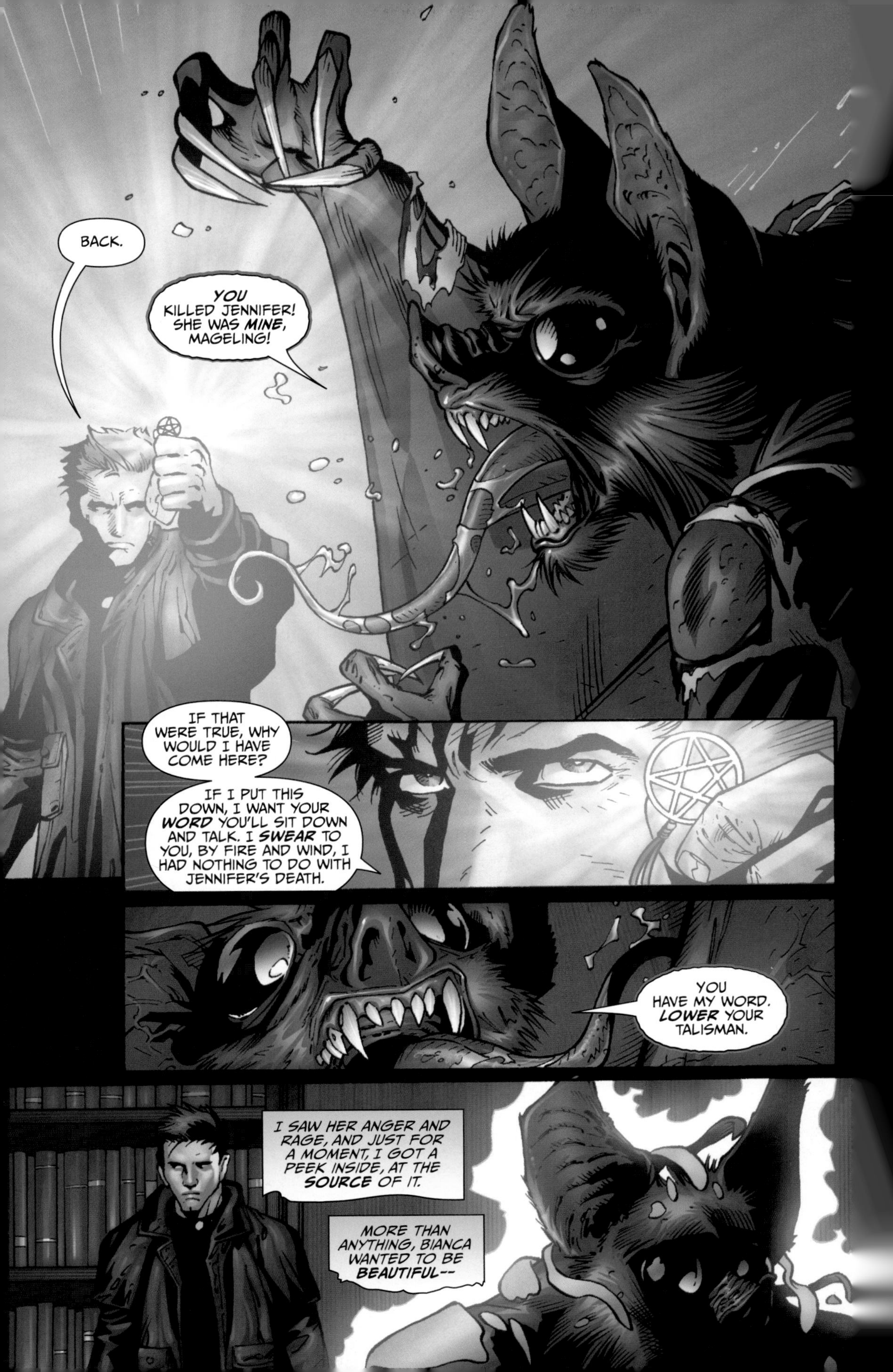
BACK.
YOU KILLED JENNIFER! SHE WAS MINE, MAGELING!
IF THAT WERE TRUE, WHY WOULD I HAVE COME HERE?
IF I PUT THIS DOWN, I WANT YOUR WORD YOU'LL SIT DOWN AND TALK. I SWEAR TO YOU, BY FIRE AND WIND, I HAD NOTHING TO DO WITH JENNIFER'S DEATH.
YOU HAVE MY WORD. LOWER YOUR TALISMAN.
I SAW HER ANGER AND RAGE, AND JUST FOR A MOMENT, I GOT A PEEK INSIDE, AT THE SOURCE OF IT.
MORE THAN ANYTHING, BIANCA WANTED TO BE BEAUTIFUL--

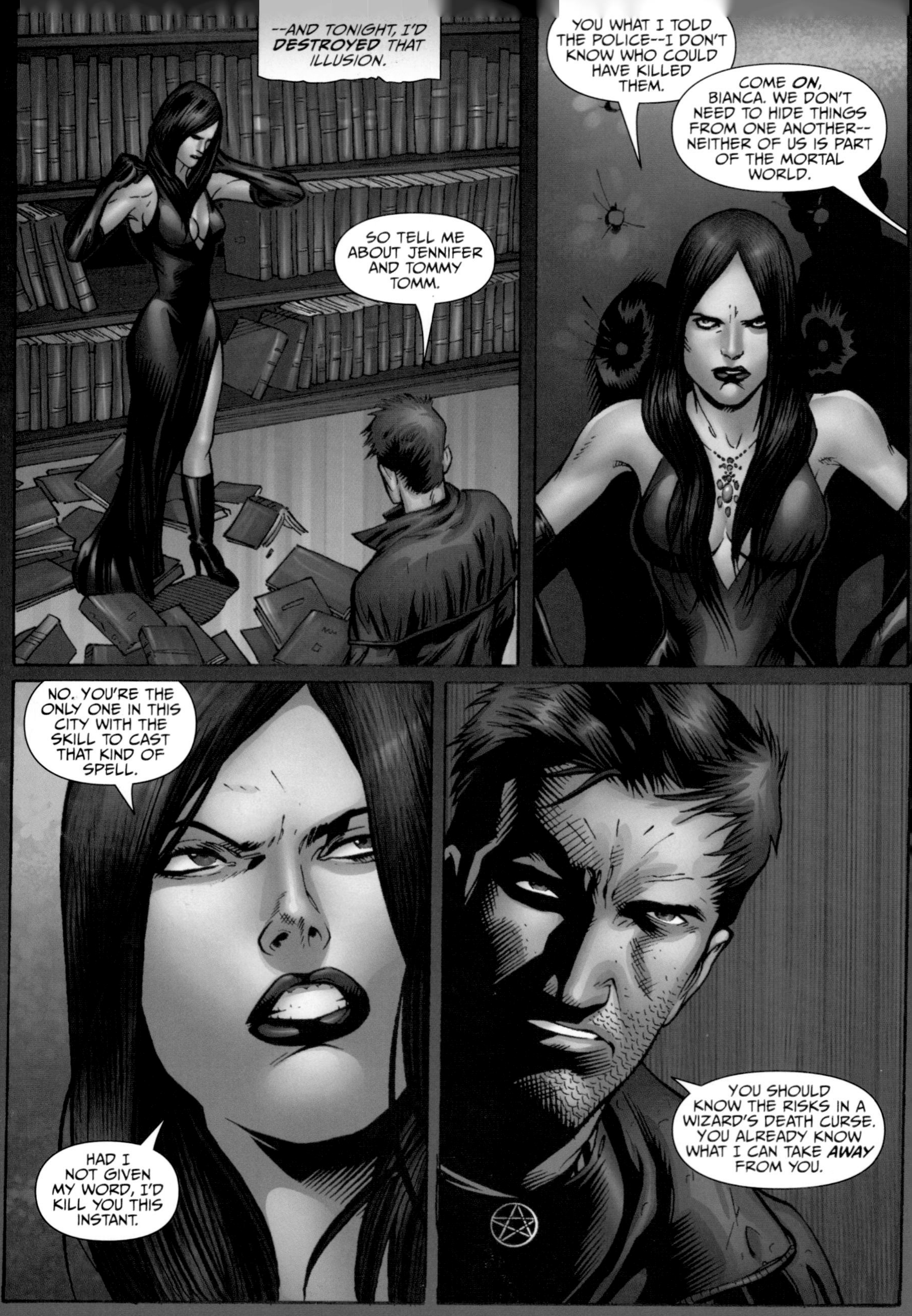
--AND TONIGHT, I'D DESTROYED THAT ILLUSION.
SO TELL ME ABOUT JENNIFER AND TOMMY TOMM.
YOU WHAT I TOLD THE POLICE--I DON'T KNOW WHO COULD HAVE KILLED THEM.
COME ON, BIANCA. WE DON'T NEED TO HIDE THINGS FROM ONE ANOTHER--NEITHER OF US IS PART OF THE MORTAL WORLD.
NO. YOU'RE THE ONLY ONE IN THIS CITY WITH THE SKILL TO CAST THAT KIND OF SPELL.
YOU SHOULD KNOW THE RISKS IN A WIZARD'S DEATH CURSE. YOU ALREADY KNOW WHAT I CAN TAKE AWAY FROM YOU.
HAD I NOT GIVEN MY WORD, I'D KILL YOU THIS INSTANT.

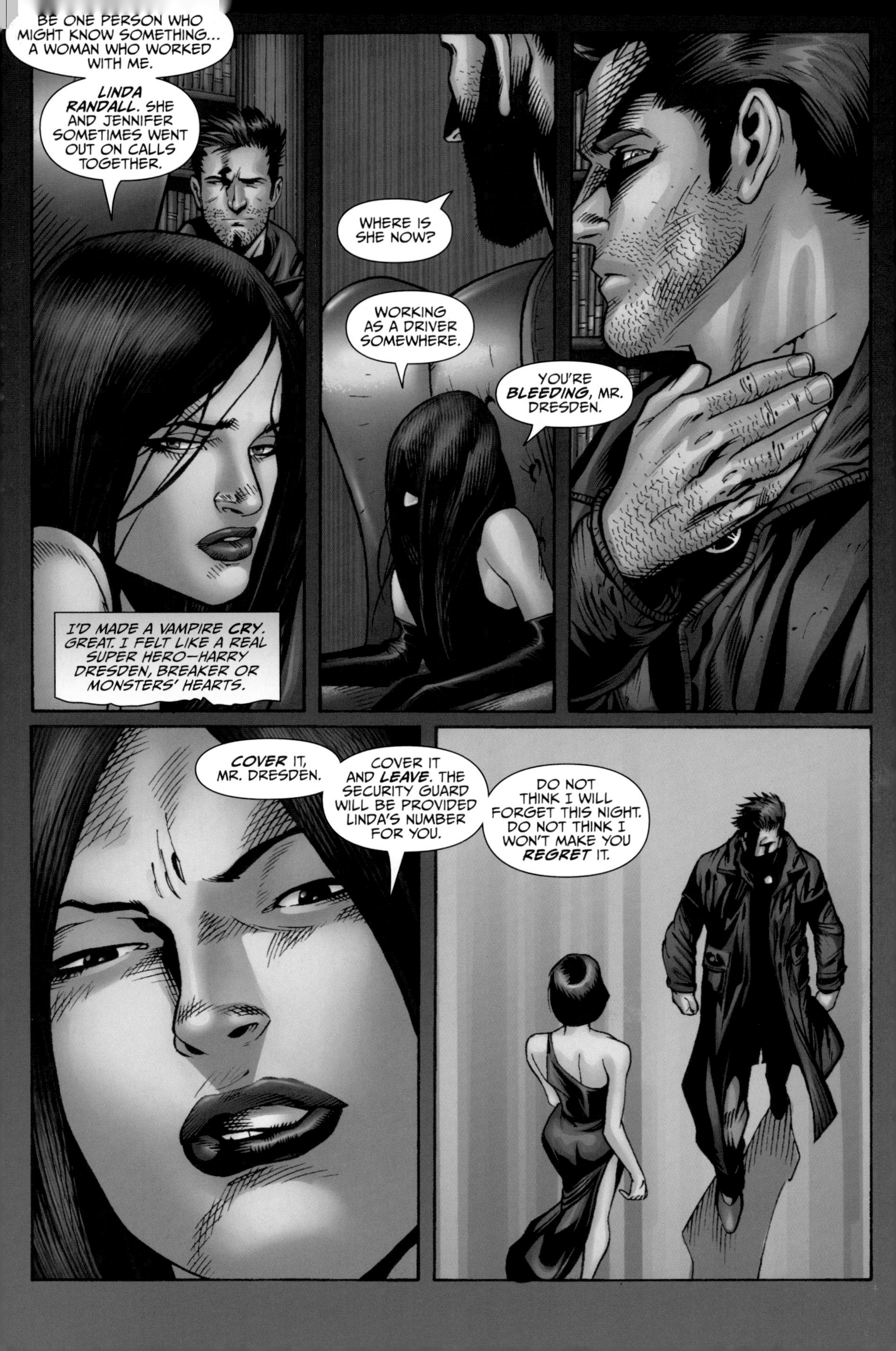
BE ONE PERSON WHO MIGHT KNOW SOMETHING... A WOMAN WHO WORKED WITH ME.
LINDA RANDALL. SHE AND JENNIFER SOMETIMES WENT OUT ON CALLS TOGETHER.
I'D MADE A VAMPIRE CRY. GREAT. I FELT LIKE A REAL SUPER HERO—HARRY DRESDEN, BREAKER OR MONSTERS' HEARTS.
WHERE IS SHE NOW?
WORKING AS A DRIVER SOMEWHERE.
YOU'RE BLEEDING, MR. DRESDEN.
COVER IT, MR. DRESDEN.
COVER IT AND LEAVE. THE SECURITY GUARD WILL BE PROVIDED LINDA'S NUMBER FOR YOU.
DO NOT THINK I WILL FORGET THIS NIGHT. DO NOT THINK I WON'T MAKE YOU REGRET IT.

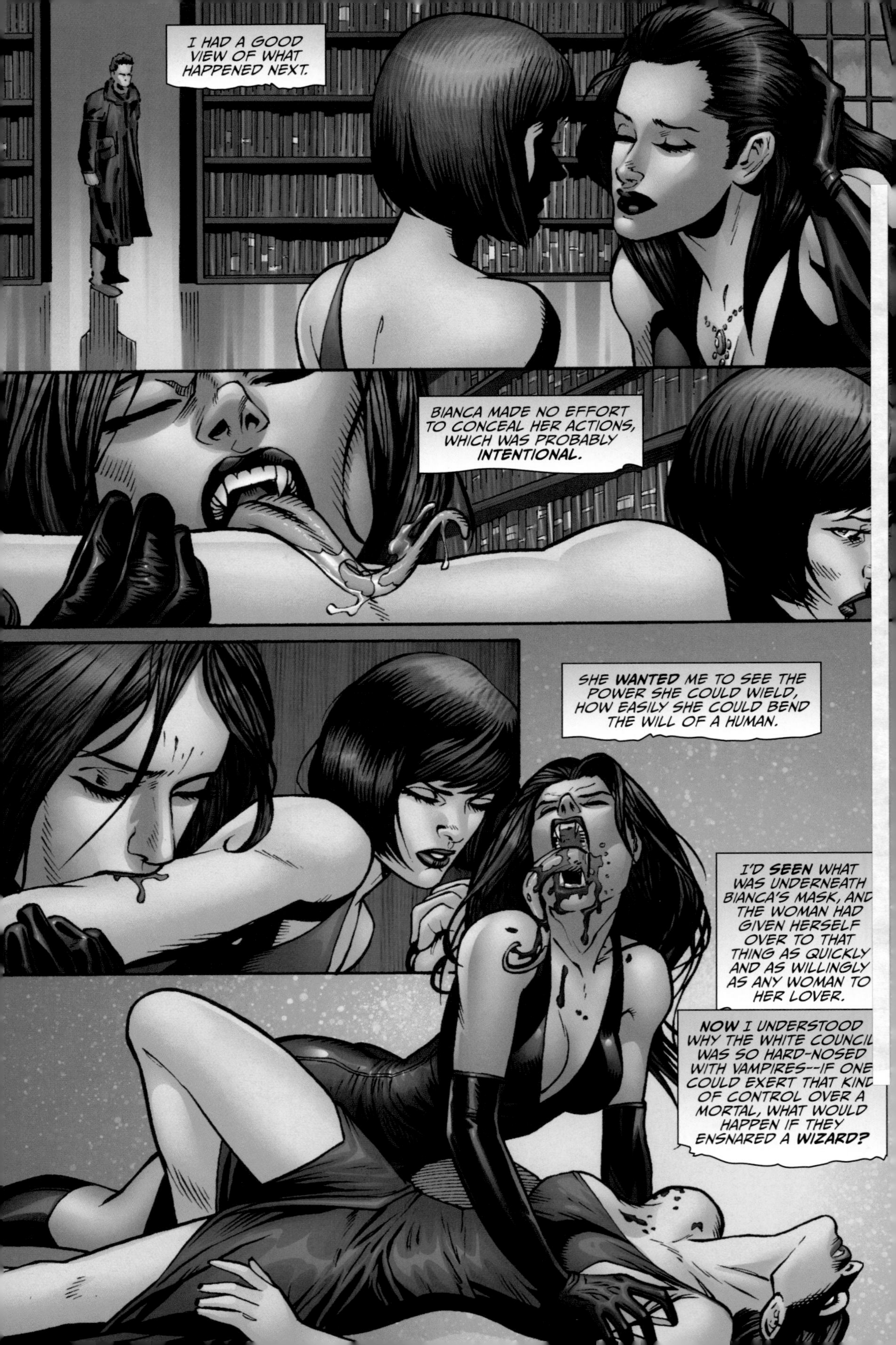
I HAD A GOOD VIEW OF WHAT HAPPENED NEXT.
BIANCA MADE NO EFFORT TO CONCEAL HER ACTIONS, WHICH WAS PROBABLY **INTENTIONAL.**
SHE **WANTED** ME TO SEE THE POWER SHE COULD WIELD, HOW EASILY SHE COULD BEND THE WILL OF A HUMAN.
I'D **SEEN** WHAT WAS UNDERNEATH BIANCA'S MASK, AND THE WOMAN HAD GIVEN HERSELF OVER TO THAT THING AS QUICKLY AND AS WILLINGLY AS ANY WOMAN TO HER LOVER.
NOW I UNDERSTOOD WHY THE WHITE COUNCIL WAS SO HARD-NOSED WITH VAMPIRES--IF ONE COULD EXERT THAT KIND OF CONTROL OVER A MORTAL, WHAT WOULD HAPPEN IF THEY ENSNARED A **WIZARD?**

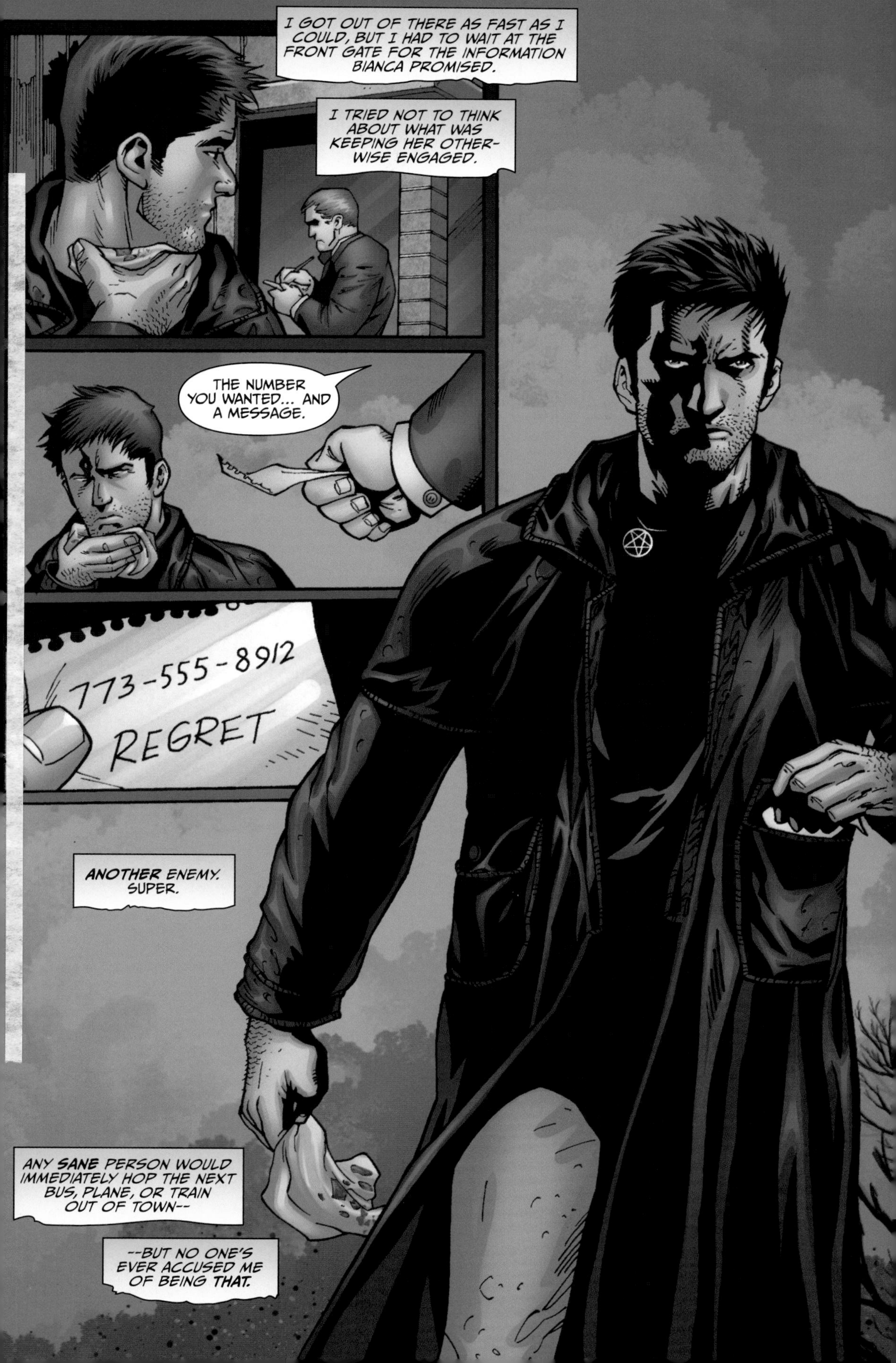
I GOT OUT OF THERE AS FAST AS I COULD, BUT I HAD TO WAIT AT THE FRONT GATE FOR THE INFORMATION BIANCA PROMISED.
I TRIED NOT TO THINK ABOUT WHAT WAS KEEPING HER OTHER-WISE ENGAGED.
THE NUMBER YOU WANTED... AND A MESSAGE.
773-555-8912
REGRET
ANOTHER ENEMY. SUPER.
ANY SANE PERSON WOULD IMMEDIATELY HOP THE NEXT BUS, PLANE, OR TRAIN OUT OF TOWN--
--BUT NO ONE'S EVER ACCUSED ME OF BEING THAT.

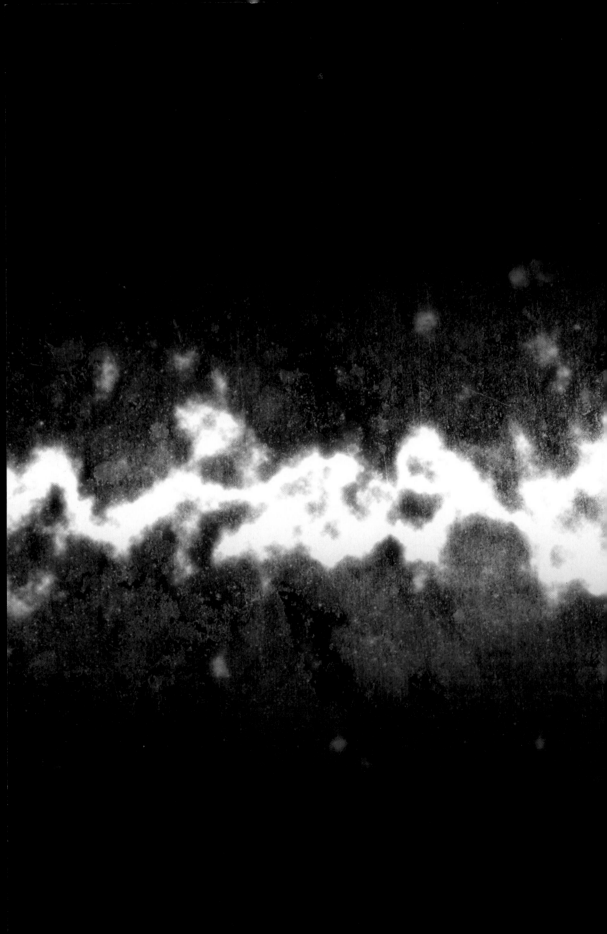

CHAPTER THREE

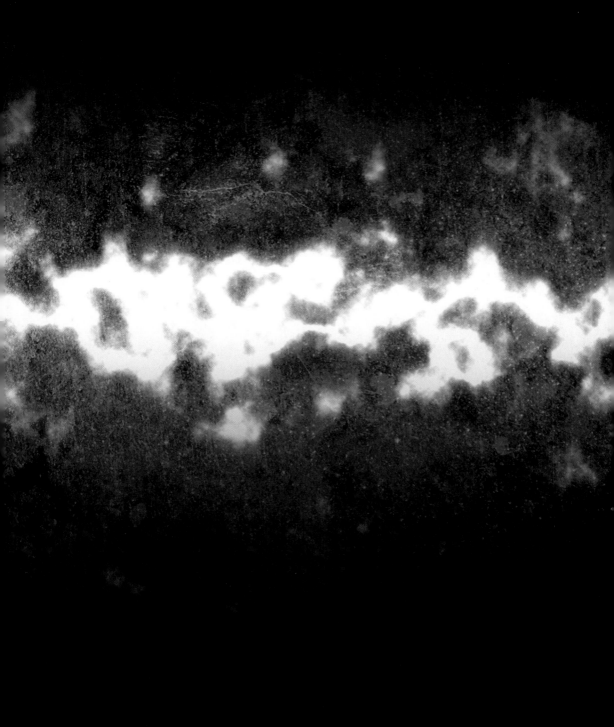

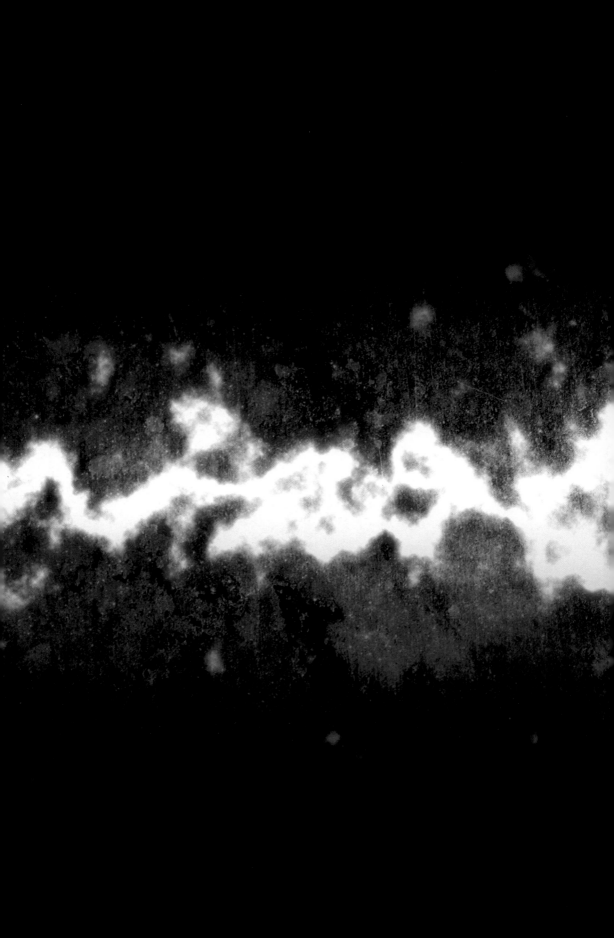

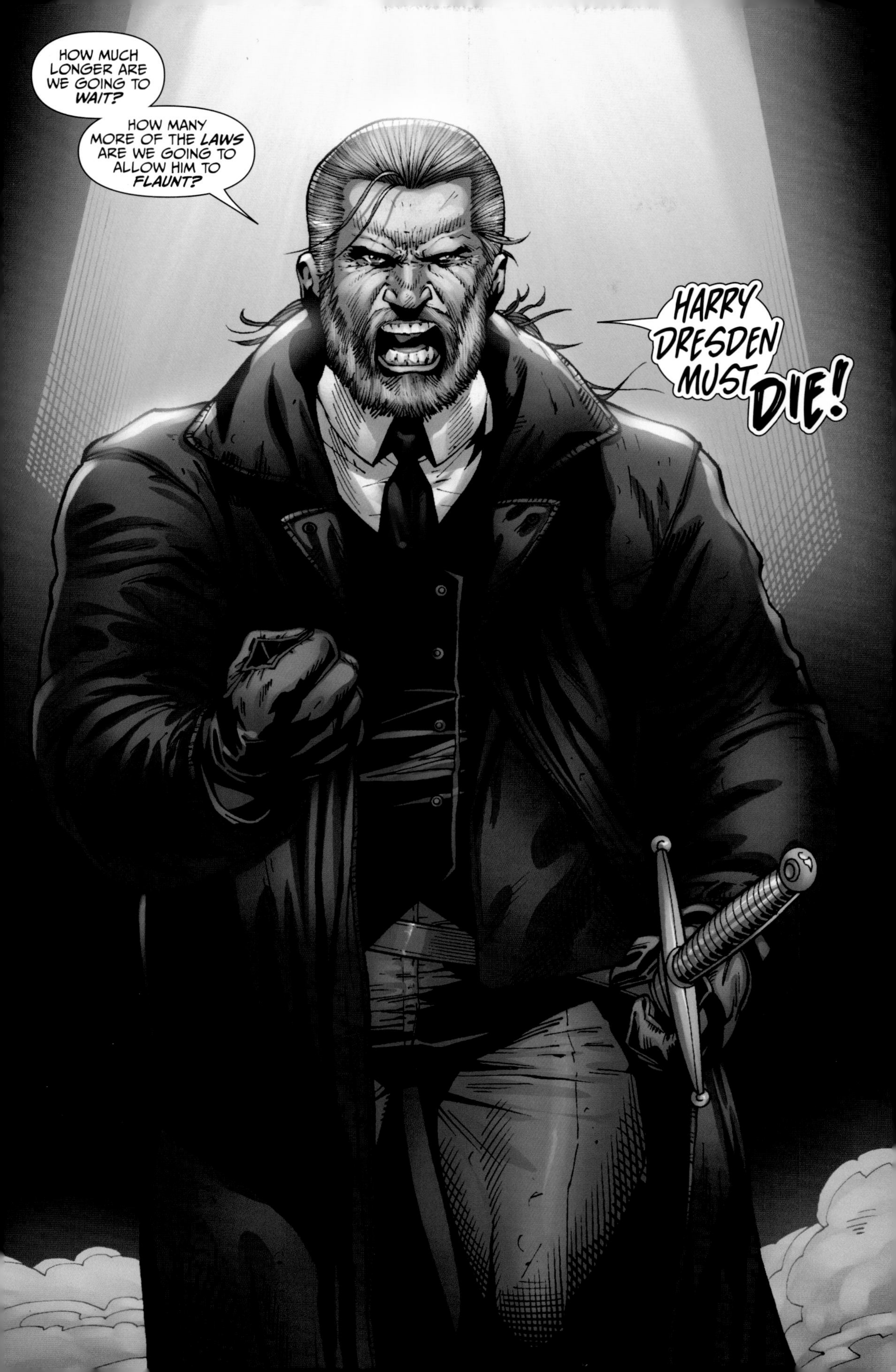
HOW MUCH LONGER ARE WE GOING TO WAIT?
HOW MANY MORE OF THE LAWS ARE WE GOING TO ALLOW HIM TO FLAUNT?
HARRY DRESDEN MUST DIE!

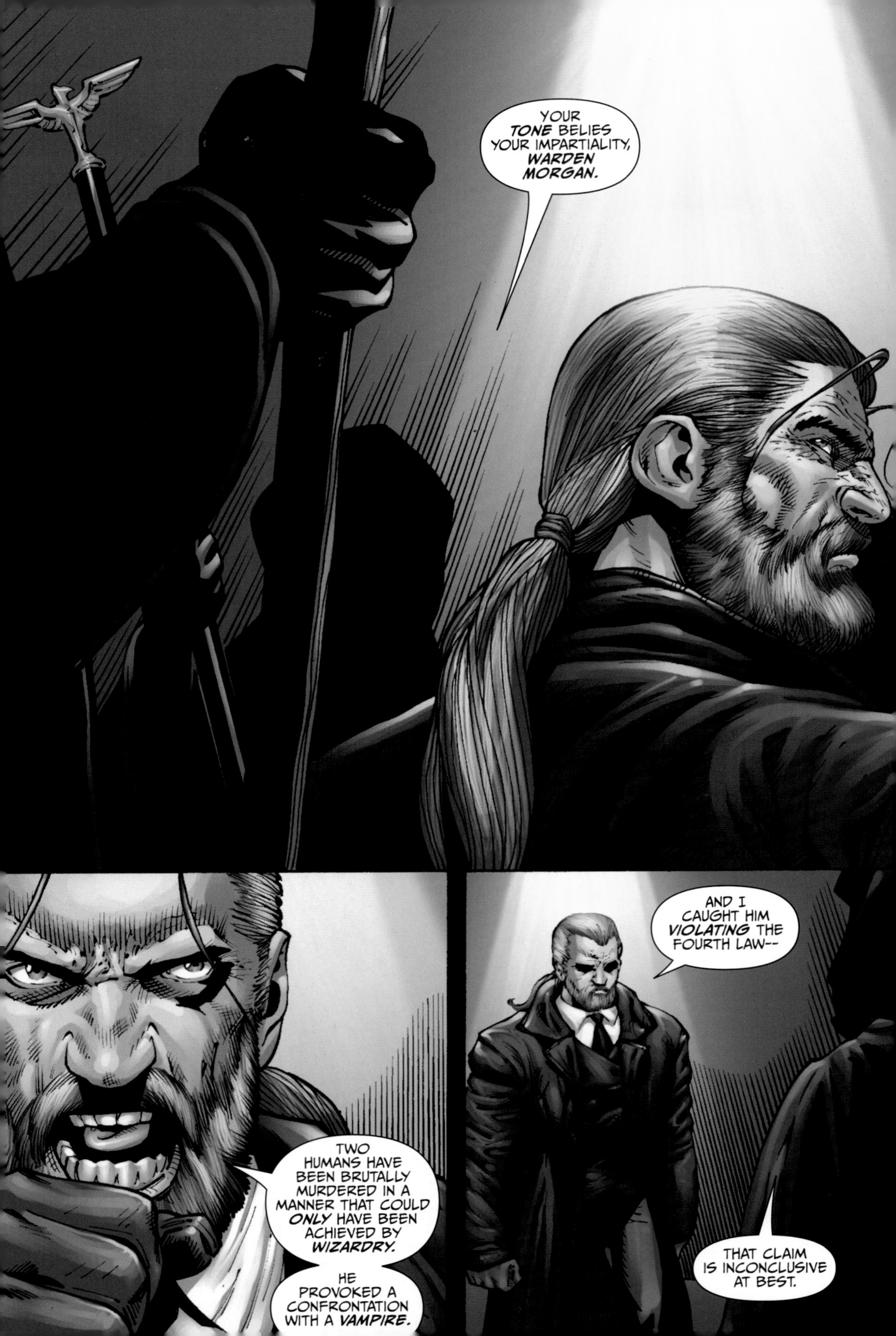
YOUR TONE BELIES YOUR IMPARTIALITY, WARDEN MORGAN.
TWO HUMANS HAVE BEEN BRUTALLY MURDERED IN A MANNER THAT COULD ONLY HAVE BEEN ACHIEVED BY WIZARDRY.
HE PROVOKED A CONFRONTATION WITH A VAMPIRE.
AND I CAUGHT HIM VIOLATING THE FOURTH LAW--
THAT CLAIM IS INCONCLUSIVE AT BEST.

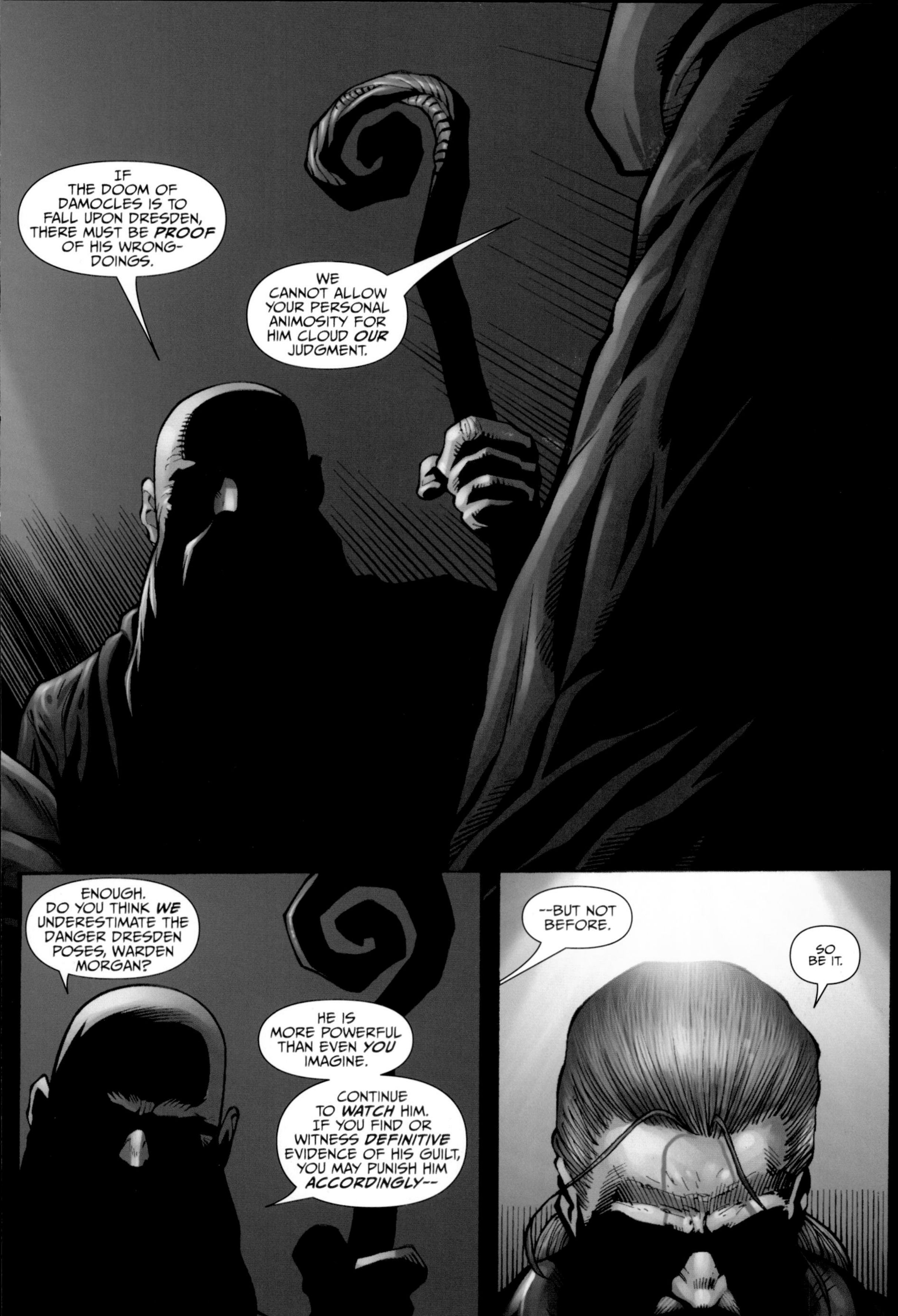
IF THE DOOM OF DAMOCLES IS TO FALL UPON DRESDEN, THERE MUST BE *PROOF* OF HIS WRONG-DOINGS.
WE CANNOT ALLOW YOUR PERSONAL ANIMOSITY FOR HIM CLOUD *OUR* JUDGMENT.
ENOUGH. DO YOU THINK *WE* UNDERESTIMATE THE DANGER DRESDEN POSES, WARDEN MORGAN?
HE IS MORE POWERFUL THAN EVEN *YOU* IMAGINE.
CONTINUE TO *WATCH* HIM. IF YOU FIND OR WITNESS *DEFINITIVE* EVIDENCE OF HIS GUILT, YOU MAY PUNISH HIM *ACCORDINGLY--*
--BUT NOT BEFORE.
SO BE IT.

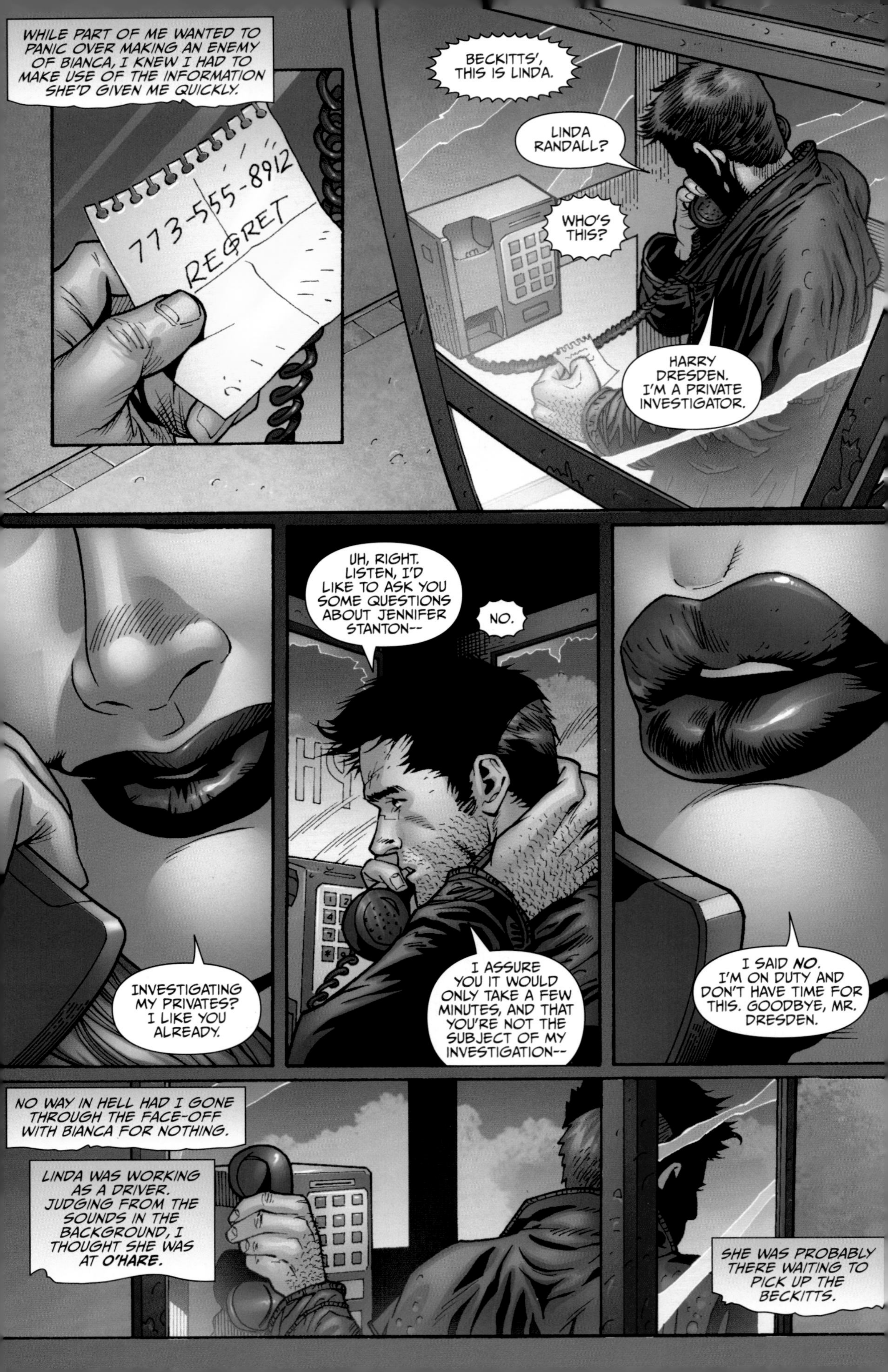
WHILE PART OF ME WANTED TO PANIC OVER MAKING AN ENEMY OF BIANCA, I KNEW I HAD TO MAKE USE OF THE INFORMATION SHE'D GIVEN ME QUICKLY.
773-555-8912
REGRET
BECKITTS', THIS IS LINDA.
LINDA RANDALL?
WHO'S THIS?
HARRY DRESDEN. I'M A PRIVATE INVESTIGATOR.
INVESTIGATING MY PRIVATES? I LIKE YOU ALREADY.
UH, RIGHT. LISTEN, I'D LIKE TO ASK YOU SOME QUESTIONS ABOUT JENNIFER STANTON--
NO.
I ASSURE YOU IT WOULD ONLY TAKE A FEW MINUTES, AND THAT YOU'RE NOT THE SUBJECT OF MY INVESTIGATION--
I SAID NO. I'M ON DUTY AND DON'T HAVE TIME FOR THIS. GOODBYE, MR. DRESDEN.
NO WAY IN HELL HAD I GONE THROUGH THE FACE-OFF WITH BIANCA FOR NOTHING.
LINDA WAS WORKING AS A DRIVER. JUDGING FROM THE SOUNDS IN THE BACKGROUND, I THOUGHT SHE WAS AT O'HARE.
SHE WAS PROBABLY THERE WAITING TO PICK UP THE BECKITTS.

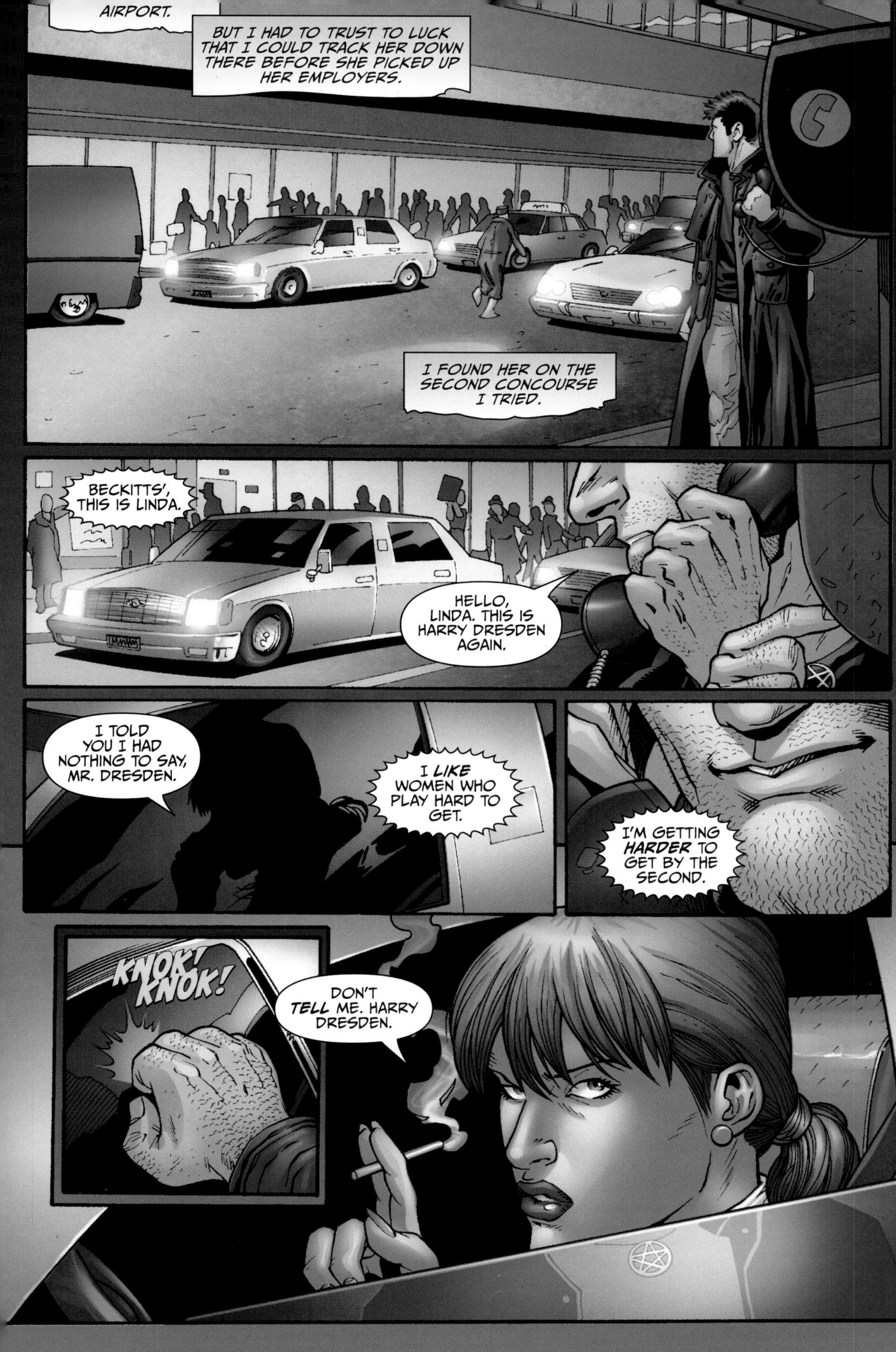

AIRPORT.
BUT I HAD TO TRUST TO LUCK THAT I COULD TRACK HER DOWN THERE BEFORE SHE PICKED UP HER EMPLOYERS.
I FOUND HER ON THE SECOND CONCOURSE I TRIED.
BECKITTS', THIS IS LINDA.
HELLO, LINDA. THIS IS HARRY DRESDEN AGAIN.
I TOLD YOU I HAD NOTHING TO SAY, MR. DRESDEN.
I *LIKE* WOMEN WHO PLAY HARD TO GET.
I'M GETTING *HARDER* TO GET BY THE SECOND.
KNOK! KNOK!
DON'T *TELL* ME. HARRY DRESDEN.

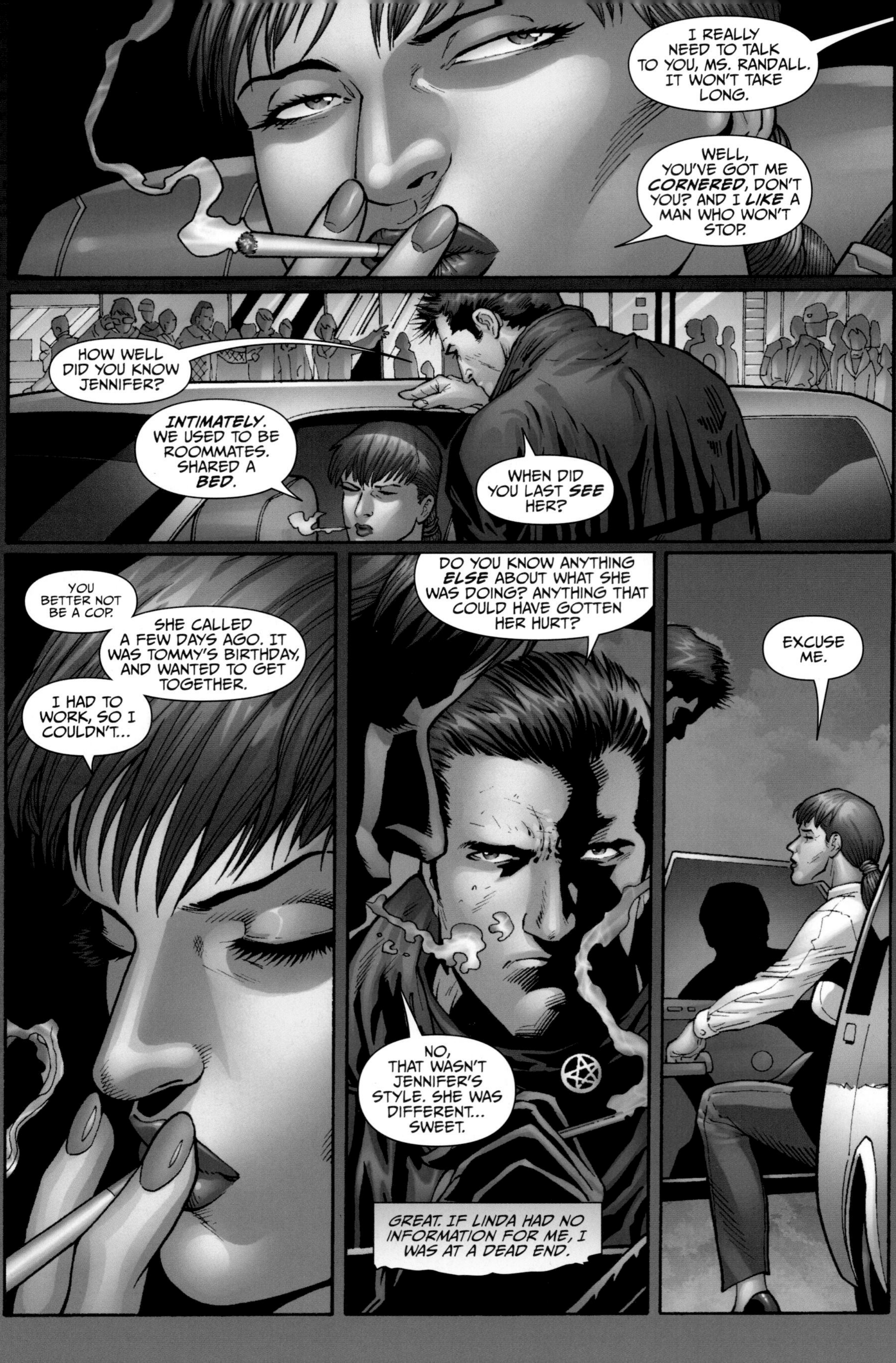
I REALLY NEED TO TALK TO YOU, MS. RANDALL. IT WON'T TAKE LONG.
WELL, YOU'VE GOT ME CORNERED, DON'T YOU? AND I LIKE A MAN WHO WON'T STOP.
HOW WELL DID YOU KNOW JENNIFER?
INTIMATELY. WE USED TO BE ROOMMATES. SHARED A BED.
WHEN DID YOU LAST SEE HER?
YOU BETTER NOT BE A COP.
SHE CALLED A FEW DAYS AGO. IT WAS TOMMY'S BIRTHDAY, AND WANTED TO GET TOGETHER.
I HAD TO WORK, SO I COULDN'T...
DO YOU KNOW ANYTHING ELSE ABOUT WHAT SHE WAS DOING? ANYTHING THAT COULD HAVE GOTTEN HER HURT?
NO, THAT WASN'T JENNIFER'S STYLE. SHE WAS DIFFERENT... SWEET.
GREAT. IF LINDA HAD NO INFORMATION FOR ME, I WAS AT A DEAD END.
EXCUSE ME.

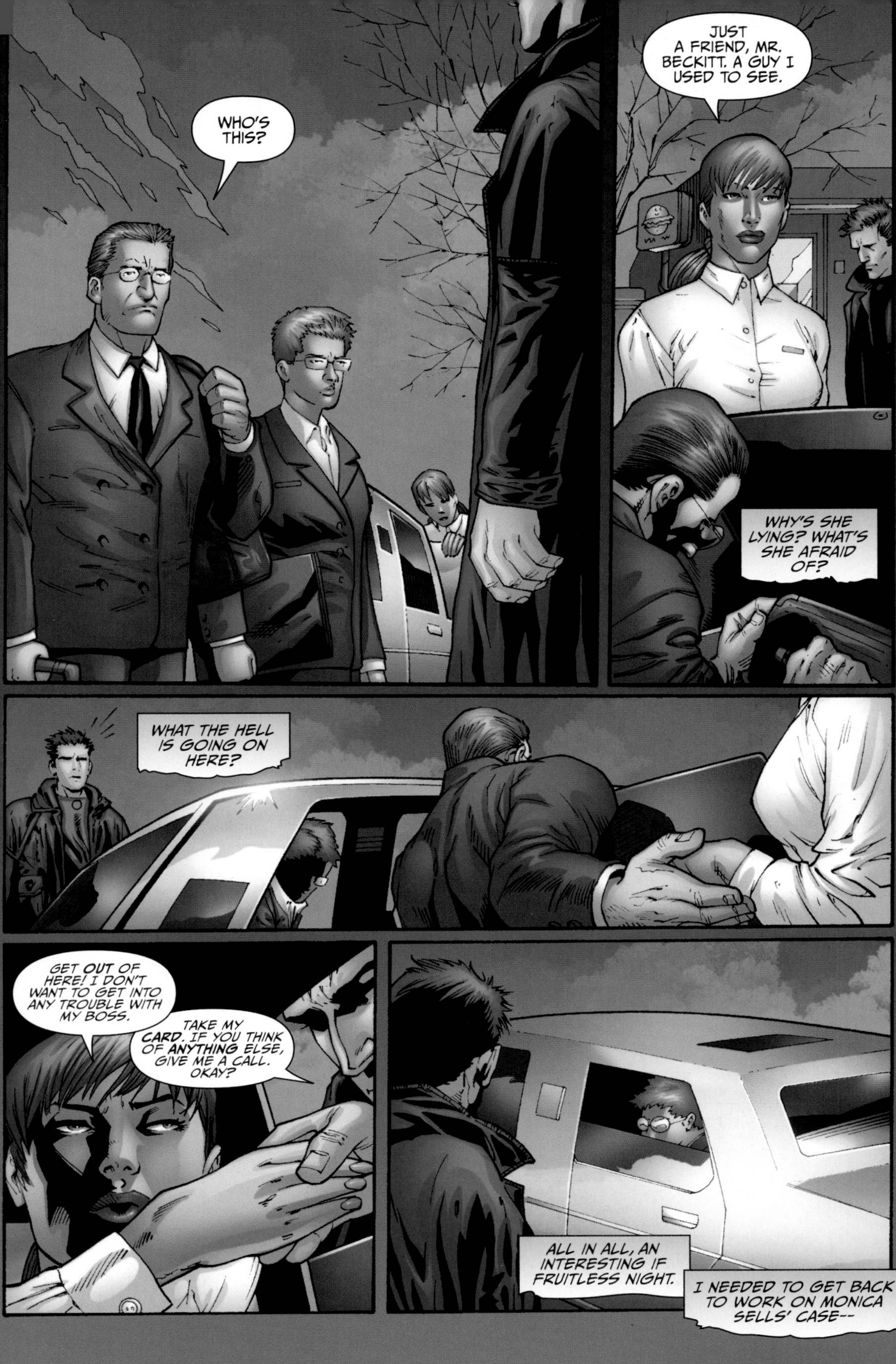
WHO'S THIS?
JUST A FRIEND, MR. BECKITT. A GUY I USED TO SEE.
WHY'S SHE LYING? WHAT'S SHE AFRAID OF?
WHAT THE HELL IS GOING ON HERE?
GET OUT OF HERE! I DON'T WANT TO GET INTO ANY TROUBLE WITH MY BOSS.
TAKE MY CARD. IF YOU THINK OF ANYTHING ELSE, GIVE ME A CALL. OKAY?
ALL IN ALL, AN INTERESTING IF FRUITLESS NIGHT.
I NEEDED TO GET BACK TO WORK ON MONICA SELLS' CASE--

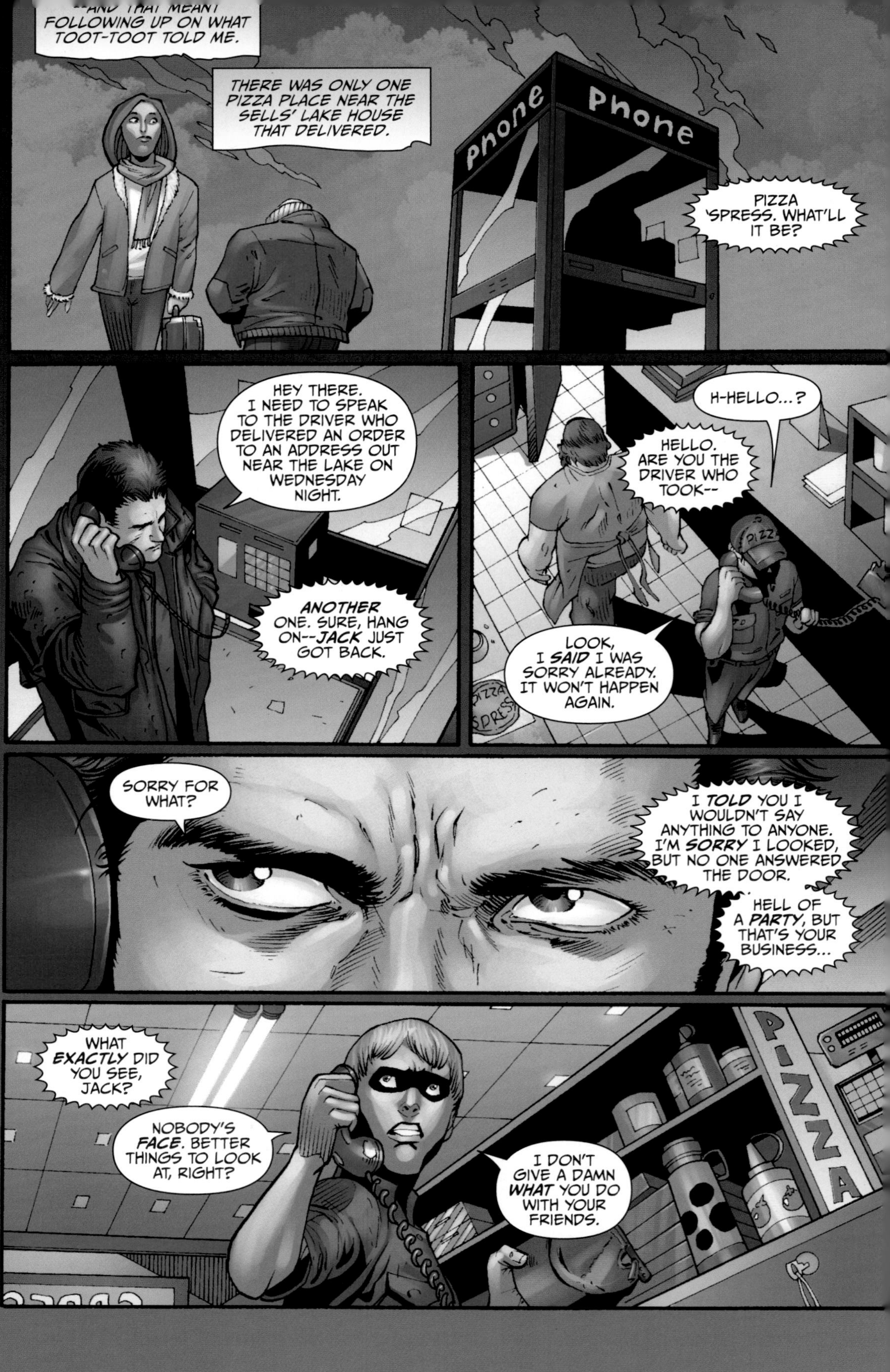
--AND THAT MEANT FOLLOWING UP ON WHAT TOOT-TOOT TOLD ME.
THERE WAS ONLY ONE PIZZA PLACE NEAR THE SELLS' LAKE HOUSE THAT DELIVERED.
Phone
Phone
PIZZA 'SPRESS. WHAT'LL IT BE?
HEY THERE. I NEED TO SPEAK TO THE DRIVER WHO DELIVERED AN ORDER TO AN ADDRESS OUT NEAR THE LAKE ON WEDNESDAY NIGHT.
ANOTHER ONE. SURE, HANG ON--JACK JUST GOT BACK.
H-HELLO...?
HELLO. ARE YOU THE DRIVER WHO TOOK--
LOOK, I SAID I WAS SORRY ALREADY. IT WON'T HAPPEN AGAIN.
PIZZA 'SPRESS
SORRY FOR WHAT?
I TOLD YOU I WOULDN'T SAY ANYTHING TO ANYONE. I'M SORRY I LOOKED, BUT NO ONE ANSWERED THE DOOR.
HELL OF A PARTY, BUT THAT'S YOUR BUSINESS...
WHAT EXACTLY DID YOU SEE, JACK?
NOBODY'S FACE. BETTER THINGS TO LOOK AT, RIGHT?
I DON'T GIVE A DAMN WHAT YOU DO WITH YOUR FRIENDS.
PIZZA

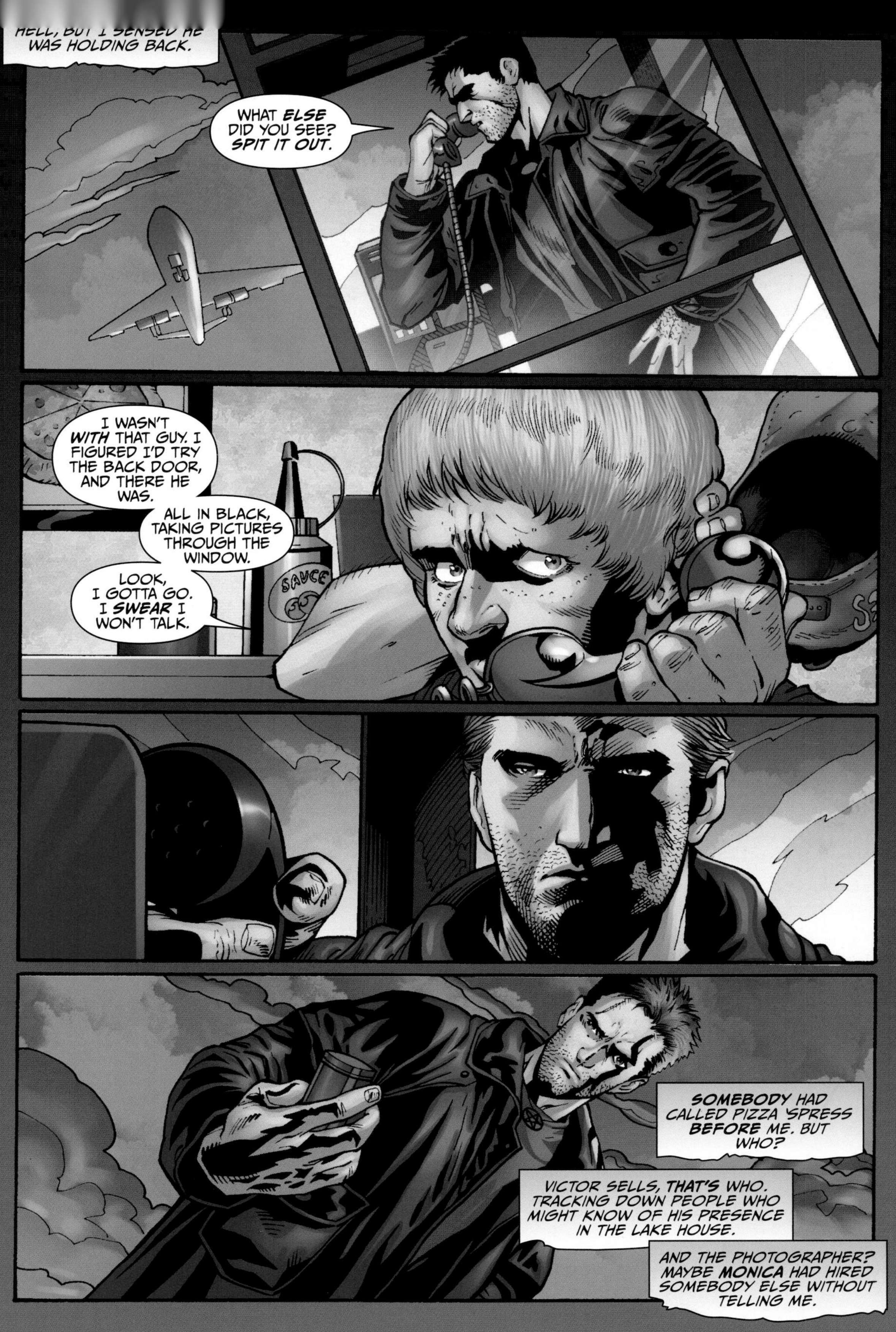
HELL, BUT I SENSED HE WAS HOLDING BACK.
WHAT ELSE DID YOU SEE? SPIT IT OUT.
I WASN'T WITH THAT GUY. I FIGURED I'D TRY THE BACK DOOR, AND THERE HE WAS.
ALL IN BLACK, TAKING PICTURES THROUGH THE WINDOW.
SAUCE
LOOK, I GOTTA GO. I SWEAR I WON'T TALK.
SOMEBODY HAD CALLED PIZZA 'SPRESS BEFORE ME. BUT WHO?
VICTOR SELLS, THAT'S WHO. TRACKING DOWN PEOPLE WHO MIGHT KNOW OF HIS PRESENCE IN THE LAKE HOUSE.
AND THE PHOTOGRAPHER? MAYBE MONICA HAD HIRED SOMEBODY ELSE WITHOUT TELLING ME.

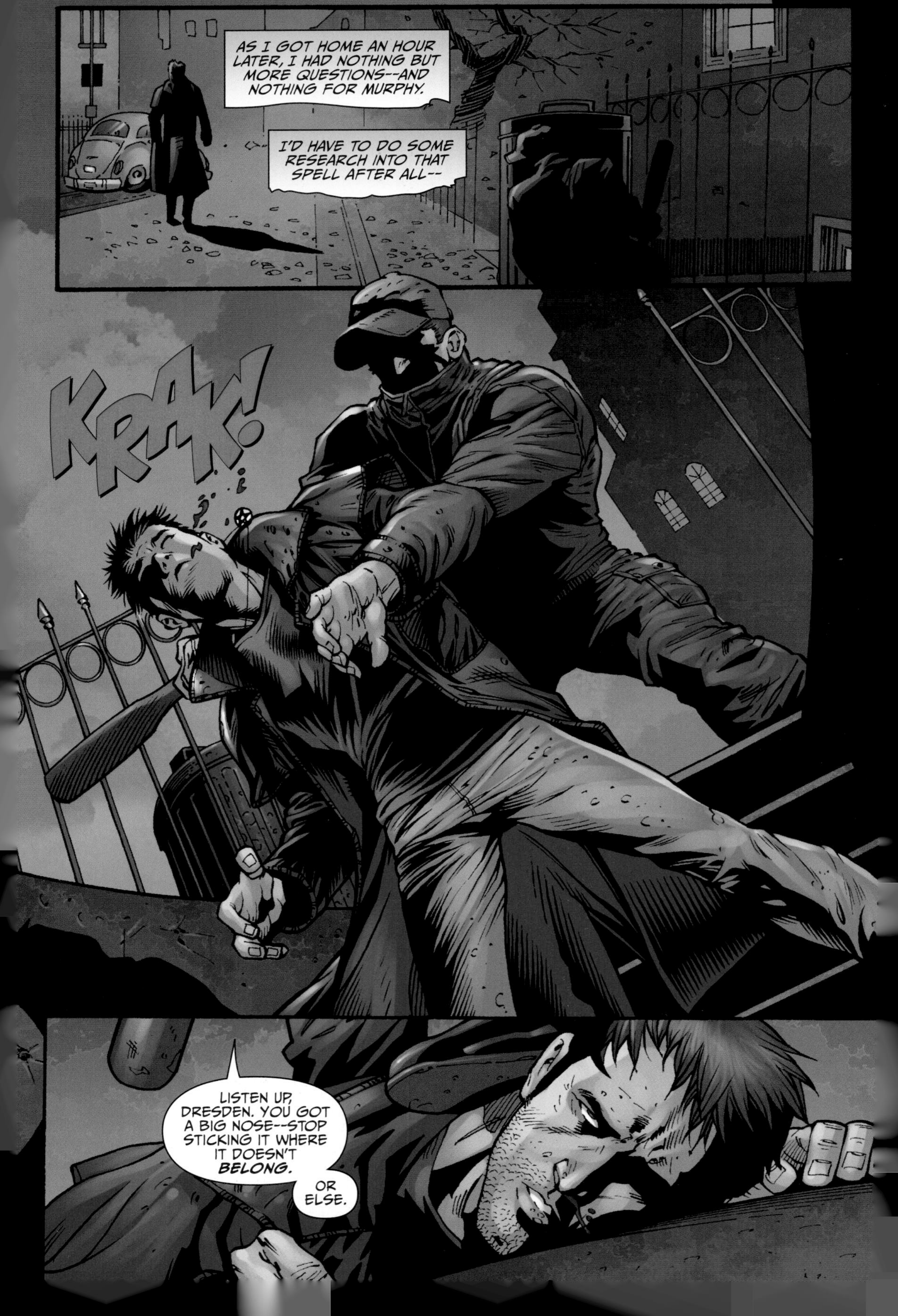

AS I GOT HOME AN HOUR LATER, I HAD NOTHING BUT MORE QUESTIONS--AND NOTHING FOR MURPHY.
I'D HAVE TO DO SOME RESEARCH INTO THAT SPELL AFTER ALL--
KRAK!
LISTEN UP, DRESDEN. YOU GOT A BIG NOSE--STOP STICKING IT WHERE IT DOESN'T **BELONG.**
OR ELSE.

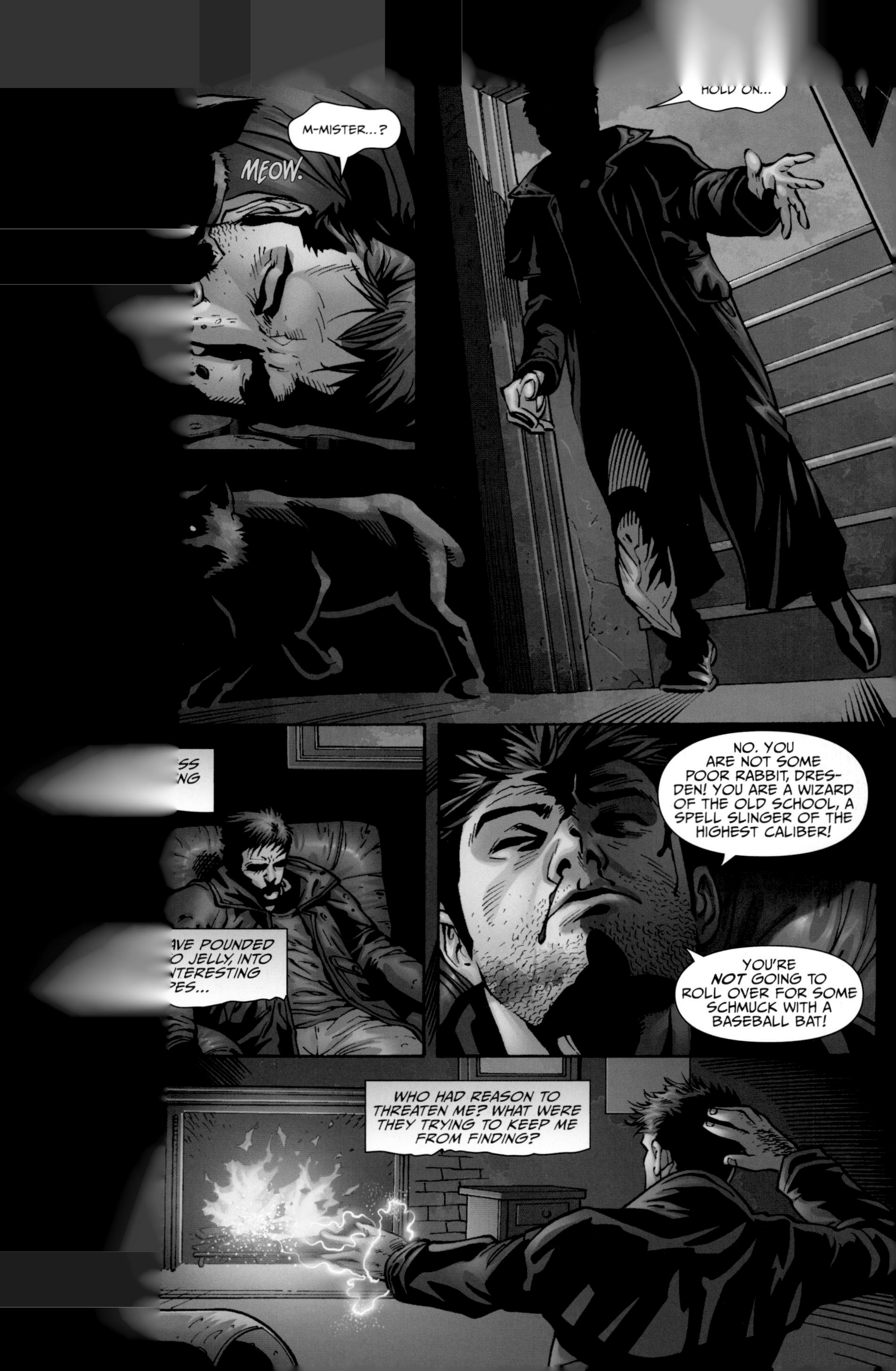
MEOW.
M-MISTER...?
HOLD ON...
AVE POUNDED
O JELLY, INTO
NTERESTING
PES...
NO. YOU ARE NOT SOME POOR RABBIT, DRES-DEN! YOU ARE A WIZARD OF THE OLD SCHOOL, A SPELL SLINGER OF THE HIGHEST CALIBER!
YOU'RE NOT GOING TO ROLL OVER FOR SOME SCHMUCK WITH A BASEBALL BAT!
WHO HAD REASON TO THREATEN ME? WHAT WERE THEY TRYING TO KEEP ME FROM FINDING?

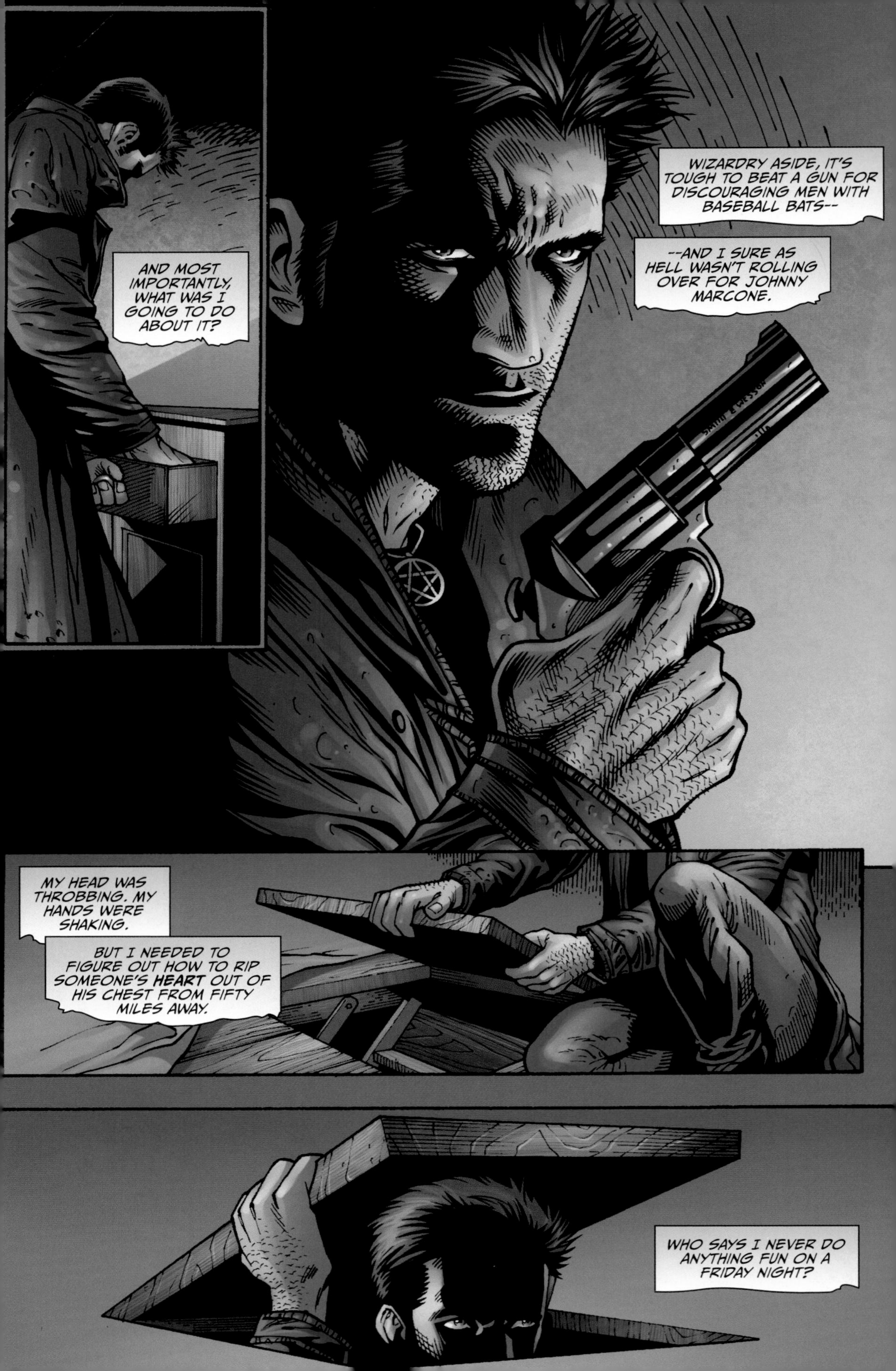
AND MOST IMPORTANTLY, WHAT WAS I GOING TO DO ABOUT IT?
WIZARDRY ASIDE, IT'S TOUGH TO BEAT A GUN FOR DISCOURAGING MEN WITH BASEBALL BATS--
--AND I SURE AS HELL WASN'T ROLLING OVER FOR JOHNNY MARCONE.
MY HEAD WAS THROBBING. MY HANDS WERE SHAKING.
BUT I NEEDED TO FIGURE OUT HOW TO RIP SOMEONE'S **HEART** OUT OF HIS CHEST FROM FIFTY MILES AWAY.
WHO SAYS I NEVER DO ANYTHING FUN ON A FRIDAY NIGHT?

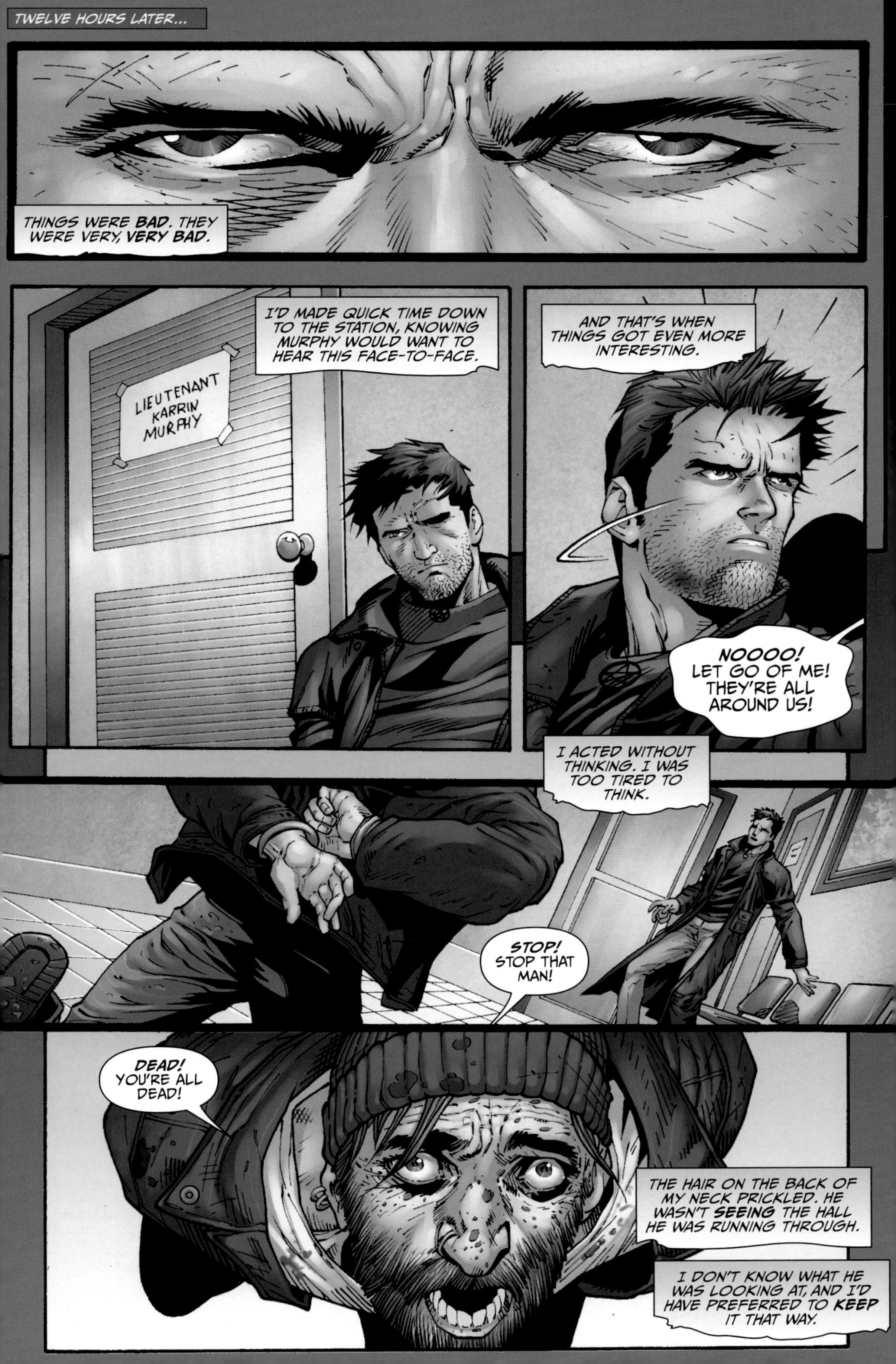
TWELVE HOURS LATER...
THINGS WERE BAD. THEY WERE VERY, VERY BAD.
LIEUTENANT KARRIN MURPHY
I'D MADE QUICK TIME DOWN TO THE STATION, KNOWING MURPHY WOULD WANT TO HEAR THIS FACE-TO-FACE.
AND THAT'S WHEN THINGS GOT EVEN MORE INTERESTING.
NOOOO! LET GO OF ME! THEY'RE ALL AROUND US!
I ACTED WITHOUT THINKING. I WAS TOO TIRED TO THINK.
STOP! STOP THAT MAN!
DEAD! YOU'RE ALL DEAD!
THE HAIR ON THE BACK OF MY NECK PRICKLED. HE WASN'T SEEING THE HALL HE WAS RUNNING THROUGH.
I DON'T KNOW WHAT HE WAS LOOKING AT, AND I'D HAVE PREFERRED TO KEEP IT THAT WAY.

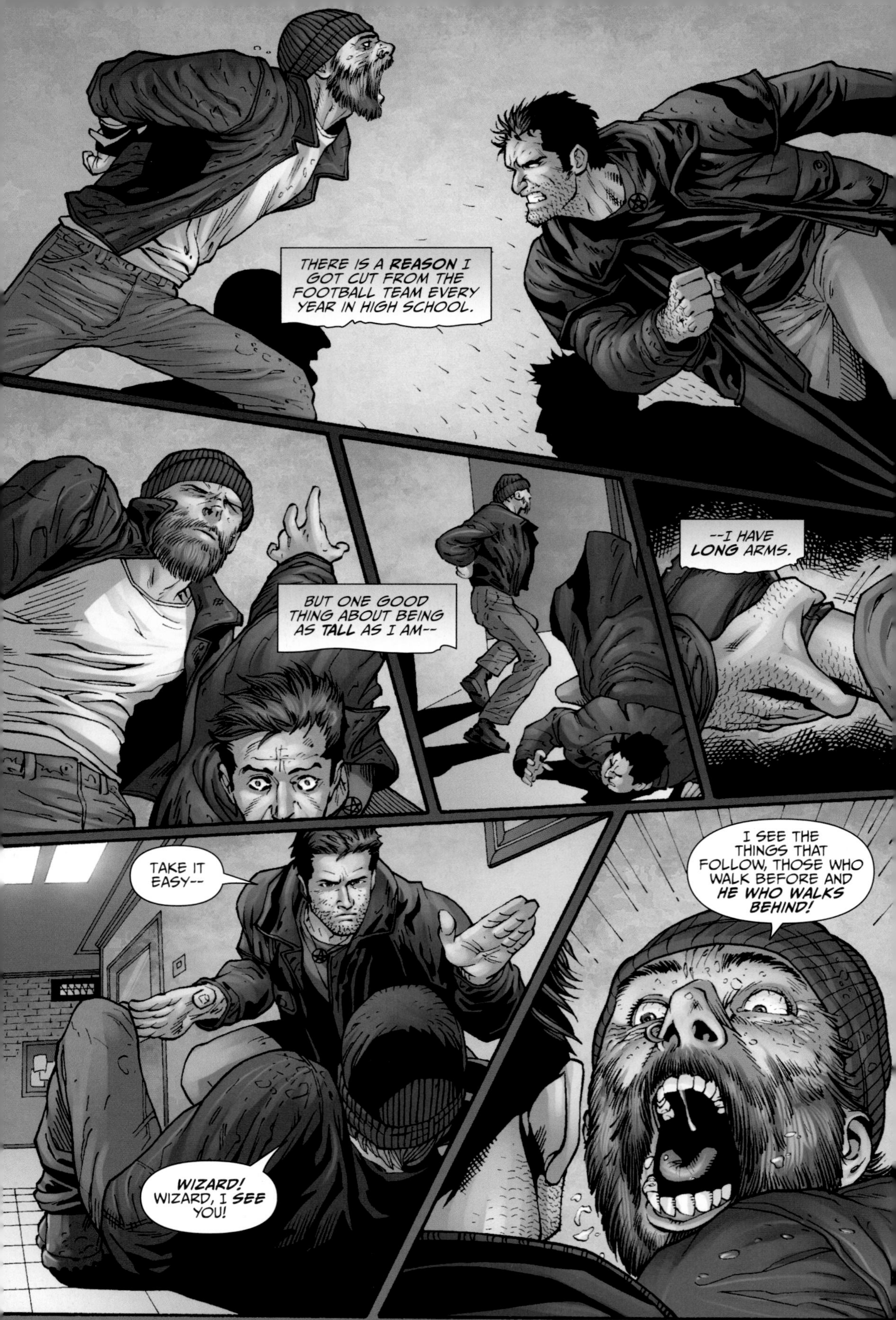
THERE IS A REASON I GOT CUT FROM THE FOOTBALL TEAM EVERY YEAR IN HIGH SCHOOL.
BUT ONE GOOD THING ABOUT BEING AS TALL AS I AM--
--I HAVE LONG ARMS.
TAKE IT EASY--
WIZARD! WIZARD, I SEE YOU!
I SEE THE THINGS THAT FOLLOW, THOSE WHO WALK BEFORE AND HE WHO WALKS BEHIND!

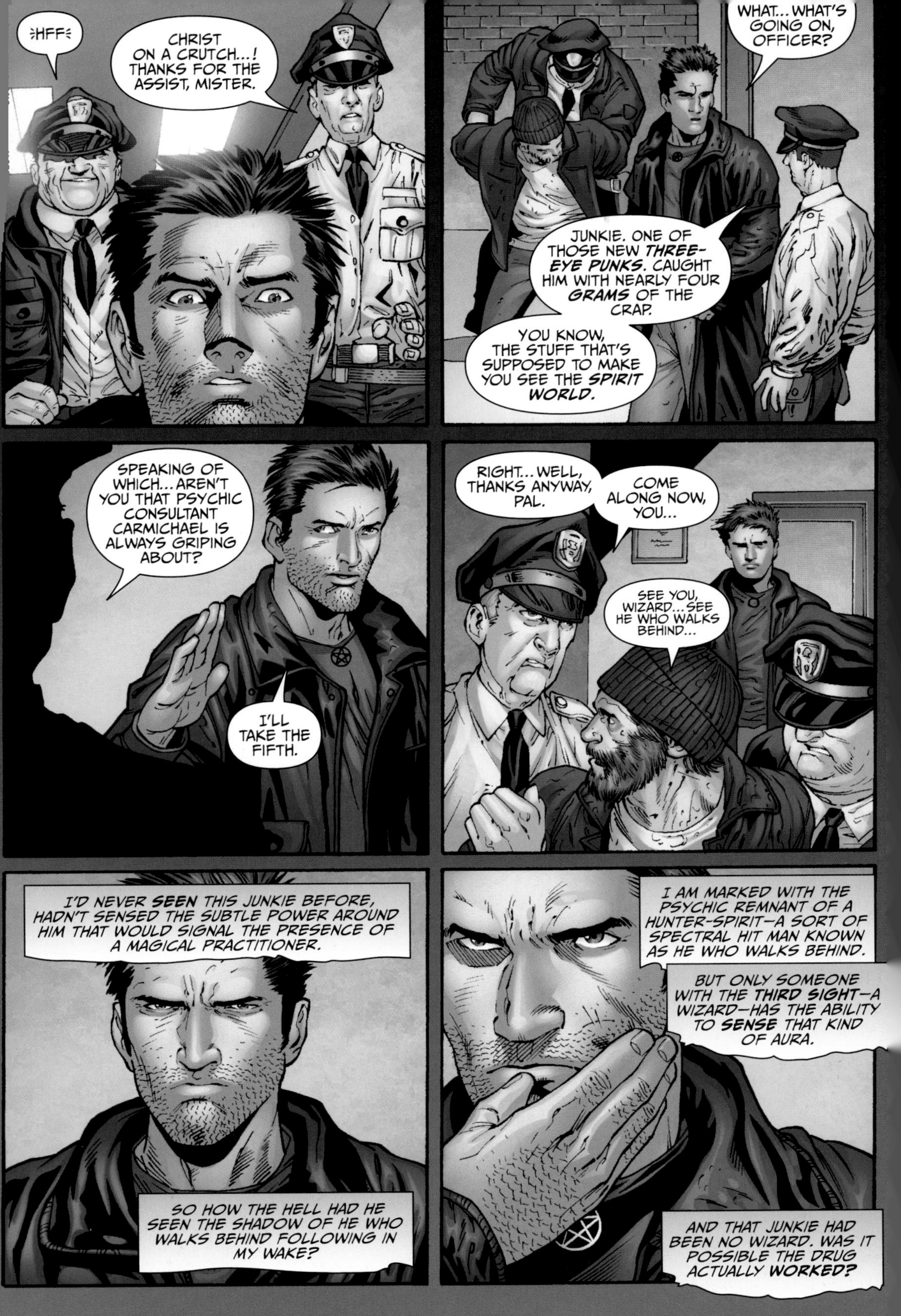

HFF
CHRIST ON A CRUTCH...! THANKS FOR THE ASSIST, MISTER.
WHAT... WHAT'S GOING ON, OFFICER?
JUNKIE. ONE OF THOSE NEW **THREE-EYE PUNKS.** CAUGHT HIM WITH NEARLY FOUR **GRAMS** OF THE CRAP.
YOU KNOW, THE STUFF THAT'S SUPPOSED TO MAKE YOU SEE THE **SPIRIT WORLD.**
SPEAKING OF WHICH... AREN'T YOU THAT PSYCHIC CONSULTANT CARMICHAEL IS ALWAYS GRIPING ABOUT?
I'LL TAKE THE FIFTH.
RIGHT... WELL, THANKS ANYWAY, PAL.
COME ALONG NOW, YOU...
SEE YOU, WIZARD... SEE HE WHO WALKS BEHIND...
I'D NEVER **SEEN** THIS JUNKIE BEFORE, HADN'T SENSED THE SUBTLE POWER AROUND HIM THAT WOULD SIGNAL THE PRESENCE OF A MAGICAL PRACTITIONER.
SO HOW THE HELL HAD HE SEEN THE SHADOW OF HE WHO WALKS BEHIND FOLLOWING IN MY WAKE?
I AM MARKED WITH THE PSYCHIC REMNANT OF A HUNTER-SPIRIT—A SORT OF SPECTRAL HIT MAN KNOWN AS HE WHO WALKS BEHIND.
BUT ONLY SOMEONE WITH THE **THIRD SIGHT**—A WIZARD—HAS THE ABILITY TO **SENSE** THAT KIND OF AURA.
AND THAT JUNKIE HAD BEEN NO WIZARD. WAS IT POSSIBLE THE DRUG ACTUALLY **WORKED?**

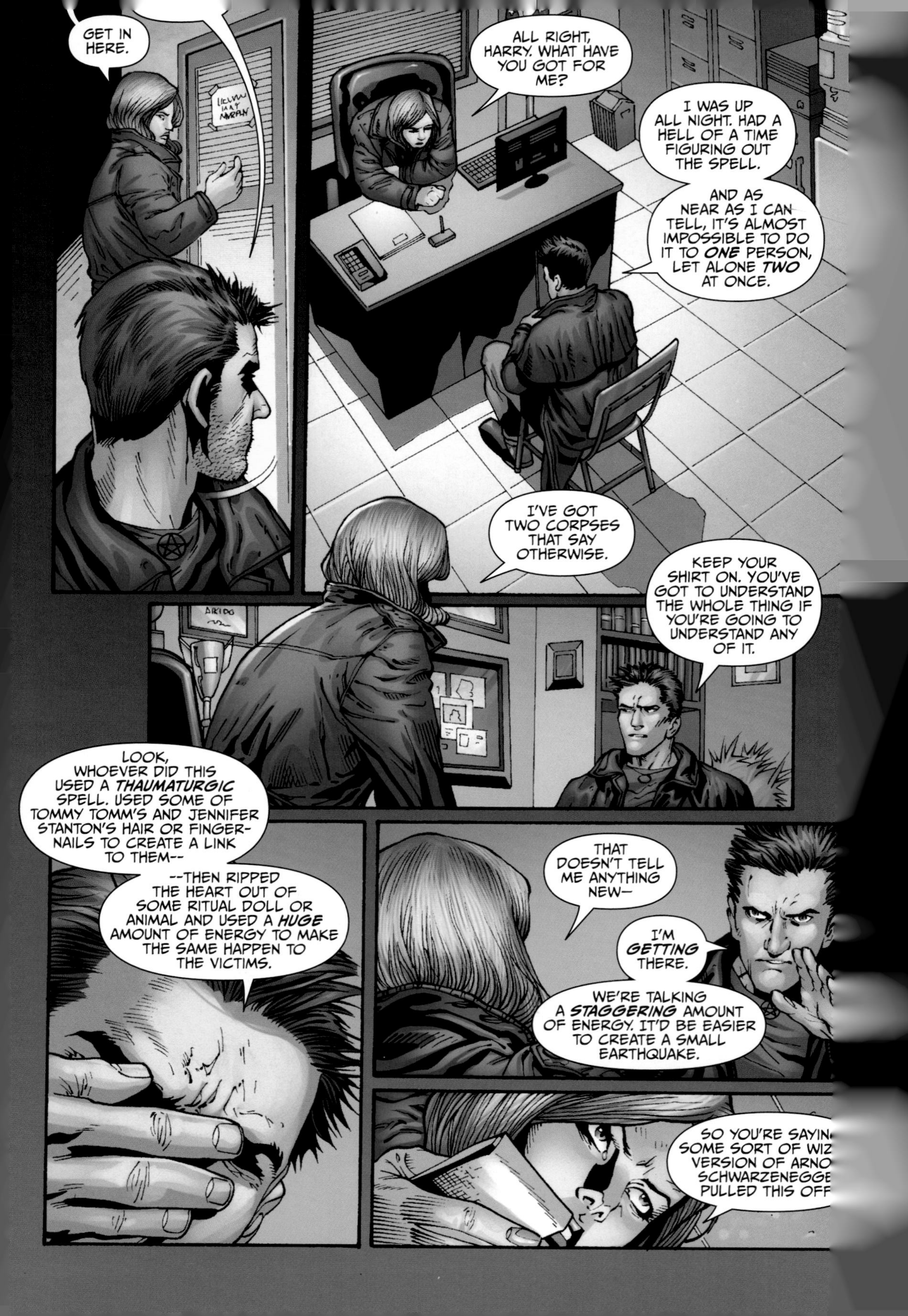
GET IN HERE.
ALL RIGHT, HARRY. WHAT HAVE YOU GOT FOR ME?
I WAS UP ALL NIGHT. HAD A HELL OF A TIME FIGURING OUT THE SPELL.
AND AS NEAR AS I CAN TELL, IT'S ALMOST IMPOSSIBLE TO DO IT TO *ONE* PERSON, LET ALONE *TWO* AT ONCE.
I'VE GOT TWO CORPSES THAT SAY OTHERWISE.
KEEP YOUR SHIRT ON. YOU'VE GOT TO UNDERSTAND THE WHOLE THING IF YOU'RE GOING TO UNDERSTAND ANY OF IT.
LOOK, WHOEVER DID THIS USED A *THAUMATURGIC* SPELL. USED SOME OF TOMMY TOMM'S AND JENNIFER STANTON'S HAIR OR FINGER-NAILS TO CREATE A LINK TO THEM--
--THEN RIPPED THE HEART OUT OF SOME RITUAL DOLL OR ANIMAL AND USED A *HUGE* AMOUNT OF ENERGY TO MAKE THE SAME HAPPEN TO THE VICTIMS.
THAT DOESN'T TELL ME ANYTHING NEW—
I'M *GETTING* THERE.
WE'RE TALKING A *STAGGERING* AMOUNT OF ENERGY. IT'D BE EASIER TO CREATE A SMALL EARTHQUAKE.
SO YOU'RE SAYIN SOME SORT OF WIZ VERSION OF ARNO SCHWARZENEGGE PULLED THIS OFF

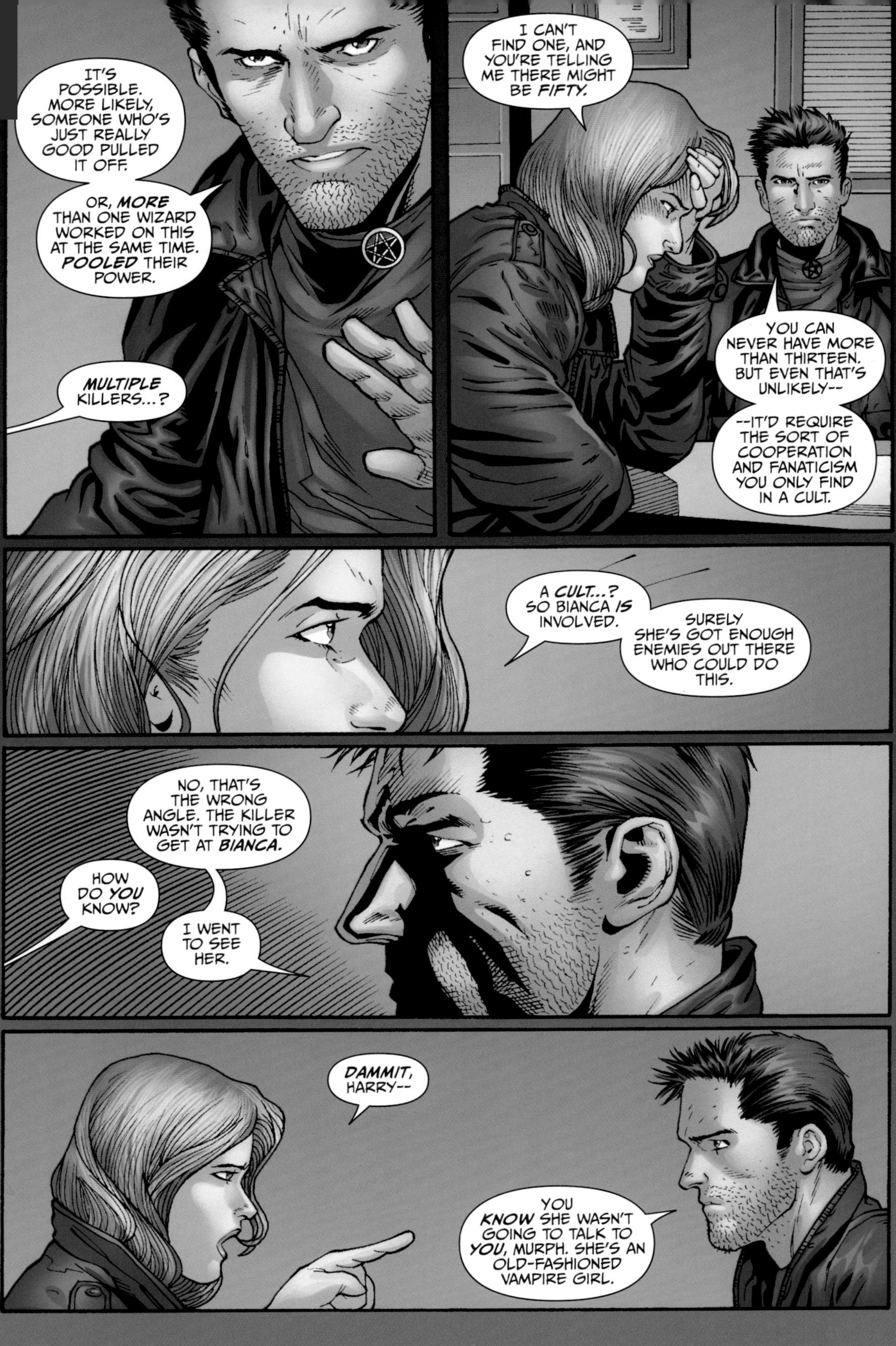
IT'S POSSIBLE. MORE LIKELY, SOMEONE WHO'S JUST REALLY GOOD PULLED IT OFF.
OR, **MORE** THAN ONE WIZARD WORKED ON THIS AT THE SAME TIME. **POOLED** THEIR POWER.
MULTIPLE KILLERS...?
I CAN'T FIND ONE, AND YOU'RE TELLING ME THERE MIGHT BE **FIFTY.**
YOU CAN NEVER HAVE MORE THAN THIRTEEN. BUT EVEN THAT'S UNLIKELY--
--IT'D REQUIRE THE SORT OF COOPERATION AND FANATICISM YOU ONLY FIND IN A CULT.
A **CULT...?** SO BIANCA **IS** INVOLVED.
SURELY SHE'S GOT ENOUGH ENEMIES OUT THERE WHO COULD DO THIS.
NO, THAT'S THE WRONG ANGLE. THE KILLER WASN'T TRYING TO GET AT **BIANCA.**
HOW DO **YOU** KNOW?
I WENT TO SEE HER.
DAMMIT, HARRY--
YOU **KNOW** SHE WASN'T GOING TO TALK TO **YOU**, MURPH. SHE'S AN OLD-FASHIONED VAMPIRE GIRL.

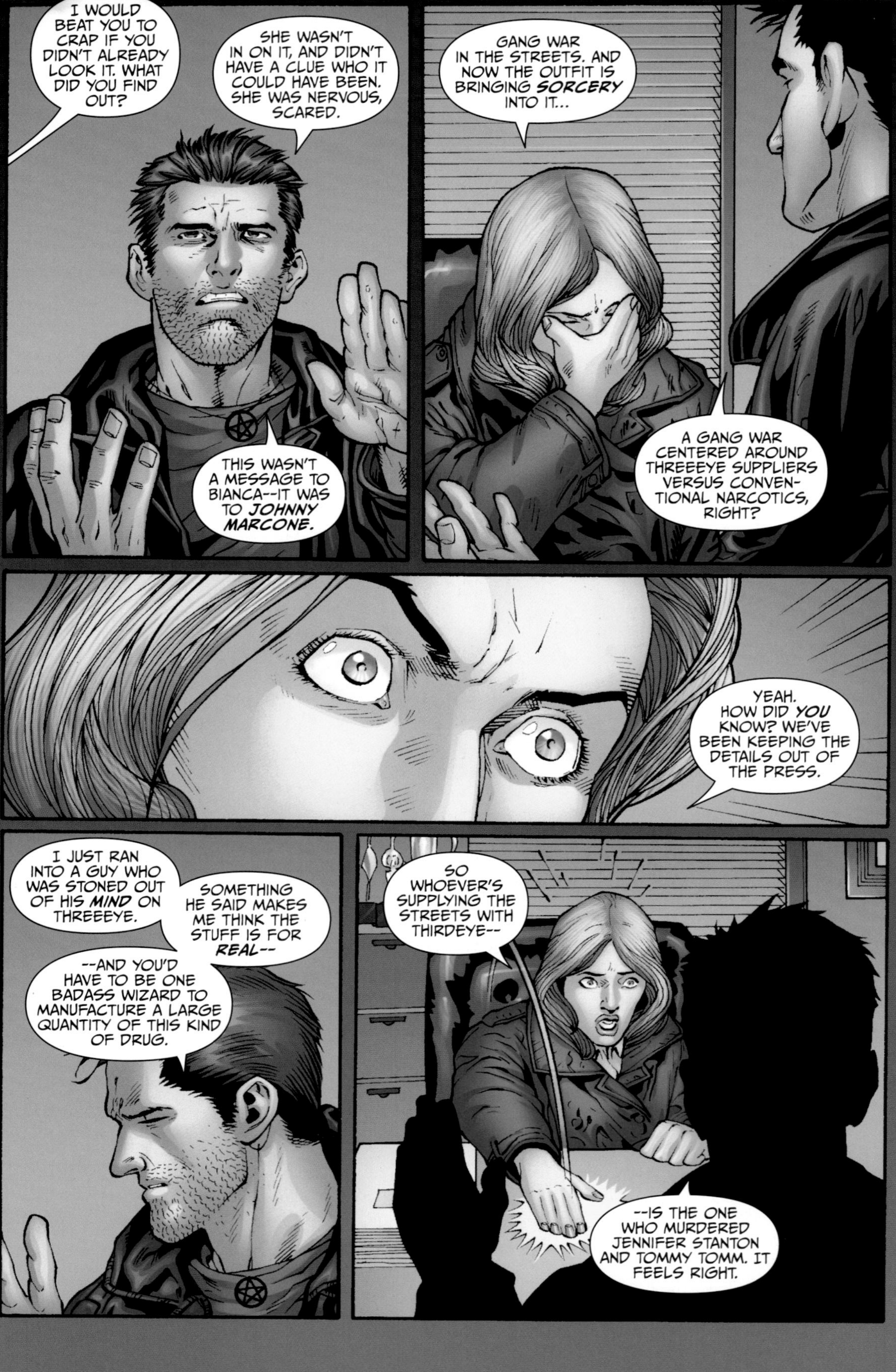
I WOULD BEAT YOU TO CRAP IF YOU DIDN'T ALREADY LOOK IT. WHAT DID YOU FIND OUT?
SHE WASN'T IN ON IT, AND DIDN'T HAVE A CLUE WHO IT COULD HAVE BEEN. SHE WAS NERVOUS, SCARED.
THIS WASN'T A MESSAGE TO BIANCA--IT WAS TO *JOHNNY MARCONE.*
GANG WAR IN THE STREETS. AND NOW THE OUTFIT IS BRINGING *SORCERY* INTO IT...
A GANG WAR CENTERED AROUND THREEEYE SUPPLIERS VERSUS CONVEN-TIONAL NARCOTICS, RIGHT?
YEAH. HOW DID *YOU* KNOW? WE'VE BEEN KEEPING THE DETAILS OUT OF THE PRESS.
I JUST RAN INTO A GUY WHO WAS STONED OUT OF HIS *MIND* ON THREEEYE.
SOMETHING HE SAID MAKES ME THINK THE STUFF IS FOR *REAL*--
--AND YOU'D HAVE TO BE ONE BADASS WIZARD TO MANUFACTURE A LARGE QUANTITY OF THIS KIND OF DRUG.
SO WHOEVER'S SUPPLYING THE STREETS WITH THIRDEYE--
--IS THE ONE WHO MURDERED JENNIFER STANTON AND TOMMY TOMM. IT FEELS RIGHT.

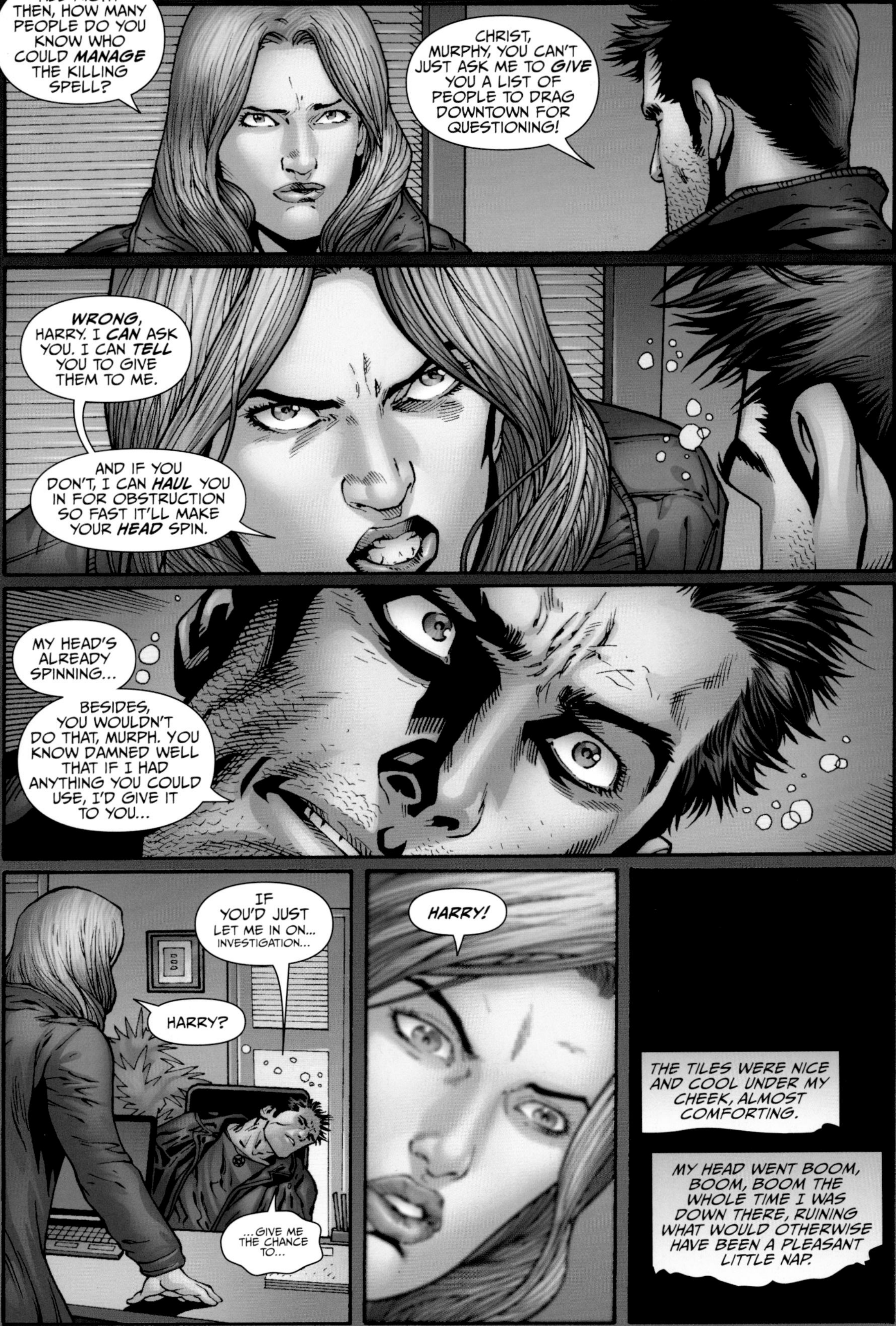
ALL RIGHT THEN, HOW MANY PEOPLE DO YOU KNOW WHO COULD MANAGE THE KILLING SPELL?
CHRIST, MURPHY, YOU CAN'T JUST ASK ME TO GIVE YOU A LIST OF PEOPLE TO DRAG DOWNTOWN FOR QUESTIONING!
WRONG, HARRY. I CAN ASK YOU. I CAN TELL YOU TO GIVE THEM TO ME.
AND IF YOU DON'T, I CAN HAUL YOU IN FOR OBSTRUCTION SO FAST IT'LL MAKE YOUR HEAD SPIN.
MY HEAD'S ALREADY SPINNING...
BESIDES, YOU WOULDN'T DO THAT, MURPH. YOU KNOW DAMNED WELL THAT IF I HAD ANYTHING YOU COULD USE, I'D GIVE IT TO YOU...
IF YOU'D JUST LET ME IN ON... INVESTIGATION...
HARRY?
...GIVE ME THE CHANCE TO...
HARRY!
THE TILES WERE NICE AND COOL UNDER MY CHEEK, ALMOST COMFORTING.
MY HEAD WENT BOOM, BOOM, BOOM THE WHOLE TIME I WAS DOWN THERE, RUINING WHAT WOULD OTHERWISE HAVE BEEN A PLEASANT LITTLE NAP.

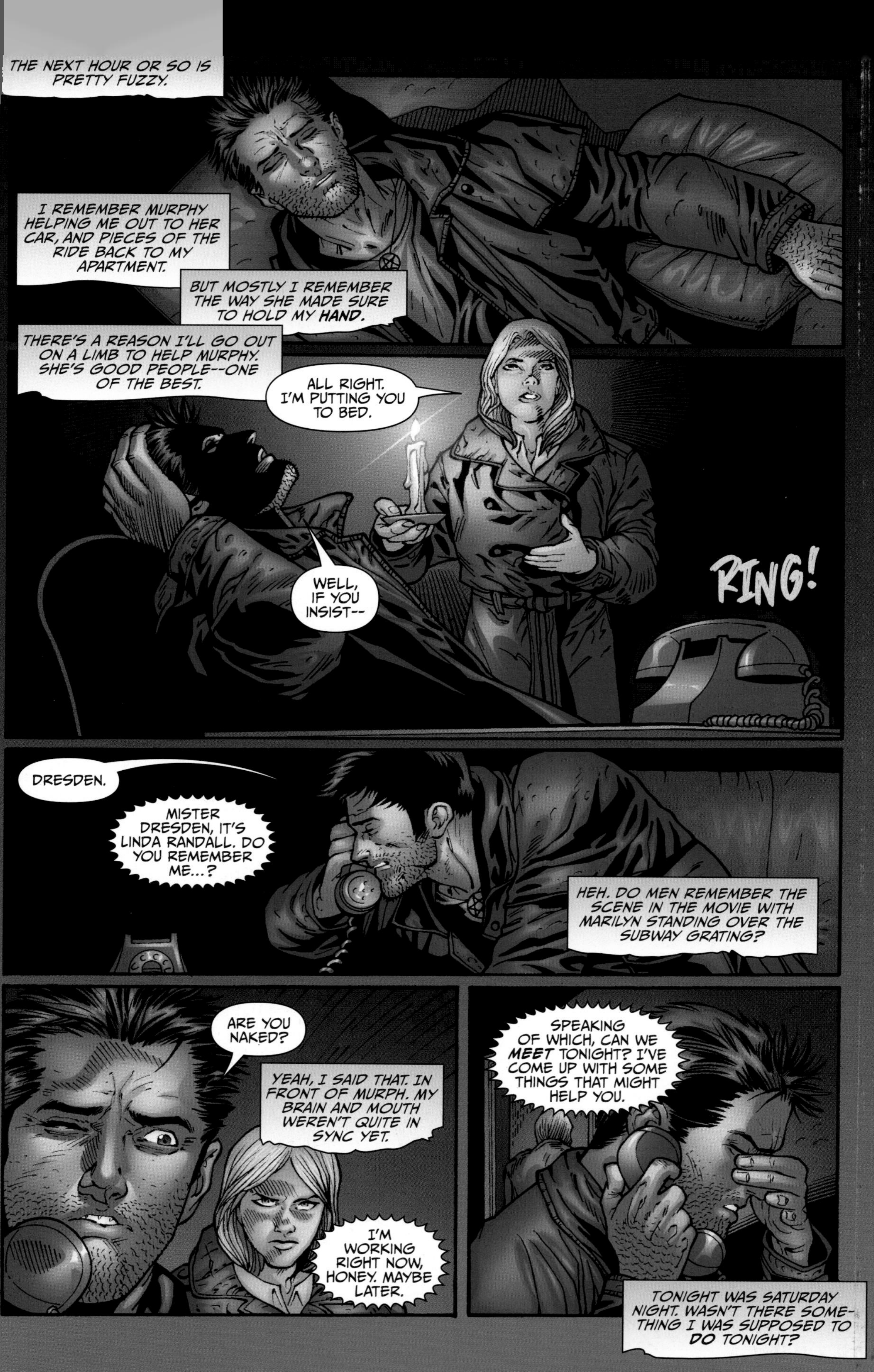

THE NEXT HOUR OR SO IS PRETTY FUZZY.
I REMEMBER MURPHY HELPING ME OUT TO HER CAR, AND PIECES OF THE RIDE BACK TO MY APARTMENT.
BUT MOSTLY I REMEMBER THE WAY SHE MADE SURE TO HOLD MY HAND.
THERE'S A REASON I'LL GO OUT ON A LIMB TO HELP MURPHY. SHE'S GOOD PEOPLE--ONE OF THE BEST.
ALL RIGHT. I'M PUTTING YOU TO BED.
WELL, IF YOU INSIST--
RING!
DRESDEN.
MISTER DRESDEN, IT'S LINDA RANDALL. DO YOU REMEMBER ME...?
HEH. DO MEN REMEMBER THE SCENE IN THE MOVIE WITH MARILYN STANDING OVER THE SUBWAY GRATING?
ARE YOU NAKED?
YEAH, I SAID THAT. IN FRONT OF MURPH. MY BRAIN AND MOUTH WEREN'T QUITE IN SYNC YET.
I'M WORKING RIGHT NOW, HONEY. MAYBE LATER.
SPEAKING OF WHICH, CAN WE MEET TONIGHT? I'VE COME UP WITH SOME THINGS THAT MIGHT HELP YOU.
TONIGHT WAS SATURDAY NIGHT. WASN'T THERE SOMETHING I WAS SUPPOSED TO DO TONIGHT?

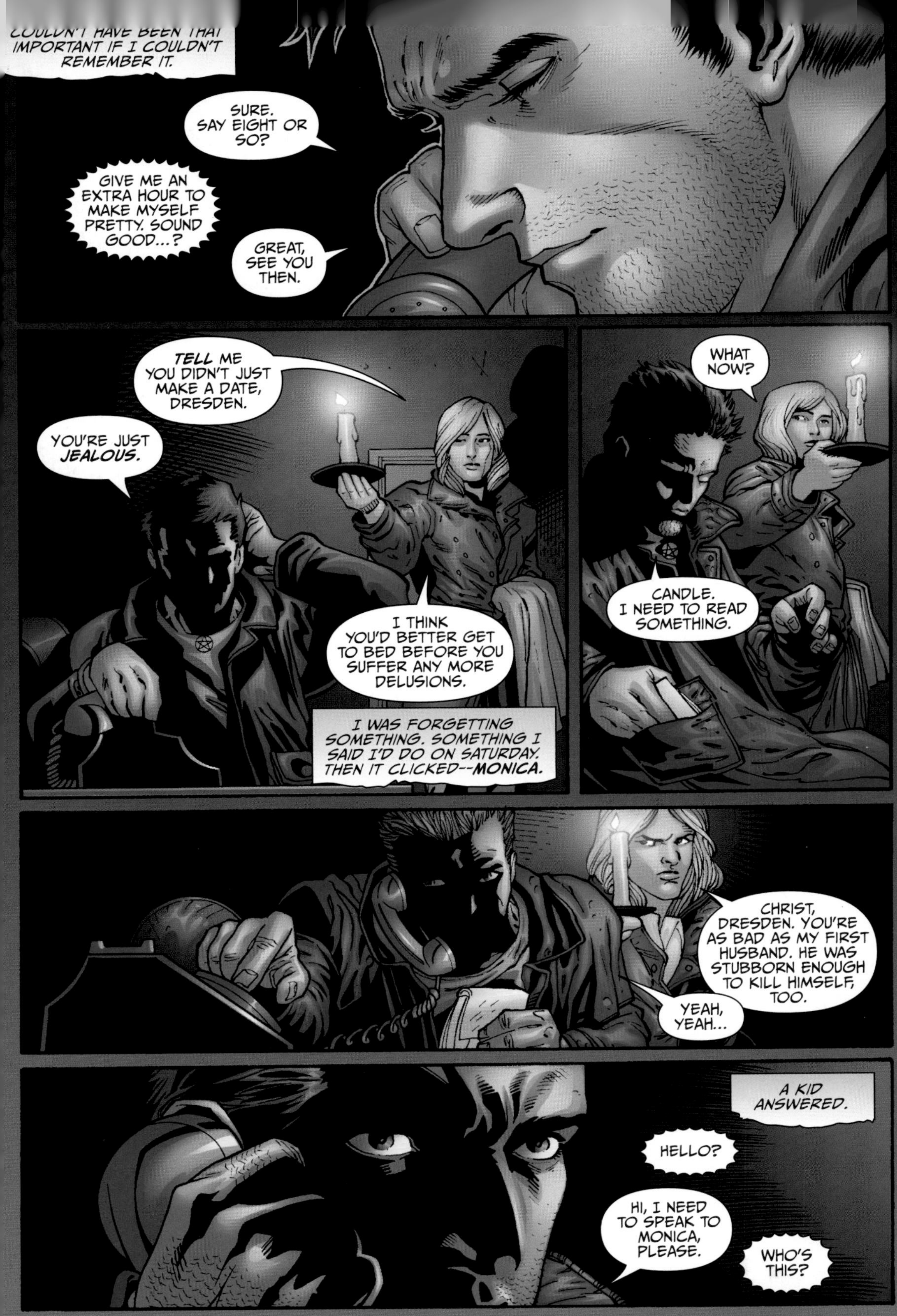

COULDN'T HAVE BEEN THAT IMPORTANT IF I COULDN'T REMEMBER IT.
SURE. SAY EIGHT OR SO?
GIVE ME AN EXTRA HOUR TO MAKE MYSELF PRETTY. SOUND GOOD...?
GREAT, SEE YOU THEN.
TELL ME YOU DIDN'T JUST MAKE A DATE, DRESDEN.
YOU'RE JUST JEALOUS.
I THINK YOU'D BETTER GET TO BED BEFORE YOU SUFFER ANY MORE DELUSIONS.
I WAS FORGETTING SOMETHING. SOMETHING I SAID I'D DO ON SATURDAY. THEN IT CLICKED--MONICA.
WHAT NOW?
CANDLE. I NEED TO READ SOMETHING.
CHRIST, DRESDEN. YOU'RE AS BAD AS MY FIRST HUSBAND. HE WAS STUBBORN ENOUGH TO KILL HIMSELF, TOO.
YEAH, YEAH...
A KID ANSWERED.
HELLO?
HI, I NEED TO SPEAK TO MONICA, PLEASE.
WHO'S THIS?

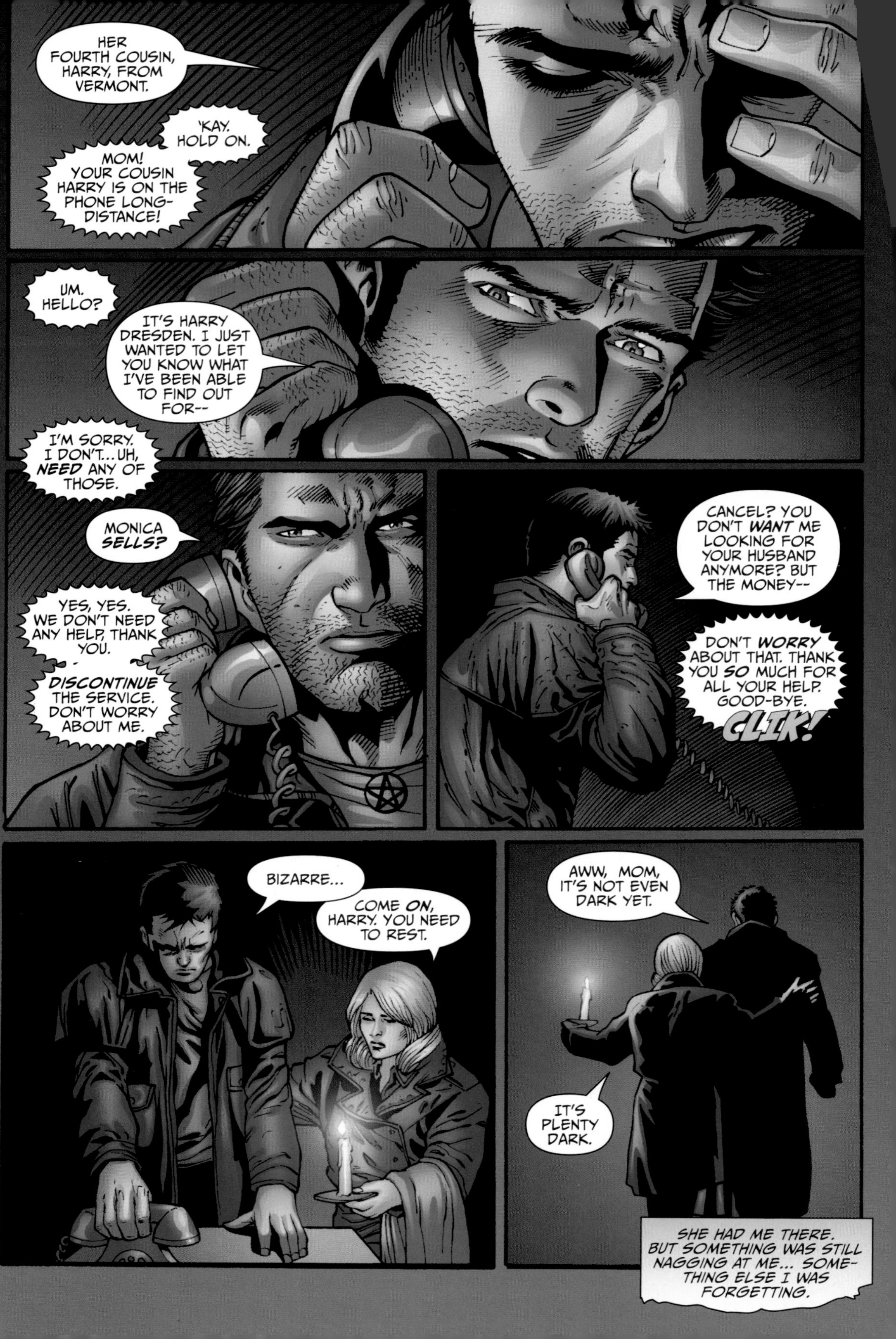
HER FOURTH COUSIN, HARRY, FROM VERMONT.
'KAY. HOLD ON.
MOM! YOUR COUSIN HARRY IS ON THE PHONE LONG-DISTANCE!
UM. HELLO?
IT'S HARRY DRESDEN. I JUST WANTED TO LET YOU KNOW WHAT I'VE BEEN ABLE TO FIND OUT FOR--
I'M SORRY. I DON'T...UH, NEED ANY OF THOSE.
MONICA SELLS?
YES, YES. WE DON'T NEED ANY HELP, THANK YOU.
DISCONTINUE THE SERVICE. DON'T WORRY ABOUT ME.
CANCEL? YOU DON'T WANT ME LOOKING FOR YOUR HUSBAND ANYMORE? BUT THE MONEY--
DON'T WORRY ABOUT THAT. THANK YOU SO MUCH FOR ALL YOUR HELP. GOOD-BYE.
CLIK!
BIZARRE...
COME ON, HARRY. YOU NEED TO REST.
AWW, MOM, IT'S NOT EVEN DARK YET.
IT'S PLENTY DARK.
SHE HAD ME THERE. BUT SOMETHING WAS STILL NAGGING AT ME... SOMETHING ELSE I WAS FORGETTING.

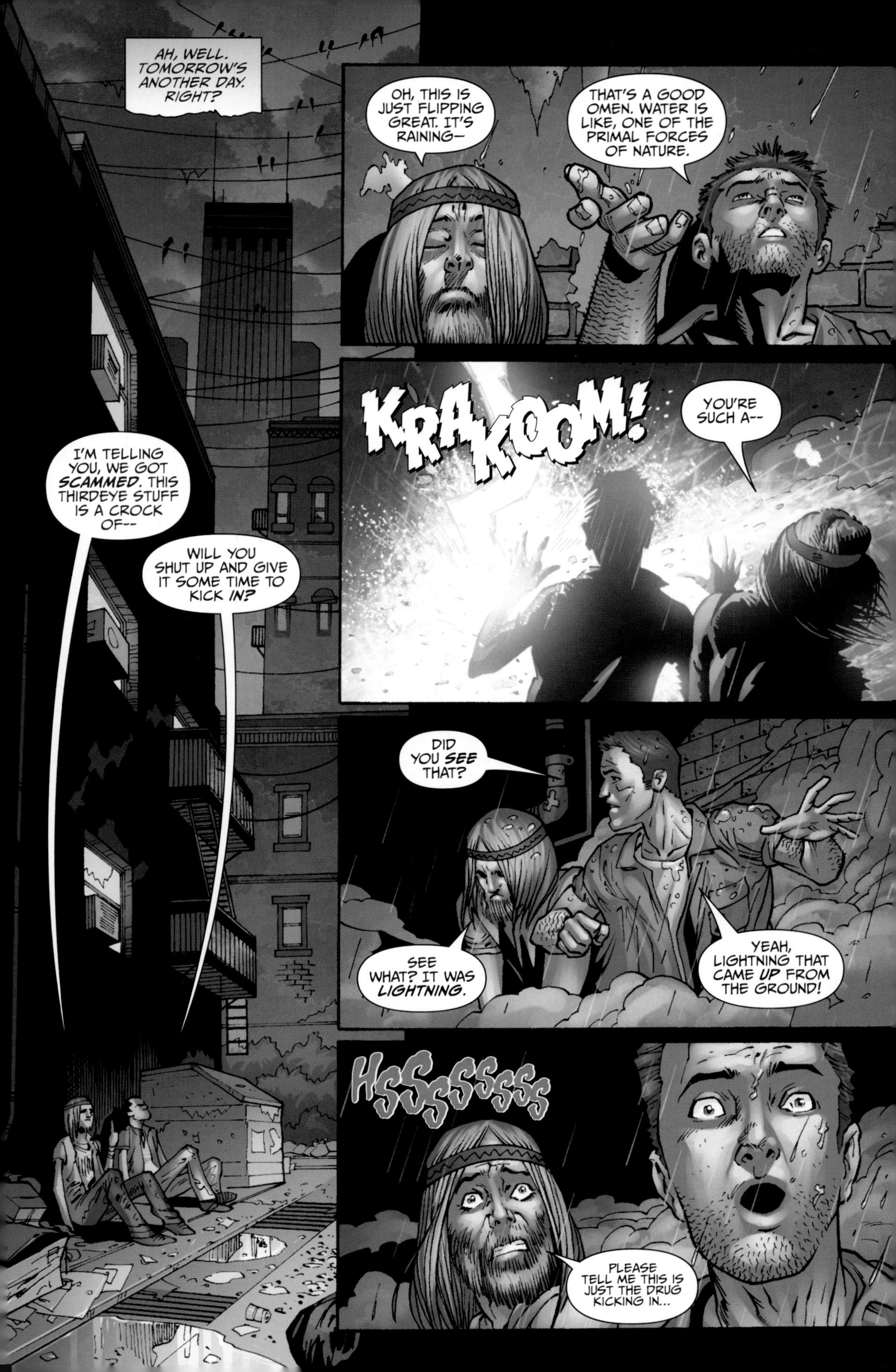
AH, WELL. TOMORROW'S ANOTHER DAY. RIGHT?
I'M TELLING YOU, WE GOT SCAMMED. THIS THIRDEYE STUFF IS A CROCK OF--
WILL YOU SHUT UP AND GIVE IT SOME TIME TO KICK IN?
OH, THIS IS JUST FLIPPING GREAT. IT'S RAINING—
THAT'S A GOOD OMEN. WATER IS LIKE, ONE OF THE PRIMAL FORCES OF NATURE.
KRAKOOM!
YOU'RE SUCH A--
DID YOU SEE THAT?
SEE WHAT? IT WAS LIGHTNING.
YEAH, LIGHTNING THAT CAME UP FROM THE GROUND!
HSSSSSSSS
PLEASE TELL ME THIS IS JUST THE DRUG KICKING IN...

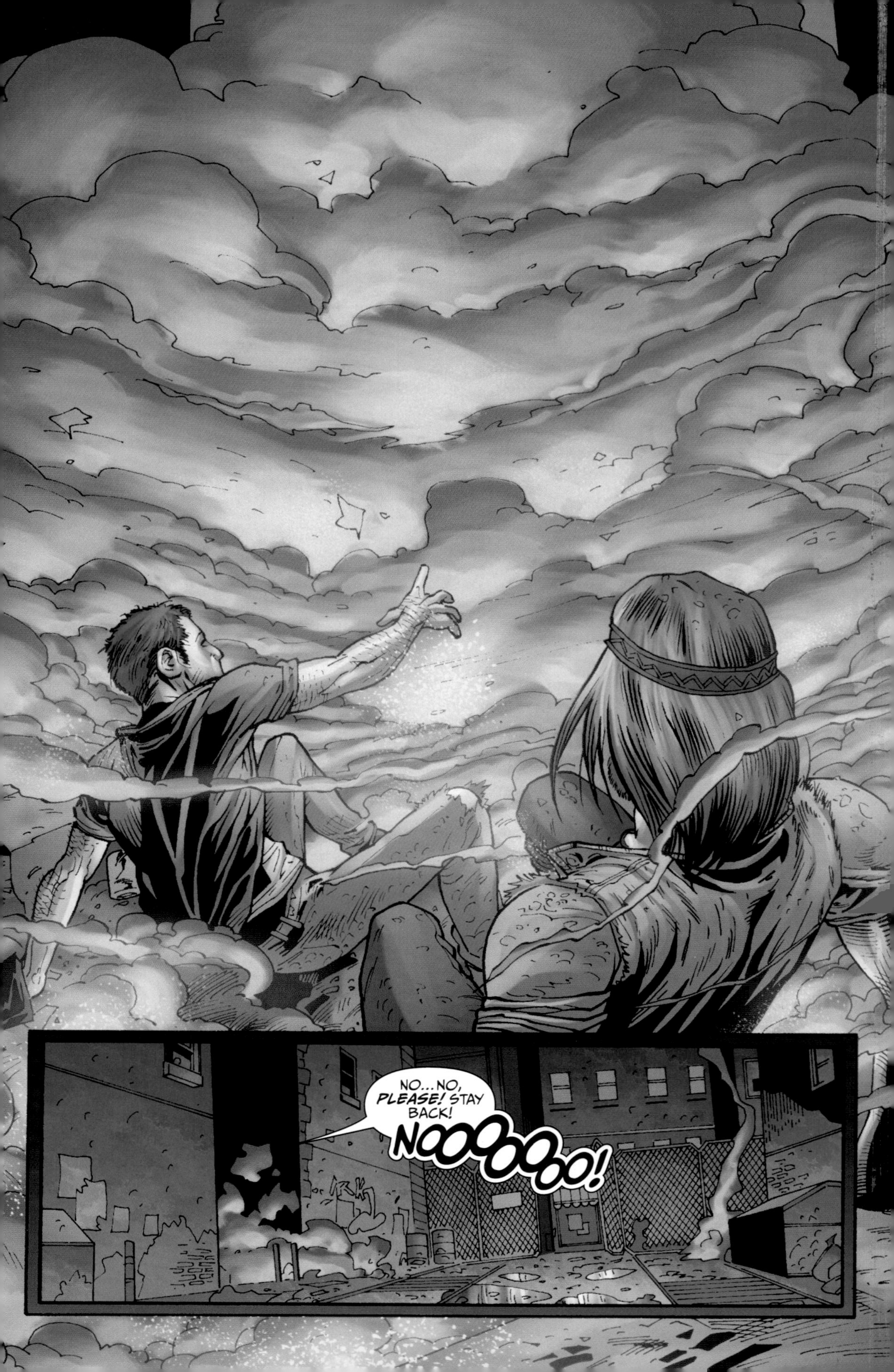
NO... NO, PLEASE! STAY BACK!
NOOOOOOO!

CHAPTER FOUR

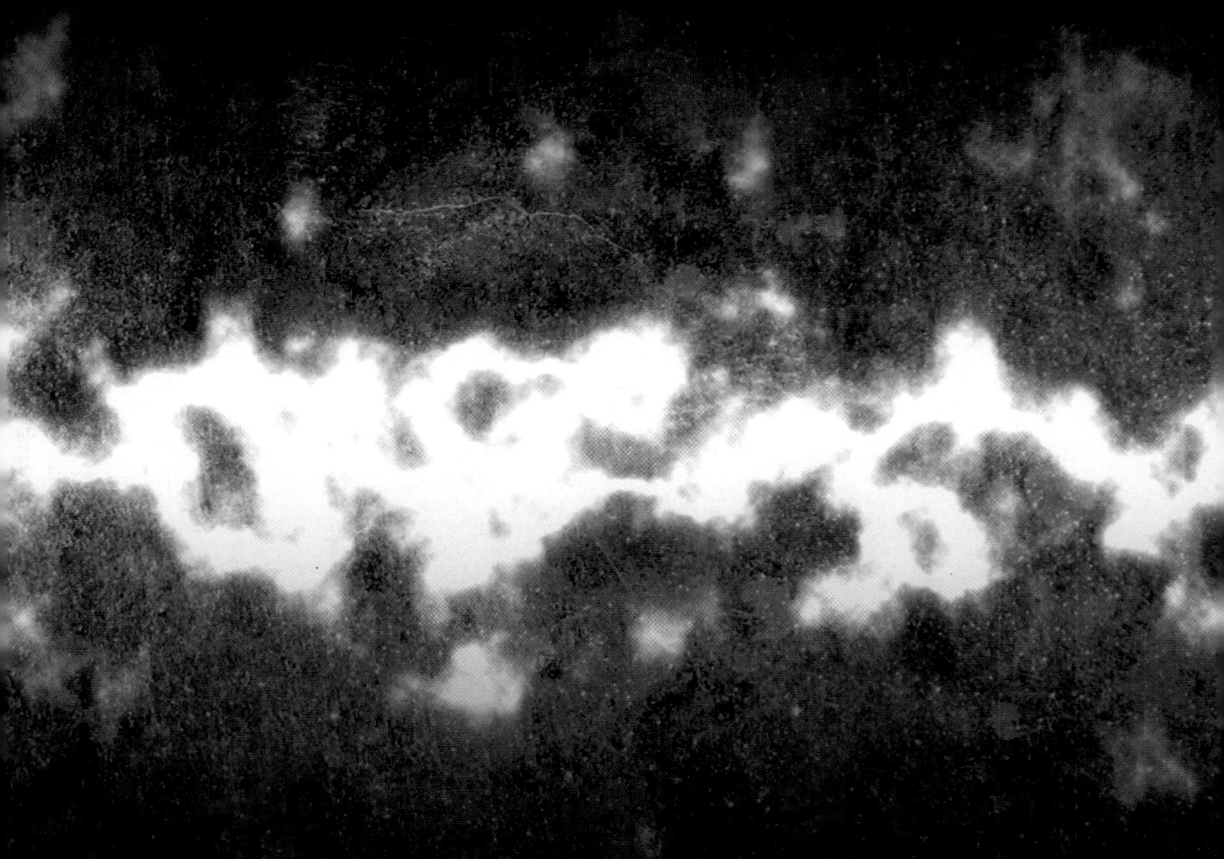

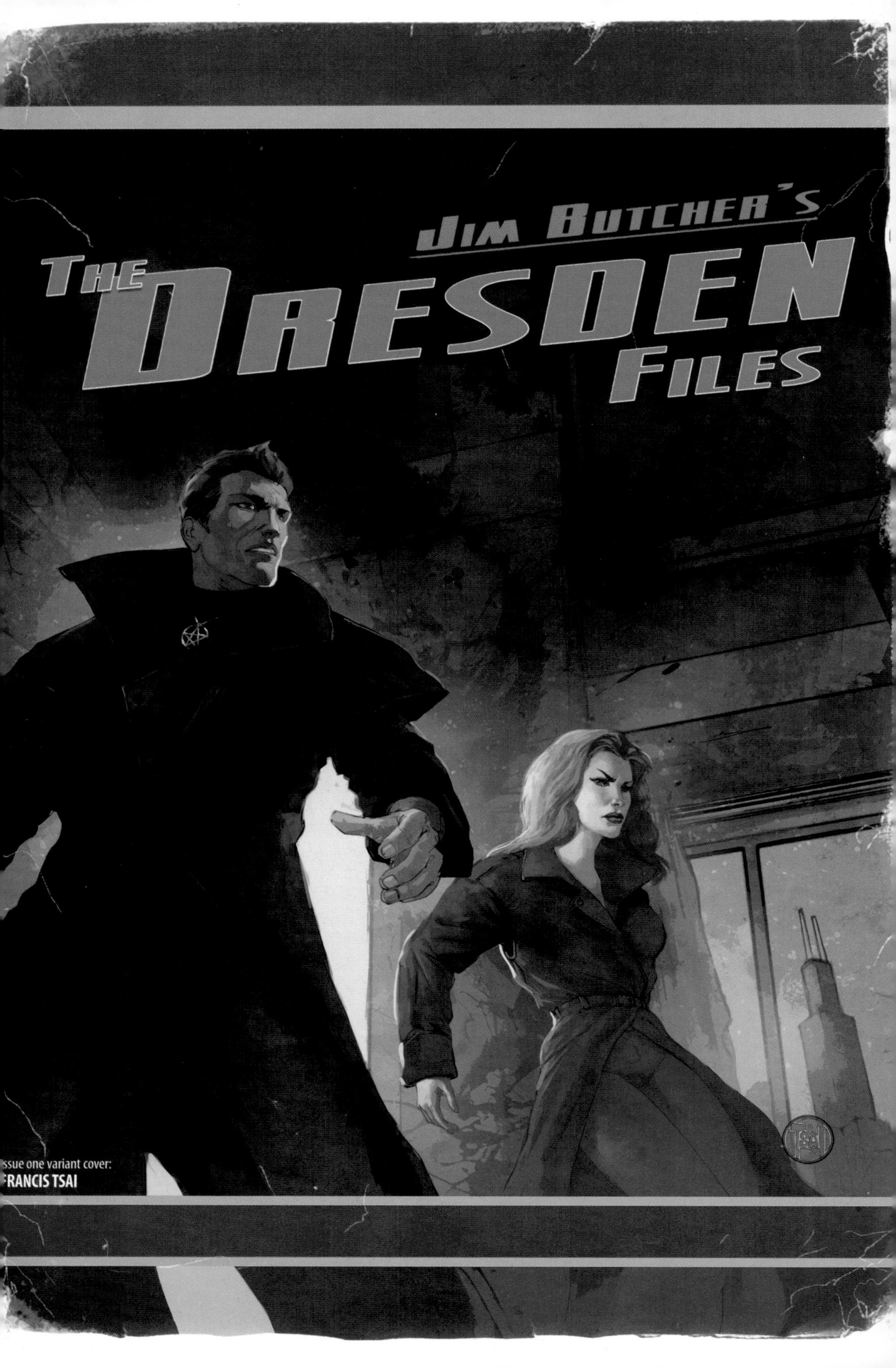
JIM BUTCHER'S
THE DRESDEN FILES
issue one variant cover:
FRANCIS TSAI

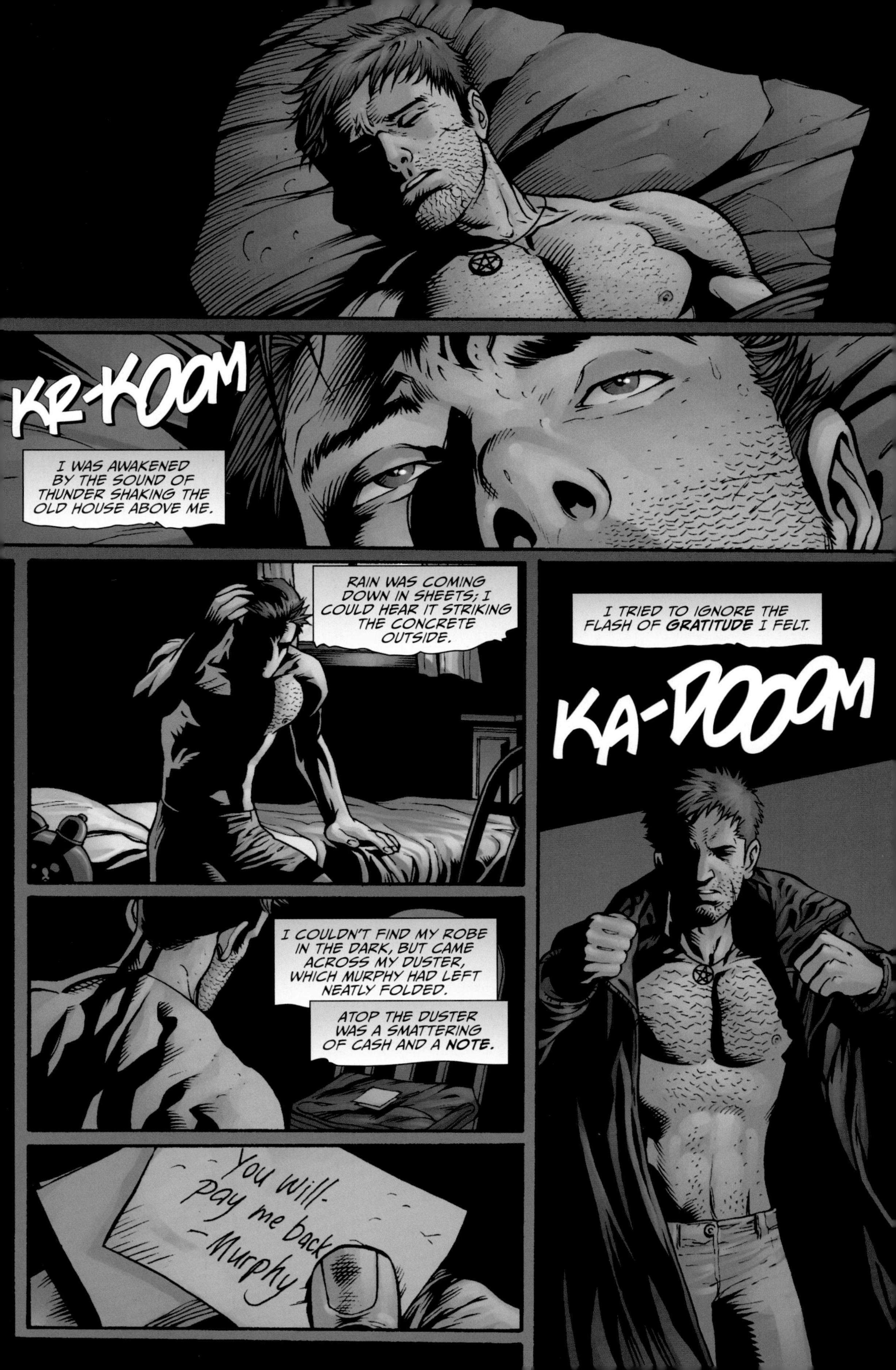
KR-KOOM
I WAS AWAKENED BY THE SOUND OF THUNDER SHAKING THE OLD HOUSE ABOVE ME.
RAIN WAS COMING DOWN IN SHEETS; I COULD HEAR IT STRIKING THE CONCRETE OUTSIDE.
I COULDN'T FIND MY ROBE IN THE DARK, BUT CAME ACROSS MY DUSTER, WHICH MURPHY HAD LEFT NEATLY FOLDED.
ATOP THE DUSTER WAS A SMATTERING OF CASH AND A NOTE.
You will-
pay me back
—Murphy
I TRIED TO IGNORE THE FLASH OF GRATITUDE I FELT.
KA-DOOOM

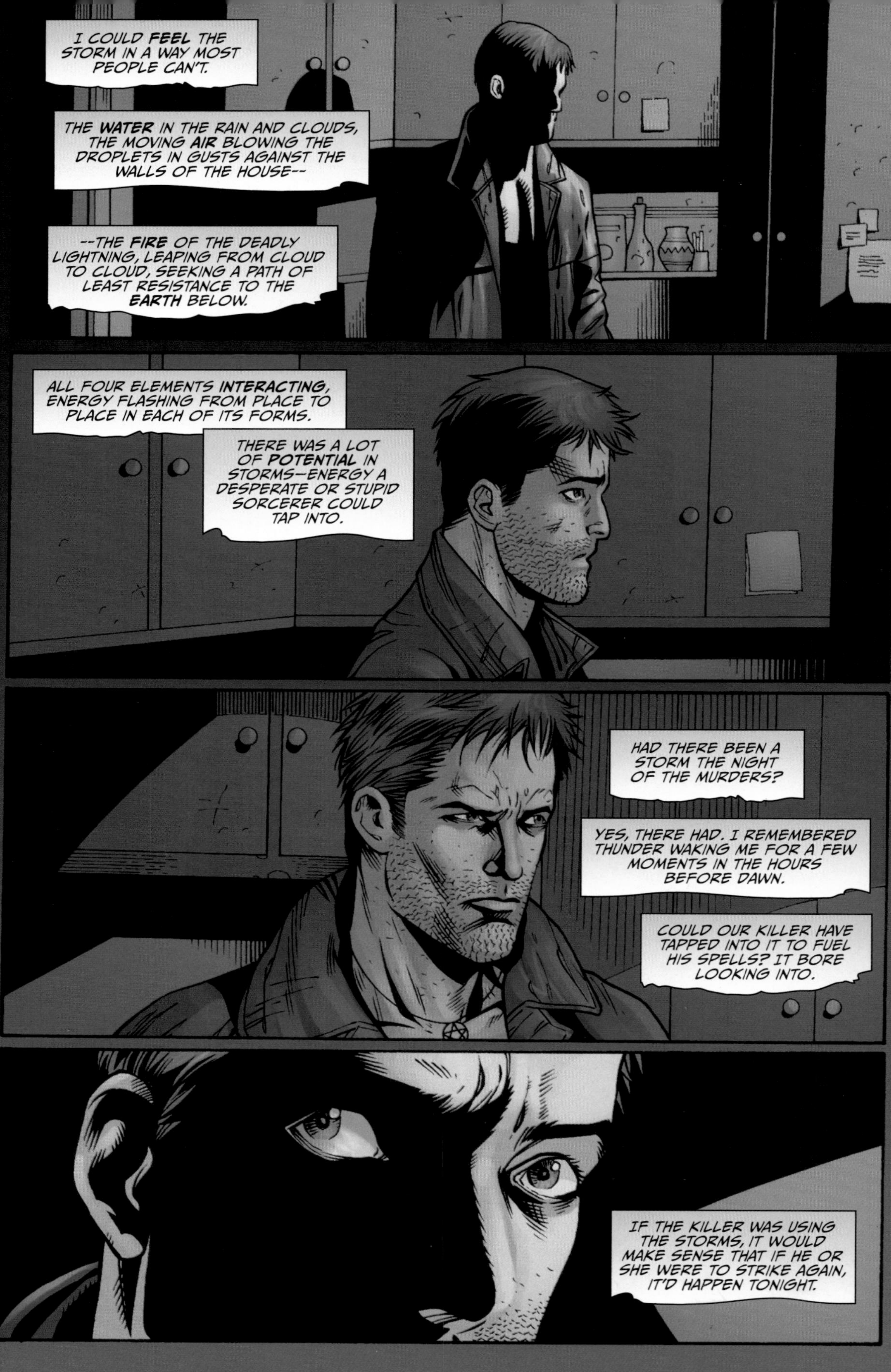
I COULD FEEL THE STORM IN A WAY MOST PEOPLE CAN'T.
THE WATER IN THE RAIN AND CLOUDS, THE MOVING AIR BLOWING THE DROPLETS IN GUSTS AGAINST THE WALLS OF THE HOUSE--
--THE FIRE OF THE DEADLY LIGHTNING, LEAPING FROM CLOUD TO CLOUD, SEEKING A PATH OF LEAST RESISTANCE TO THE EARTH BELOW.
ALL FOUR ELEMENTS INTERACTING, ENERGY FLASHING FROM PLACE TO PLACE IN EACH OF ITS FORMS.
THERE WAS A LOT OF POTENTIAL IN STORMS—ENERGY A DESPERATE OR STUPID SORCERER COULD TAP INTO.
HAD THERE BEEN A STORM THE NIGHT OF THE MURDERS?
YES, THERE HAD. I REMEMBERED THUNDER WAKING ME FOR A FEW MOMENTS IN THE HOURS BEFORE DAWN.
COULD OUR KILLER HAVE TAPPED INTO IT TO FUEL HIS SPELLS? IT BORE LOOKING INTO.
IF THE KILLER WAS USING THE STORMS, IT WOULD MAKE SENSE THAT IF HE OR SHE WERE TO STRIKE AGAIN, IT'D HAPPEN TONIGHT.

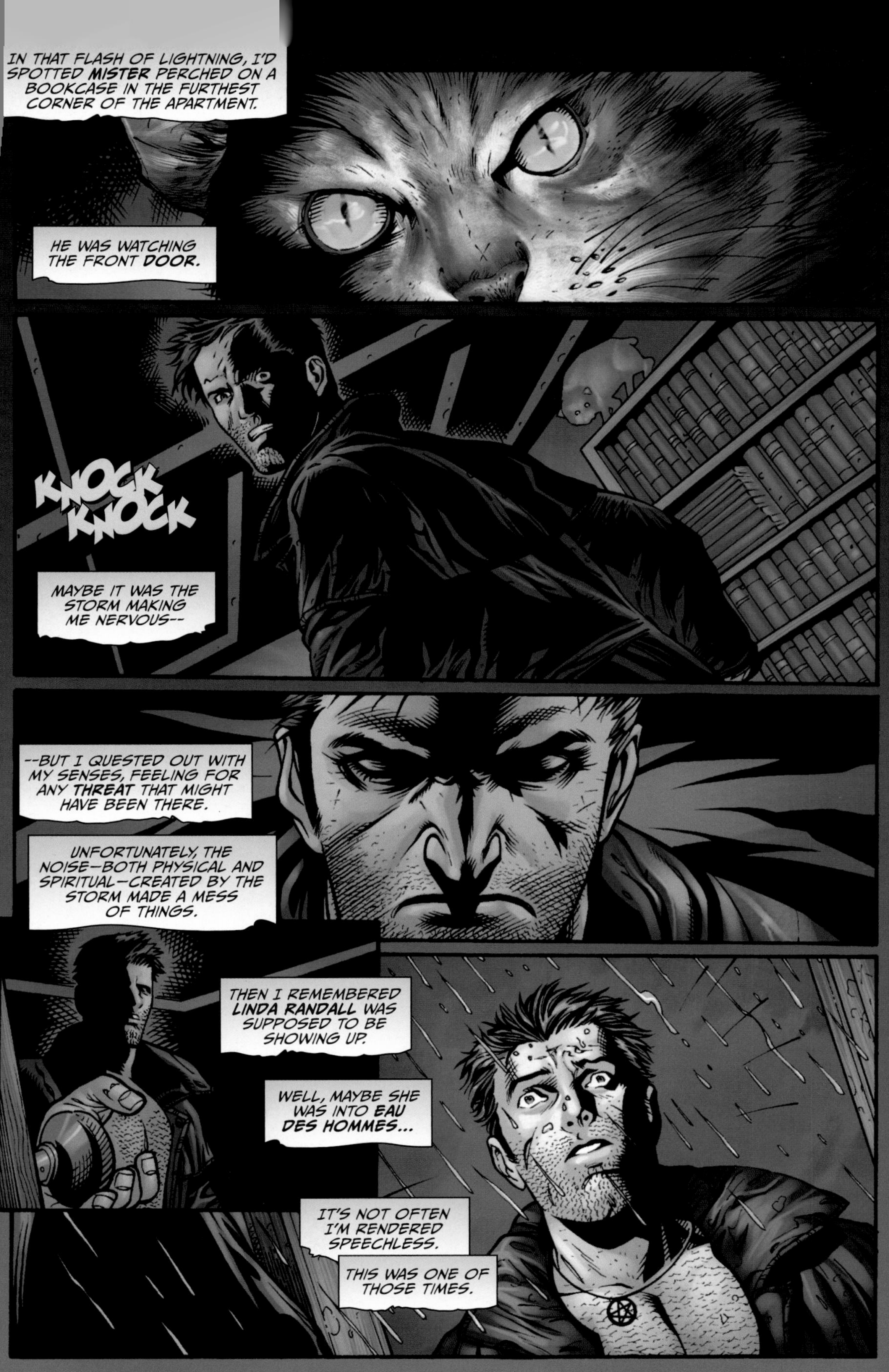
IN THAT FLASH OF LIGHTNING, I'D SPOTTED MISTER PERCHED ON A BOOKCASE IN THE FURTHEST CORNER OF THE APARTMENT.
HE WAS WATCHING THE FRONT DOOR.
KNOCK KNOCK
MAYBE IT WAS THE STORM MAKING ME NERVOUS--
--BUT I QUESTED OUT WITH MY SENSES, FEELING FOR ANY THREAT THAT MIGHT HAVE BEEN THERE.
UNFORTUNATELY, THE NOISE—BOTH PHYSICAL AND SPIRITUAL—CREATED BY THE STORM MADE A MESS OF THINGS.
THEN I REMEMBERED LINDA RANDALL WAS SUPPOSED TO BE SHOWING UP.
WELL, MAYBE SHE WAS INTO EAU DES HOMMES...
IT'S NOT OFTEN I'M RENDERED SPEECHLESS.
THIS WAS ONE OF THOSE TIMES.

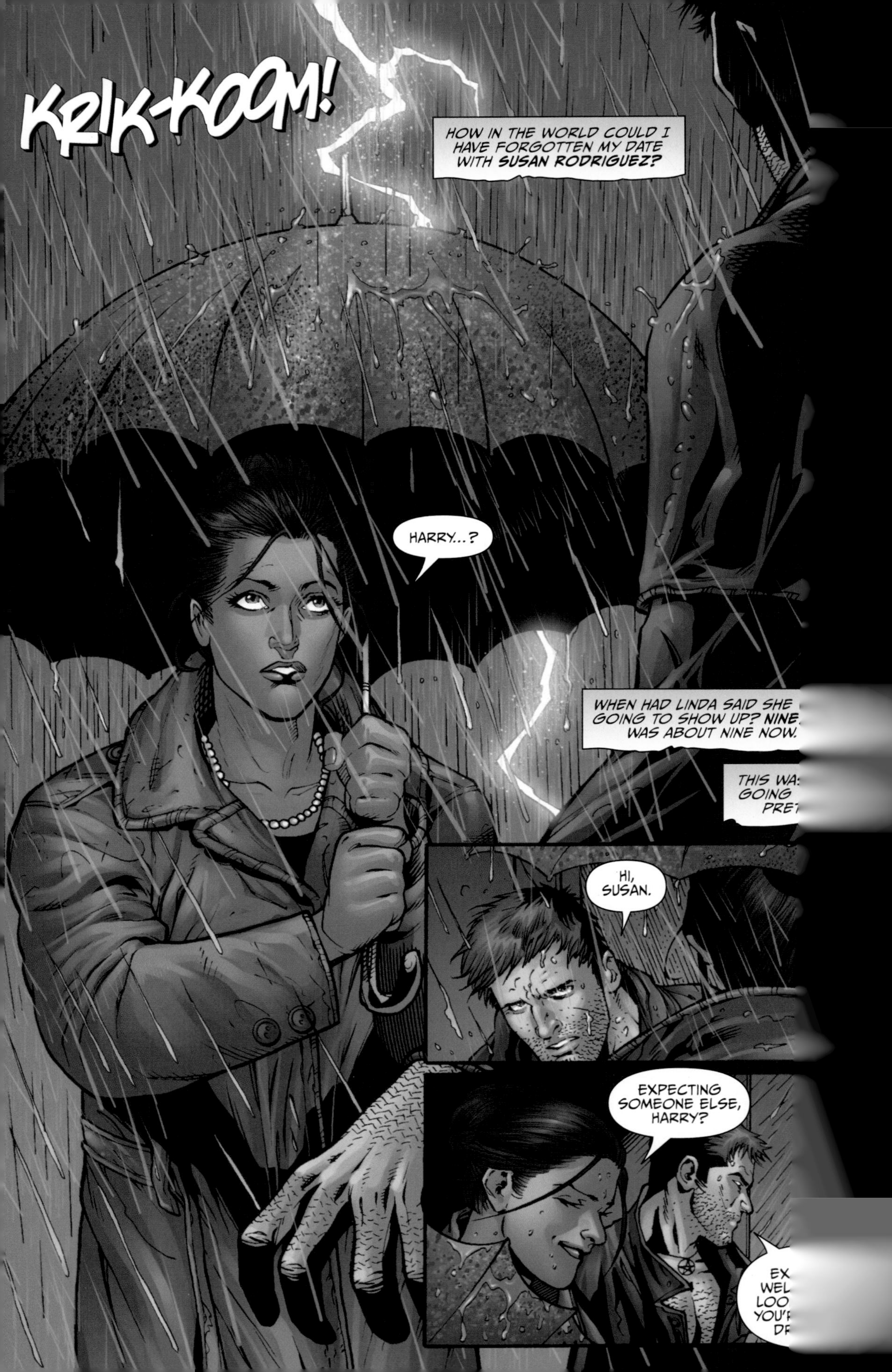
KRIK-KOOM!
HOW IN THE WORLD COULD I HAVE FORGOTTEN MY DATE WITH SUSAN RODRIGUEZ?
HARRY...?
WHEN HAD LINDA SAID SHE GOING TO SHOW UP? NINE. WAS ABOUT NINE NOW.
THIS WAS GOING PRET
HI, SUSAN.
EXPECTING SOMEONE ELSE, HARRY?
EX WEL LOO YOU'R DR

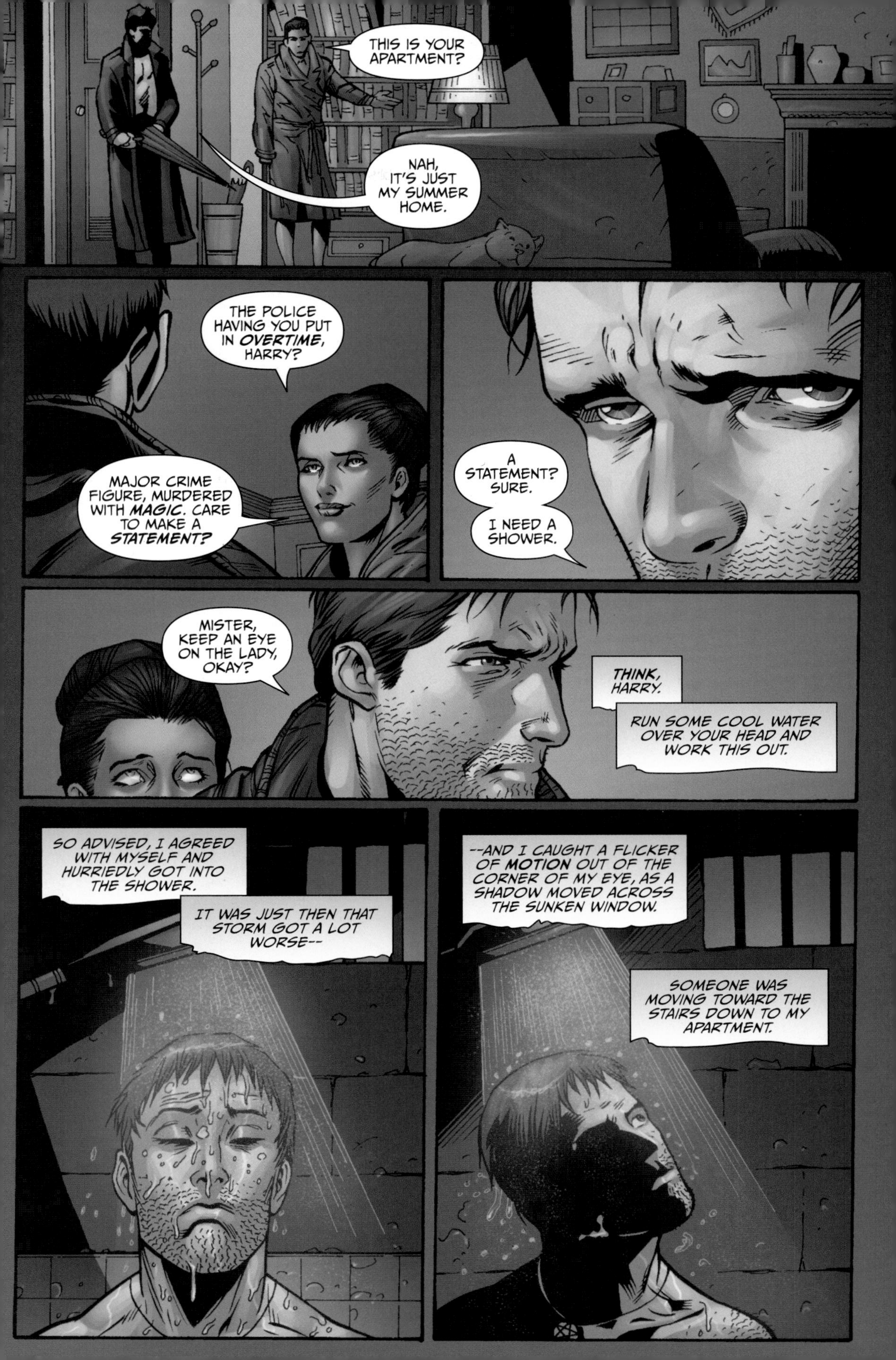
THIS IS YOUR APARTMENT?
NAH, IT'S JUST MY SUMMER HOME.
THE POLICE HAVING YOU PUT IN OVERTIME, HARRY?
MAJOR CRIME FIGURE, MURDERED WITH MAGIC. CARE TO MAKE A STATEMENT?
A STATEMENT? SURE.
I NEED A SHOWER.
MISTER, KEEP AN EYE ON THE LADY, OKAY?
THINK, HARRY.
RUN SOME COOL WATER OVER YOUR HEAD AND WORK THIS OUT.
SO ADVISED, I AGREED WITH MYSELF AND HURRIEDLY GOT INTO THE SHOWER.
IT WAS JUST THEN THAT STORM GOT A LOT WORSE--
--AND I CAUGHT A FLICKER OF MOTION OUT OF THE CORNER OF MY EYE, AS A SHADOW MOVED ACROSS THE SUNKEN WINDOW.
SOMEONE WAS MOVING TOWARD THE STAIRS DOWN TO MY APARTMENT.

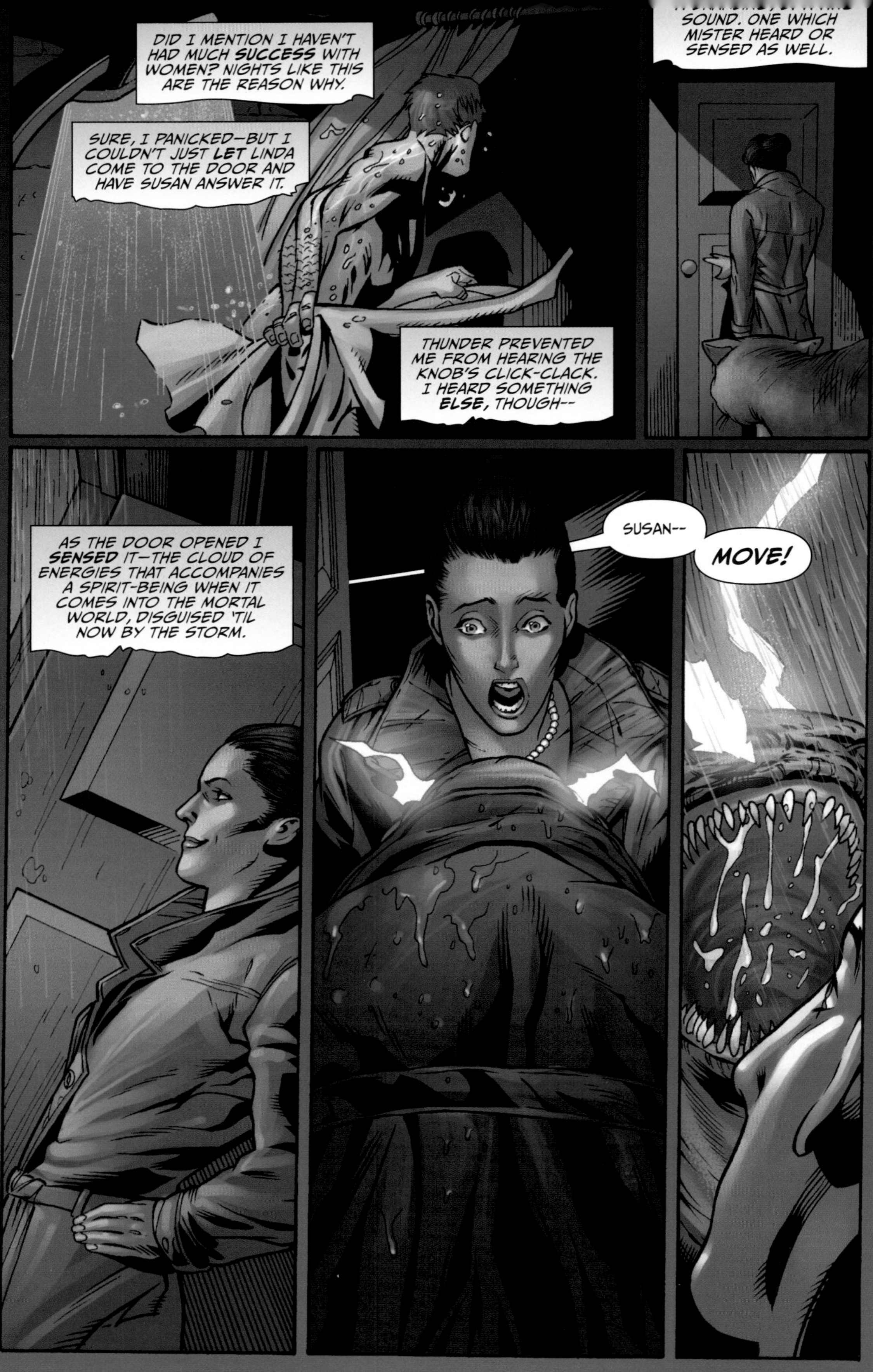
DID I MENTION I HAVEN'T HAD MUCH SUCCESS WITH WOMEN? NIGHTS LIKE THIS ARE THE REASON WHY.
SURE, I PANICKED—BUT I COULDN'T JUST LET LINDA COME TO THE DOOR AND HAVE SUSAN ANSWER IT.
THUNDER PREVENTED ME FROM HEARING THE KNOB'S CLICK-CLACK. I HEARD SOMETHING ELSE, THOUGH--
SOUND. ONE WHICH MISTER HEARD OR SENSED AS WELL.
AS THE DOOR OPENED I SENSED IT—THE CLOUD OF ENERGIES THAT ACCOMPANIES A SPIRIT-BEING WHEN IT COMES INTO THE MORTAL WORLD, DISGUISED 'TIL NOW BY THE STORM.
SUSAN--
MOVE!

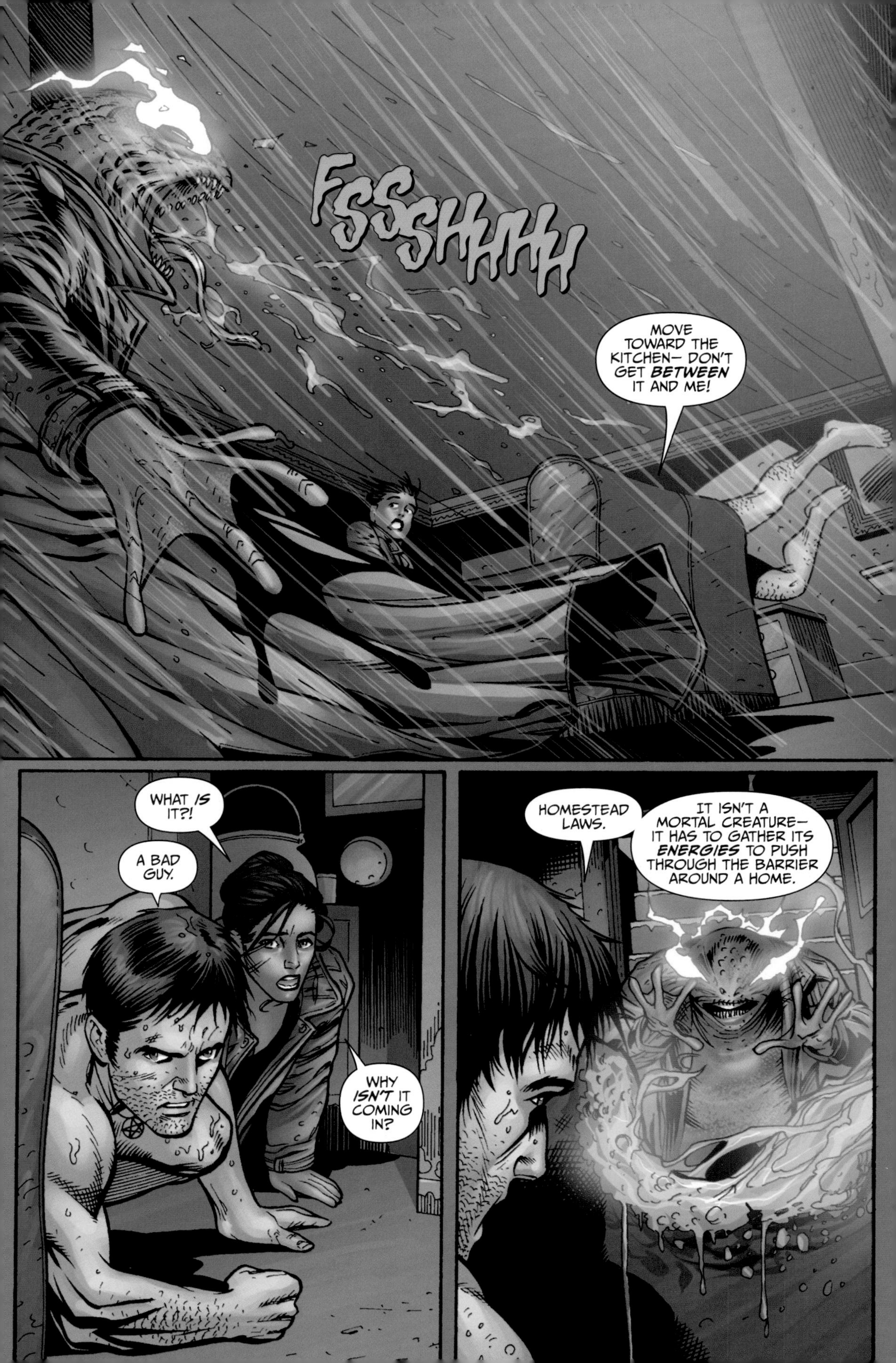
FSSSHHHH
MOVE TOWARD THE KITCHEN— DON'T GET *BETWEEN* IT AND ME!
WHAT *IS* IT?!
A BAD GUY.
WHY *ISN'T* IT COMING IN?
HOMESTEAD LAWS.
IT ISN'T A MORTAL CREATURE— IT HAS TO GATHER ITS *ENERGIES* TO PUSH THROUGH THE BARRIER AROUND A HOME.

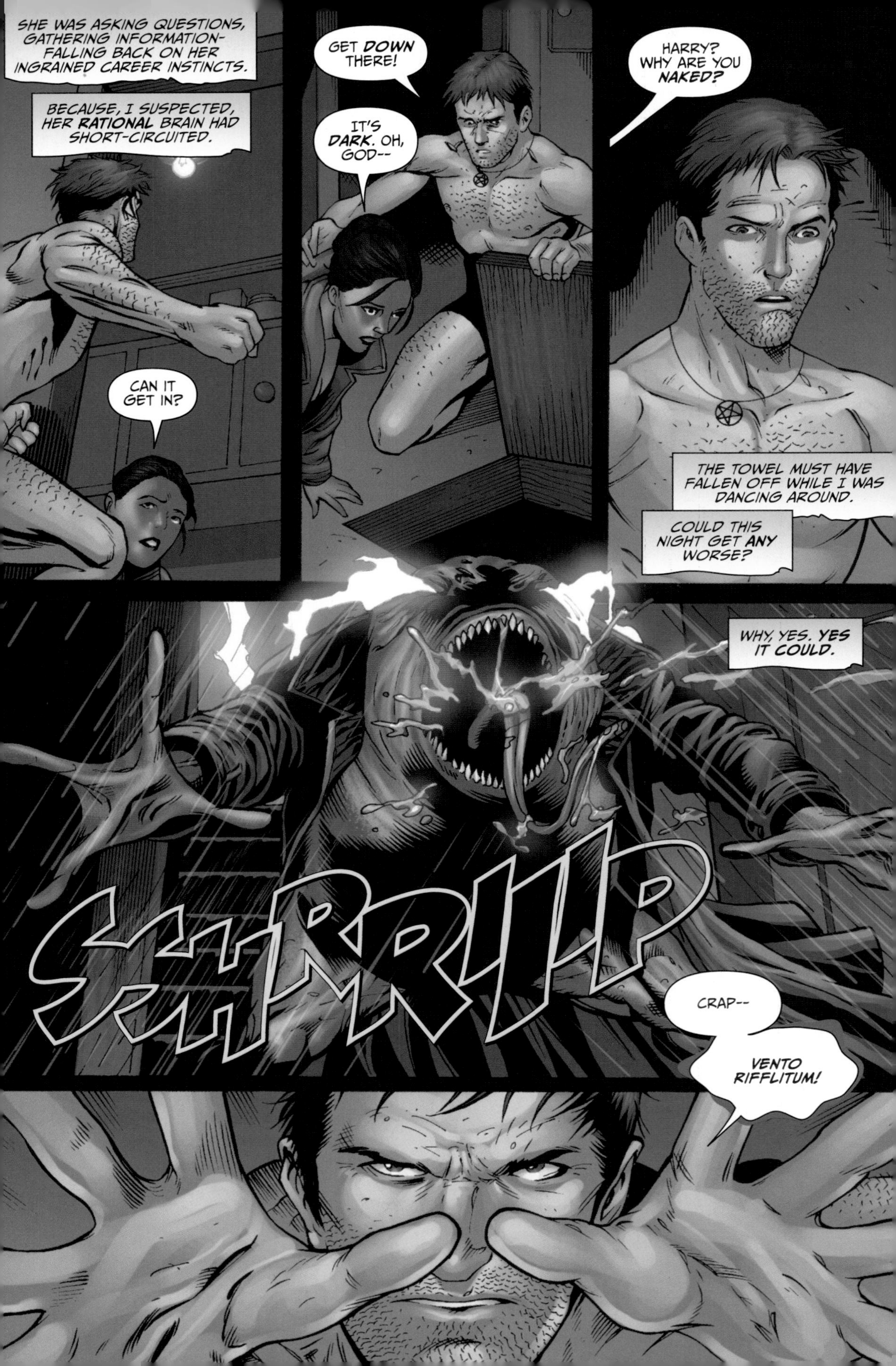
SHE WAS ASKING QUESTIONS, GATHERING INFORMATION- FALLING BACK ON HER INGRAINED CAREER INSTINCTS.
BECAUSE, I SUSPECTED, HER RATIONAL BRAIN HAD SHORT-CIRCUITED.
CAN IT GET IN?
GET DOWN THERE!
IT'S DARK. OH, GOD--
HARRY? WHY ARE YOU NAKED?
THE TOWEL MUST HAVE FALLEN OFF WHILE I WAS DANCING AROUND.
COULD THIS NIGHT GET ANY WORSE?
WHY, YES. YES IT COULD.
SCHRIIIP
CRAP--
VENTO RIFFLITUM!

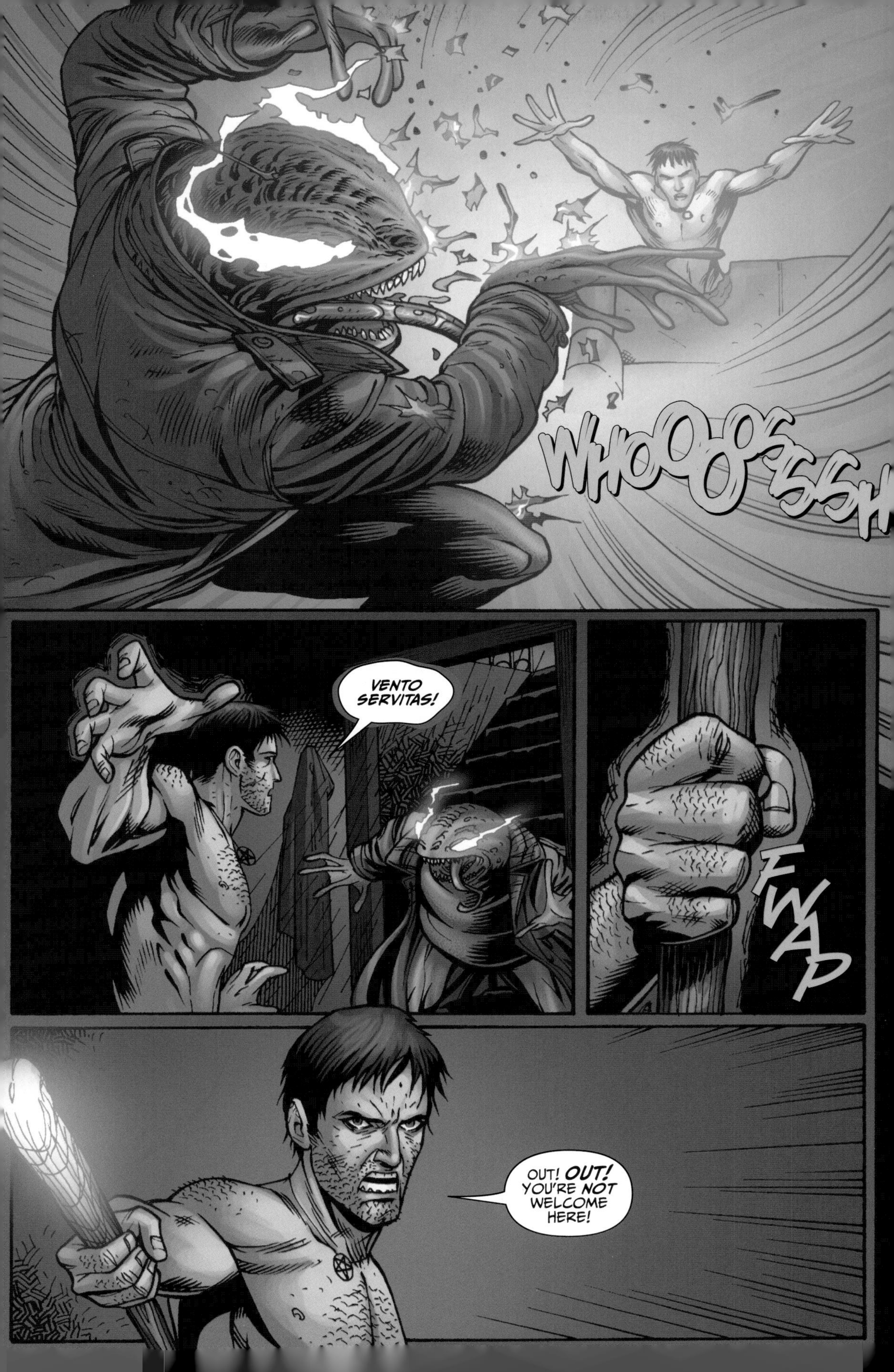
WHOOOOSSSH
VENTO SERVITAS!
FWAP
OUT! OUT! YOU'RE NOT WELCOME HERE!

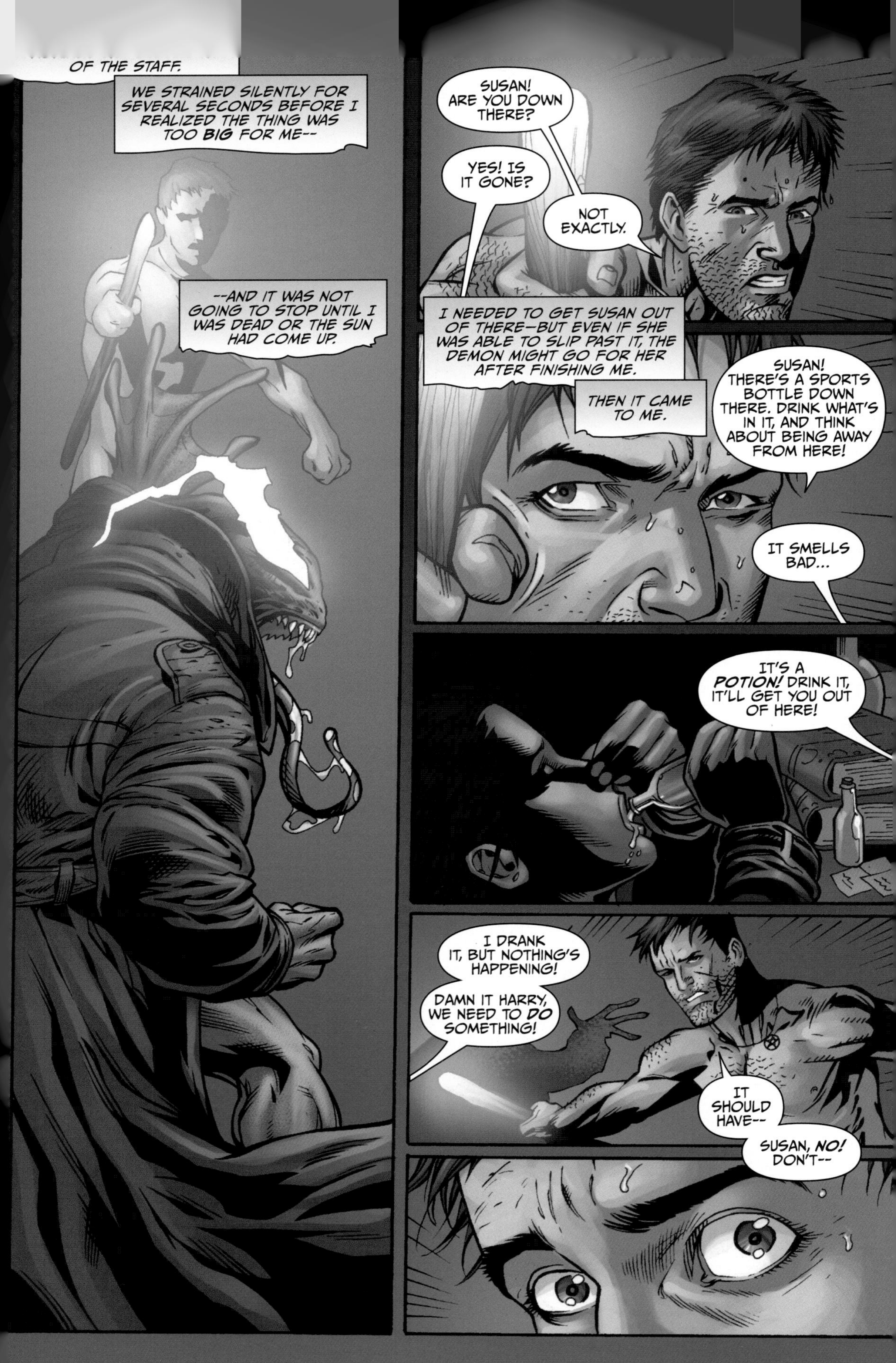
OF THE STAFF.
WE STRAINED SILENTLY FOR SEVERAL SECONDS BEFORE I REALIZED THE THING WAS TOO BIG FOR ME--
--AND IT WAS NOT GOING TO STOP UNTIL I WAS DEAD OR THE SUN HAD COME UP.
SUSAN! ARE YOU DOWN THERE?
YES! IS IT GONE?
NOT EXACTLY.
I NEEDED TO GET SUSAN OUT OF THERE--BUT EVEN IF SHE WAS ABLE TO SLIP PAST IT, THE DEMON MIGHT GO FOR HER AFTER FINISHING ME.
THEN IT CAME TO ME.
SUSAN! THERE'S A SPORTS BOTTLE DOWN THERE. DRINK WHAT'S IN IT, AND THINK ABOUT BEING AWAY FROM HERE!
IT SMELLS BAD...
IT'S A POTION! DRINK IT, IT'LL GET YOU OUT OF HERE!
I DRANK IT, BUT NOTHING'S HAPPENING!
DAMN IT HARRY, WE NEED TO DO SOMETHING!
IT SHOULD HAVE--
SUSAN, NO! DON'T--

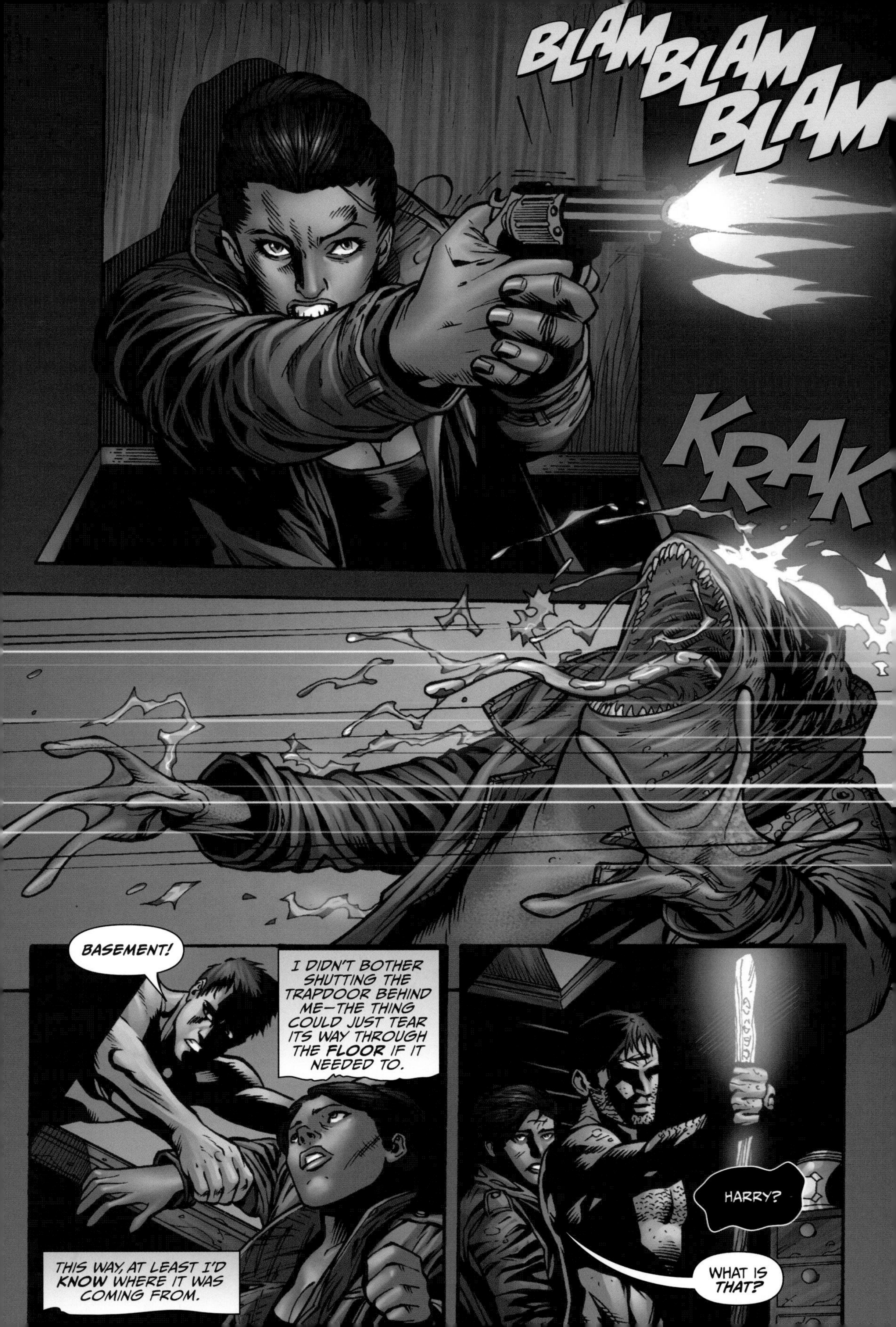
BLAM BLAM BLAM
KRAK
BASEMENT!
I DIDN'T BOTHER SHUTTING THE TRAPDOOR BEHIND ME—THE THING COULD JUST TEAR ITS WAY THROUGH THE FLOOR IF IT NEEDED TO.
THIS WAY, AT LEAST I'D KNOW WHERE IT WAS COMING FROM.
HARRY?
WHAT IS THAT?

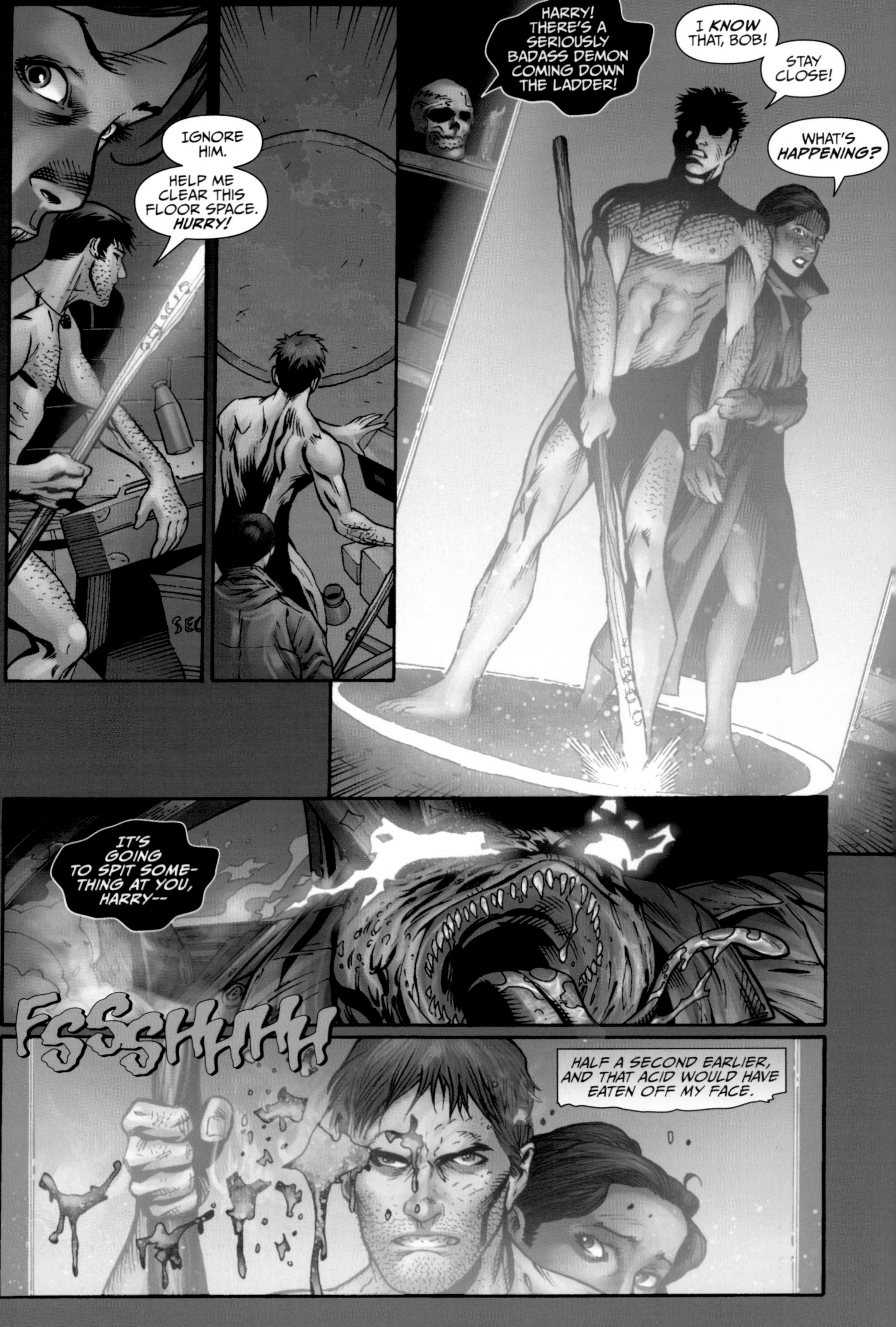
IGNORE HIM.
HELP ME CLEAR THIS FLOOR SPACE. *HURRY!*
HARRY! THERE'S A SERIOUSLY BADASS DEMON COMING DOWN THE LADDER!
I *KNOW* THAT, BOB!
STAY CLOSE!
WHAT'S *HAPPENING?*
IT'S GOING TO SPIT SOME-THING AT YOU, HARRY--
FSSSHHHH
HALF A SECOND EARLIER, AND THAT ACID WOULD HAVE EATEN OFF MY FACE.

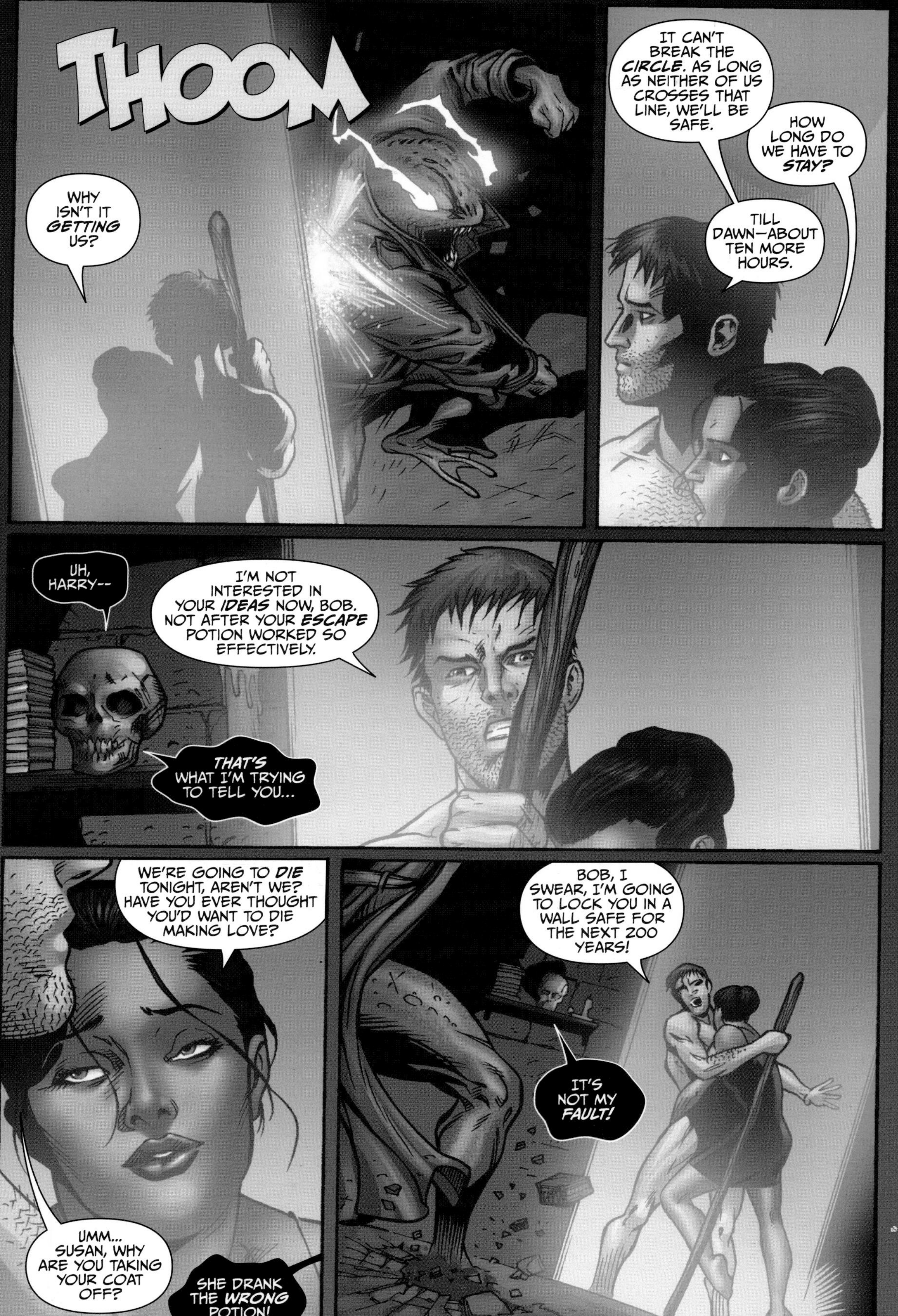
THOOM
WHY ISN'T IT GETTING US?
IT CAN'T BREAK THE CIRCLE. AS LONG AS NEITHER OF US CROSSES THAT LINE, WE'LL BE SAFE.
HOW LONG DO WE HAVE TO STAY?
TILL DAWN—ABOUT TEN MORE HOURS.
UH, HARRY--
I'M NOT INTERESTED IN YOUR IDEAS NOW, BOB. NOT AFTER YOUR ESCAPE POTION WORKED SO EFFECTIVELY.
THAT'S WHAT I'M TRYING TO TELL YOU...
WE'RE GOING TO DIE TONIGHT, AREN'T WE? HAVE YOU EVER THOUGHT YOU'D WANT TO DIE MAKING LOVE?
UMM... SUSAN, WHY ARE YOU TAKING YOUR COAT OFF?
SHE DRANK THE WRONG POTION!
BOB, I SWEAR, I'M GOING TO LOCK YOU IN A WALL SAFE FOR THE NEXT 200 YEARS!
IT'S NOT MY FAULT!

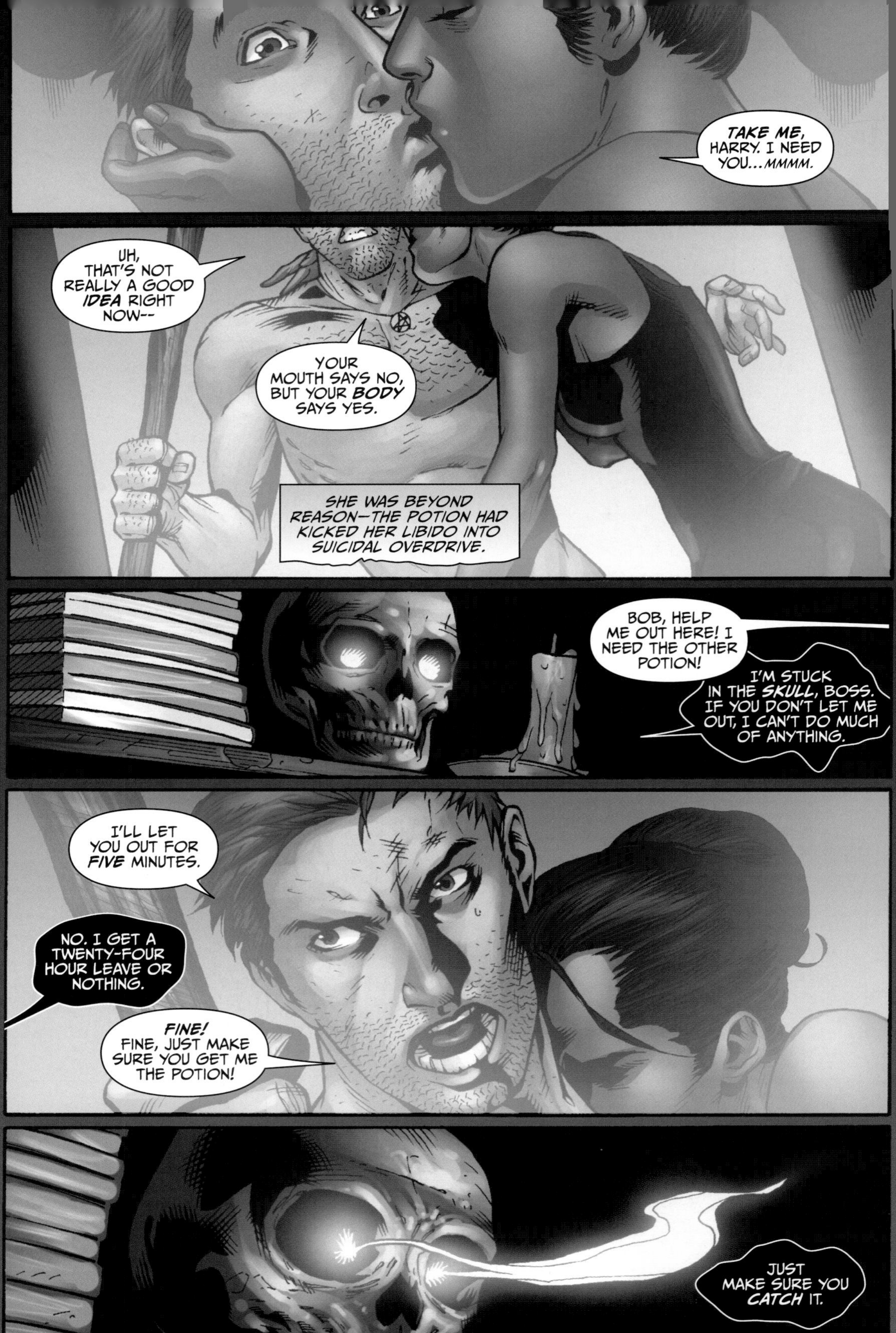
TAKE ME, HARRY. I NEED YOU...MMMM.
UH, THAT'S NOT REALLY A GOOD IDEA RIGHT NOW--
YOUR MOUTH SAYS NO, BUT YOUR BODY SAYS YES.
SHE WAS BEYOND REASON—THE POTION HAD KICKED HER LIBIDO INTO SUICIDAL OVERDRIVE.
BOB, HELP ME OUT HERE! I NEED THE OTHER POTION!
I'M STUCK IN THE SKULL, BOSS. IF YOU DON'T LET ME OUT, I CAN'T DO MUCH OF ANYTHING.
I'LL LET YOU OUT FOR FIVE MINUTES.
NO. I GET A TWENTY-FOUR HOUR LEAVE OR NOTHING.
FINE! FINE, JUST MAKE SURE YOU GET ME THE POTION!
JUST MAKE SURE YOU CATCH IT.

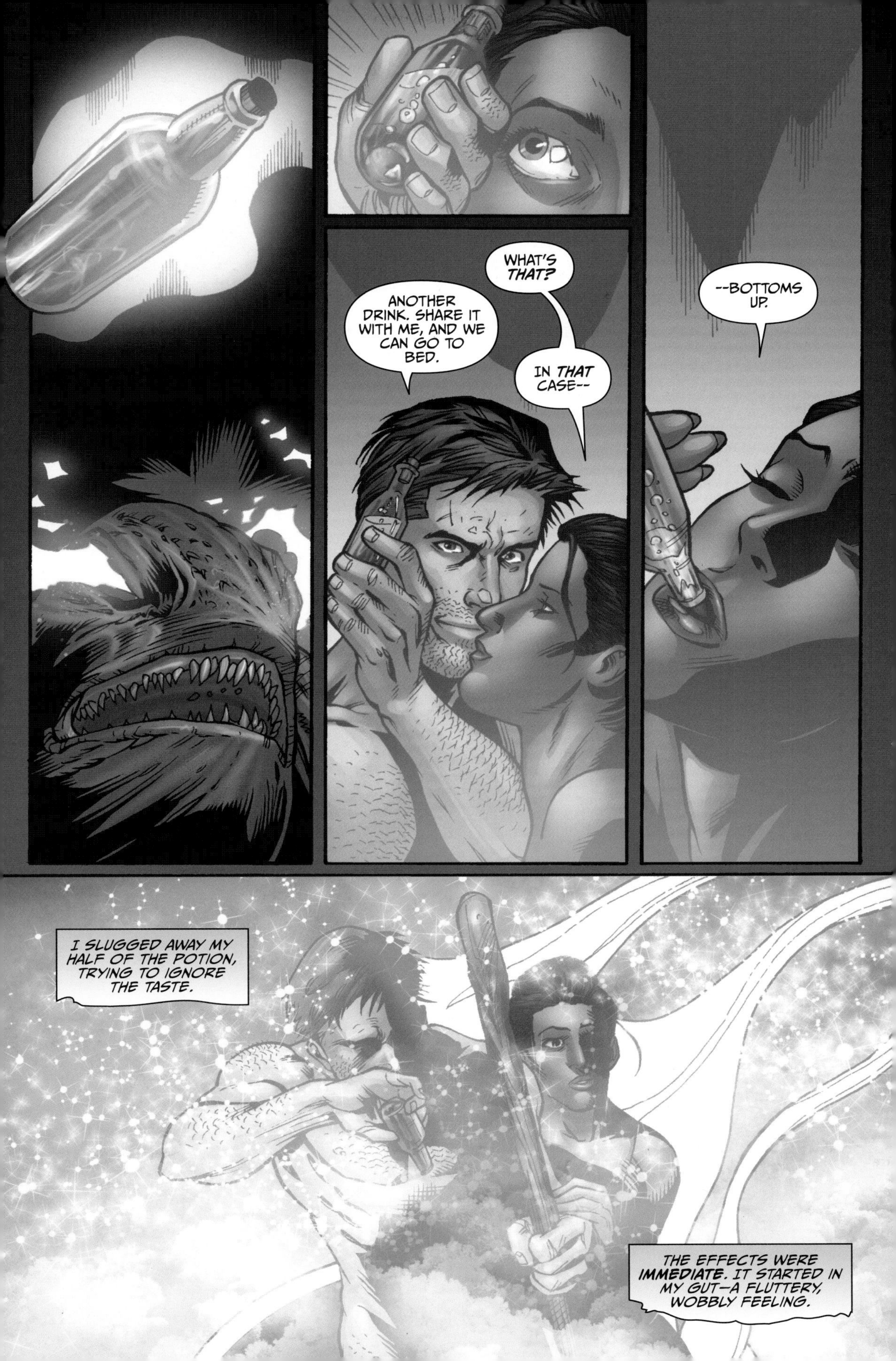
WHAT'S *THAT?*
ANOTHER DRINK. SHARE IT WITH ME, AND WE CAN GO TO BED.
IN *THAT* CASE--
--BOTTOMS UP.
I SLUGGED AWAY MY HALF OF THE POTION, TRYING TO IGNORE THE TASTE.
THE EFFECTS WERE ***IMMEDIATE****. IT STARTED IN MY GUT—A FLUTTERY, WOBBLY FEELING.*

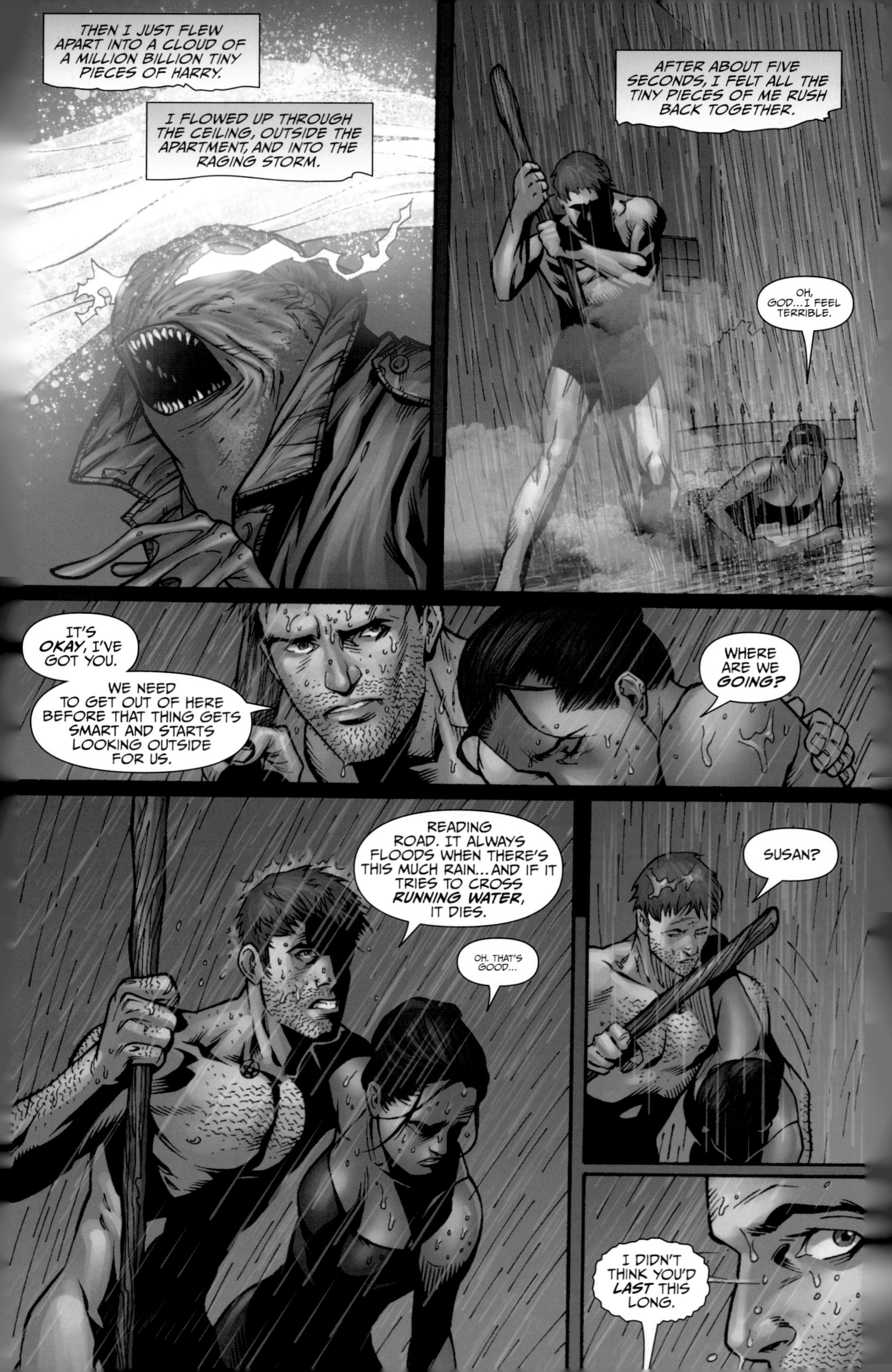
THEN I JUST FLEW APART INTO A CLOUD OF A MILLION BILLION TINY PIECES OF HARRY.
I FLOWED UP THROUGH THE CEILING, OUTSIDE THE APARTMENT, AND INTO THE RAGING STORM.
AFTER ABOUT FIVE SECONDS, I FELT ALL THE TINY PIECES OF ME RUSH BACK TOGETHER.
OH, GOD...I FEEL TERRIBLE.
IT'S OKAY, I'VE GOT YOU.
WE NEED TO GET OUT OF HERE BEFORE THAT THING GETS SMART AND STARTS LOOKING OUTSIDE FOR US.
WHERE ARE WE GOING?
READING ROAD. IT ALWAYS FLOODS WHEN THERE'S THIS MUCH RAIN...AND IF IT TRIES TO CROSS RUNNING WATER, IT DIES.
OH. THAT'S GOOD...
SUSAN?
I DIDN'T THINK YOU'D LAST THIS LONG.

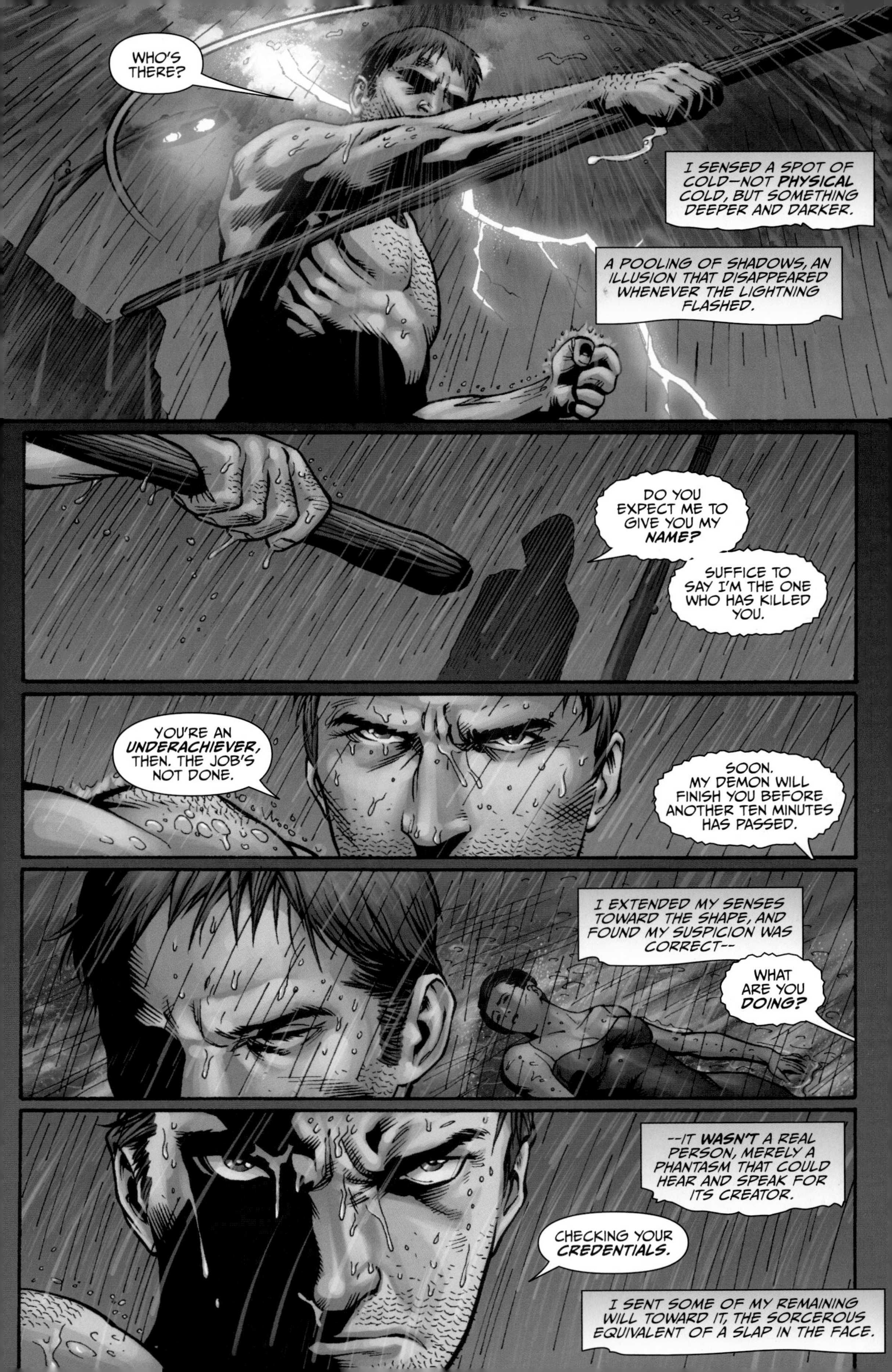
WHO'S THERE?
I SENSED A SPOT OF COLD—NOT PHYSICAL COLD, BUT SOMETHING DEEPER AND DARKER.
A POOLING OF SHADOWS, AN ILLUSION THAT DISAPPEARED WHENEVER THE LIGHTNING FLASHED.
DO YOU EXPECT ME TO GIVE YOU MY NAME?
SUFFICE TO SAY I'M THE ONE WHO HAS KILLED YOU.
YOU'RE AN UNDERACHIEVER, THEN. THE JOB'S NOT DONE.
SOON. MY DEMON WILL FINISH YOU BEFORE ANOTHER TEN MINUTES HAS PASSED.
I EXTENDED MY SENSES TOWARD THE SHAPE, AND FOUND MY SUSPICION WAS CORRECT--
WHAT ARE YOU DOING?
--IT WASN'T A REAL PERSON, MERELY A PHANTASM THAT COULD HEAR AND SPEAK FOR ITS CREATOR.
CHECKING YOUR CREDENTIALS.
I SENT SOME OF MY REMAINING WILL TOWARD IT, THE SORCEROUS EQUIVALENT OF A SLAP IN THE FACE.

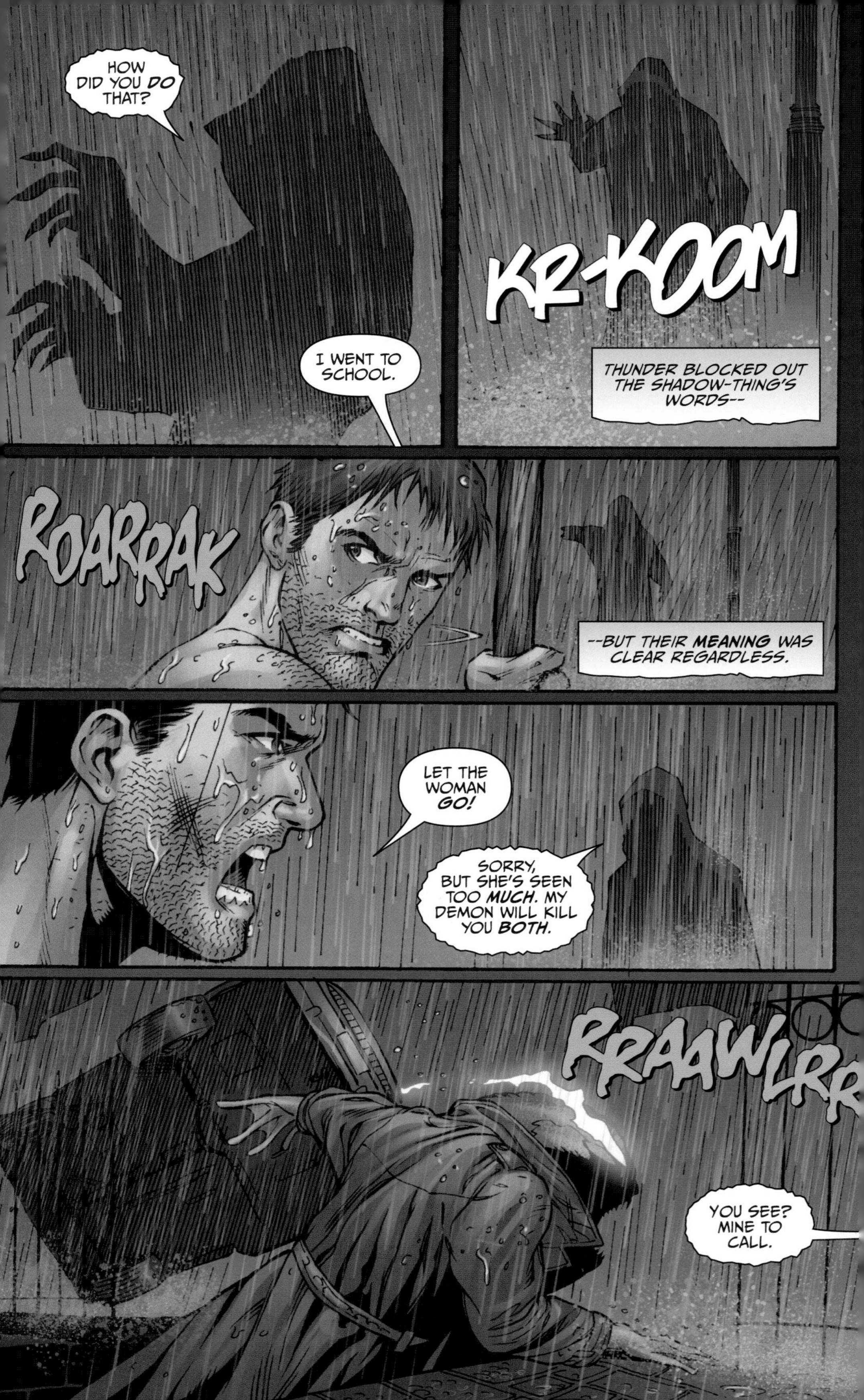
HOW DID YOU DO THAT?
I WENT TO SCHOOL.
KR-KOOM
THUNDER BLOCKED OUT THE SHADOW-THING'S WORDS--
ROARRAK
--BUT THEIR MEANING WAS CLEAR REGARDLESS.
LET THE WOMAN GO!
SORRY, BUT SHE'S SEEN TOO MUCH. MY DEMON WILL KILL YOU BOTH.
RRAAWLRR
YOU SEE? MINE TO CALL.

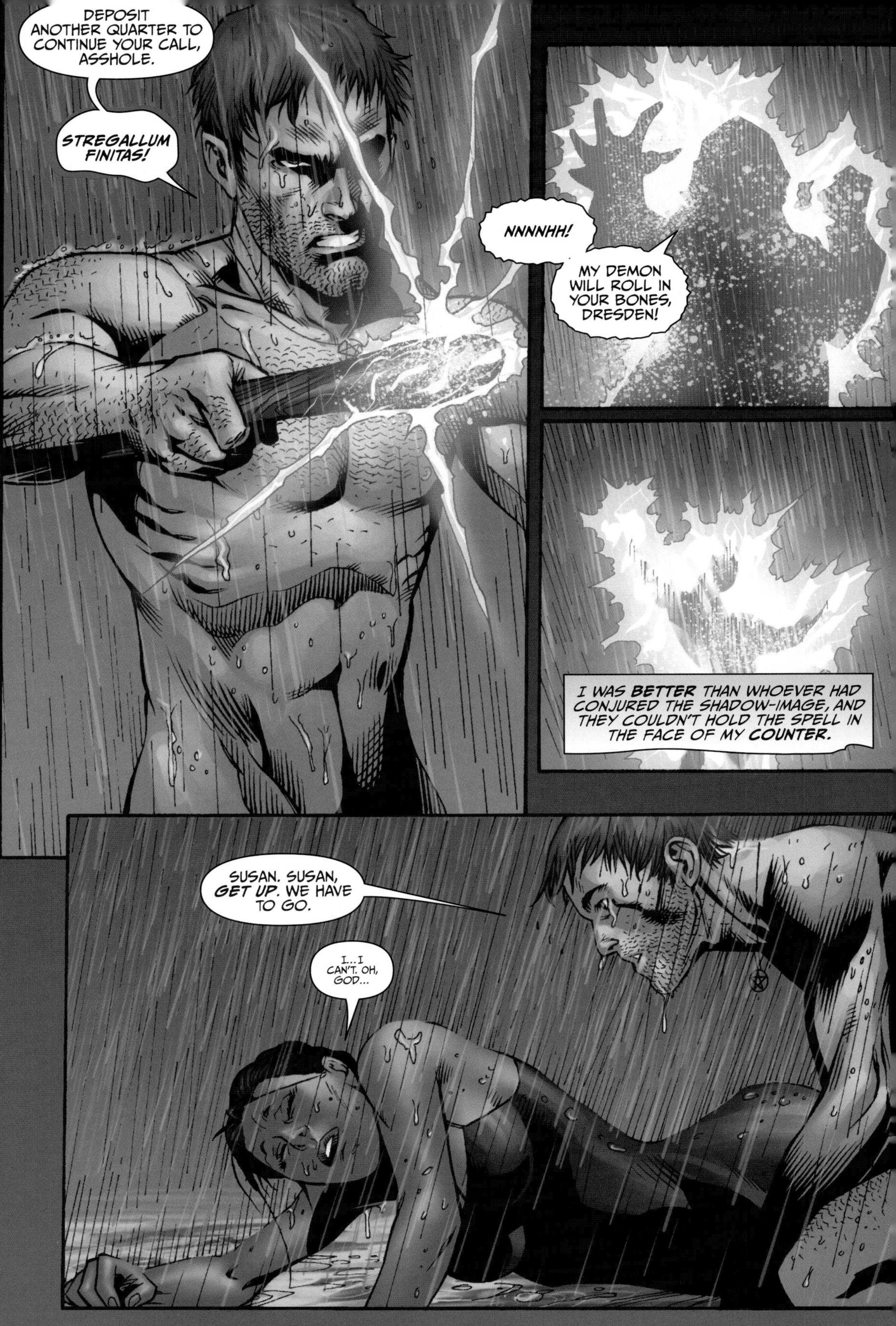

DEPOSIT ANOTHER QUARTER TO CONTINUE YOUR CALL, ASSHOLE.
STREGALLUM FINITAS!
NNNNHH!
MY DEMON WILL ROLL IN YOUR BONES, DRESDEN!
I WAS BETTER THAN WHOEVER HAD CONJURED THE SHADOW-IMAGE, AND THEY COULDN'T HOLD THE SPELL IN THE FACE OF MY COUNTER.
SUSAN. SUSAN, GET UP. WE HAVE TO GO.
I... I CAN'T. OH, GOD...

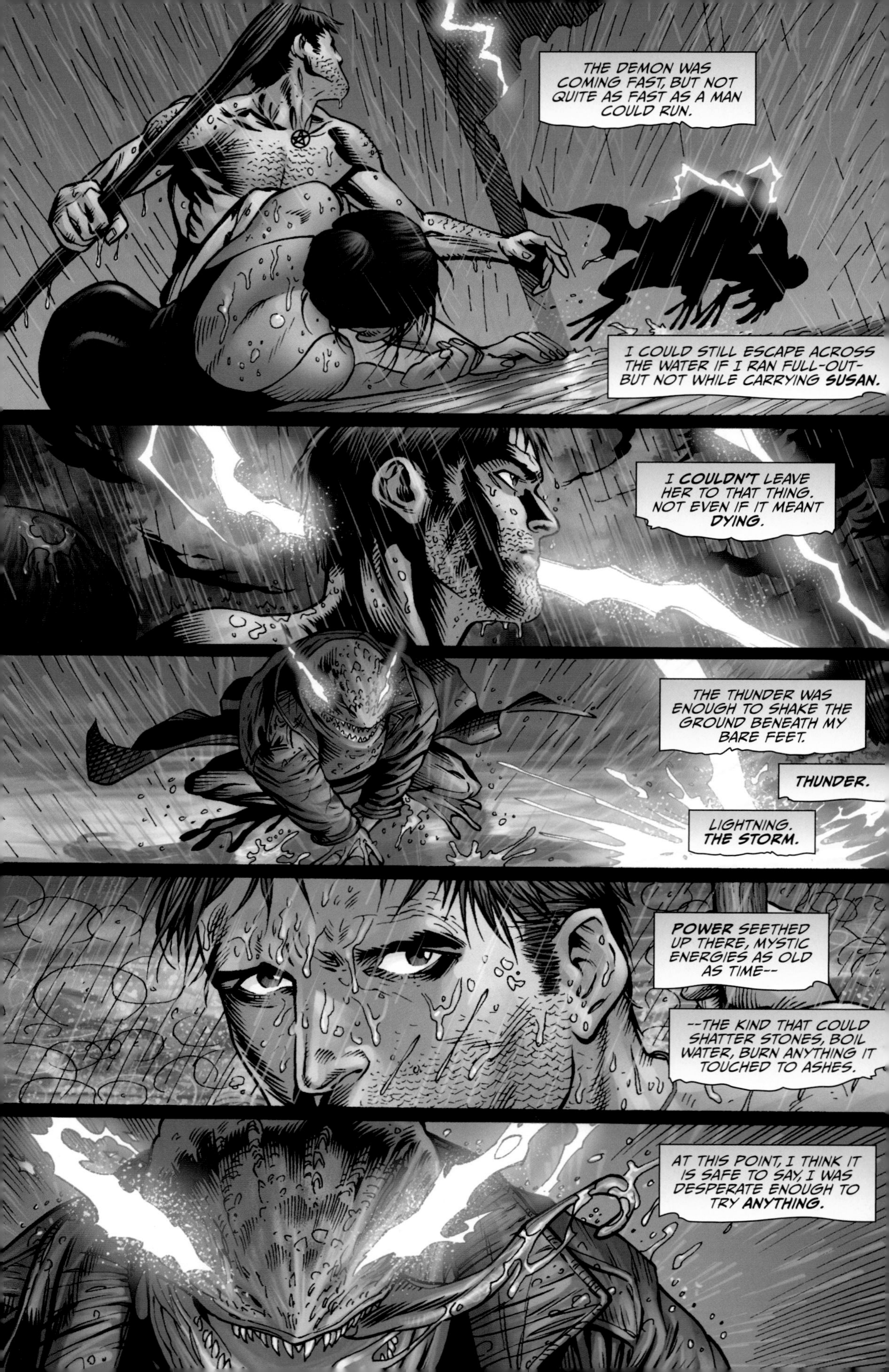
THE DEMON WAS COMING FAST, BUT NOT QUITE AS FAST AS A MAN COULD RUN.
I COULD STILL ESCAPE ACROSS THE WATER IF I RAN FULL-OUT-BUT NOT WHILE CARRYING SUSAN.
I COULDN'T LEAVE HER TO THAT THING. NOT EVEN IF IT MEANT DYING.
THE THUNDER WAS ENOUGH TO SHAKE THE GROUND BENEATH MY BARE FEET.
THUNDER.
LIGHTNING. THE STORM.
POWER SEETHED UP THERE, MYSTIC ENERGIES AS OLD AS TIME--
--THE KIND THAT COULD SHATTER STONES, BOIL WATER, BURN ANYTHING IT TOUCHED TO ASHES.
AT THIS POINT, I THINK IT IS SAFE TO SAY, I WAS DESPERATE ENOUGH TO TRY ANYTHING.

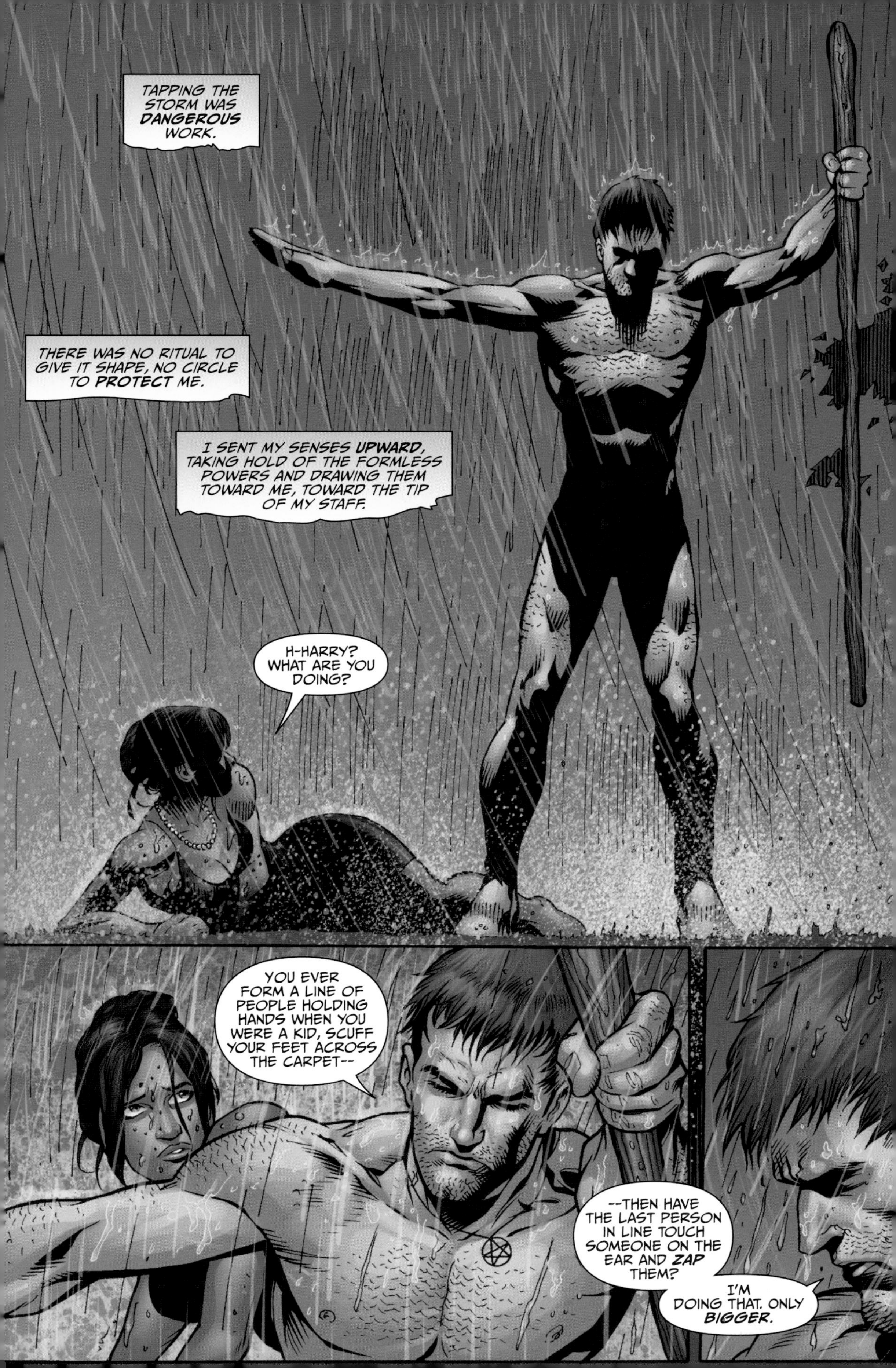
TAPPING THE STORM WAS DANGEROUS WORK.
THERE WAS NO RITUAL TO GIVE IT SHAPE, NO CIRCLE TO PROTECT ME.
I SENT MY SENSES UPWARD, TAKING HOLD OF THE FORMLESS POWERS AND DRAWING THEM TOWARD ME, TOWARD THE TIP OF MY STAFF.
H-HARRY? WHAT ARE YOU DOING?
YOU EVER FORM A LINE OF PEOPLE HOLDING HANDS WHEN YOU WERE A KID, SCUFF YOUR FEET ACROSS THE CARPET--
--THEN HAVE THE LAST PERSON IN LINE TOUCH SOMEONE ON THE EAR AND ZAP THEM?
I'M DOING THAT. ONLY BIGGER.

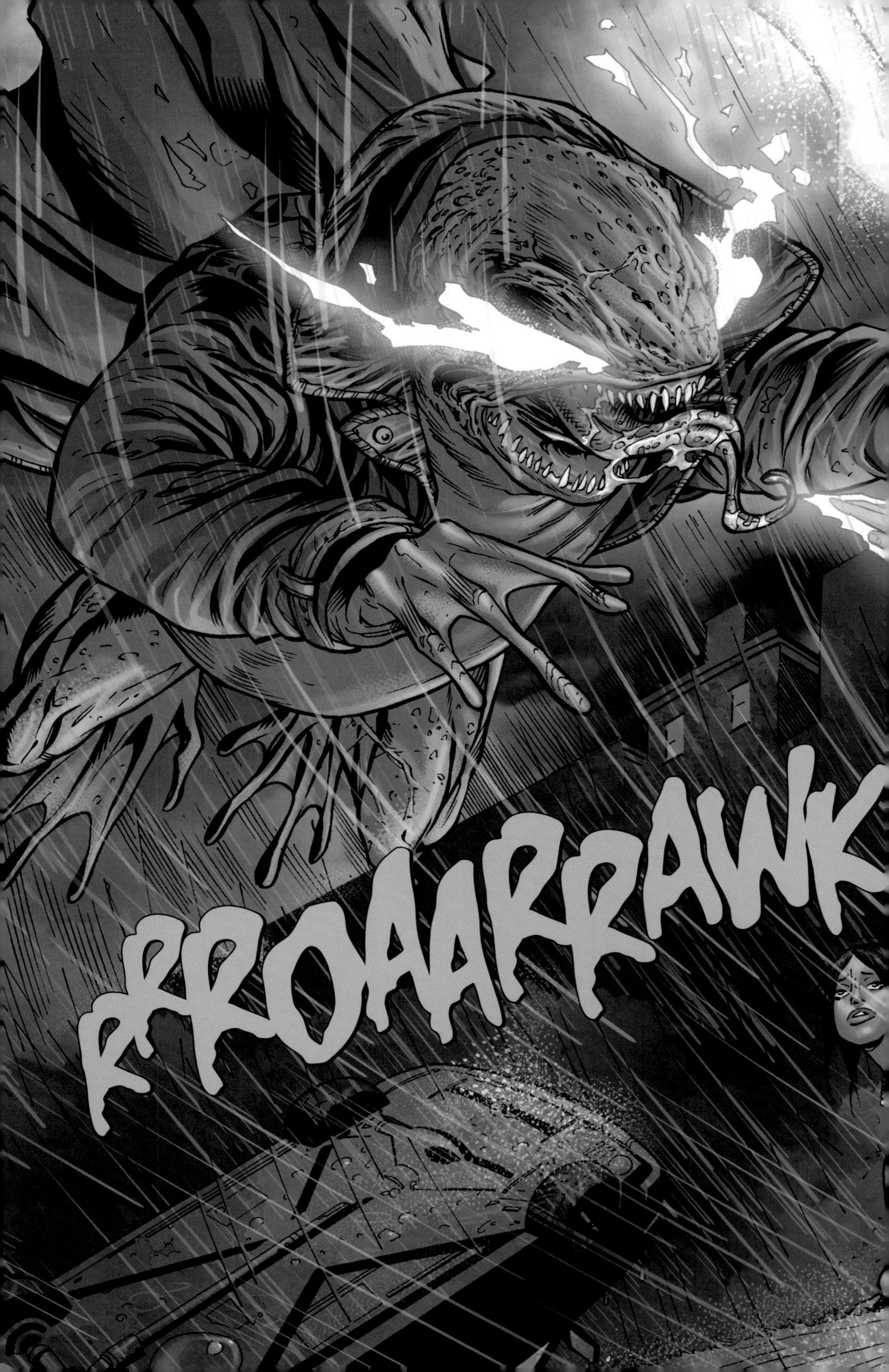
RRROAARRAWK

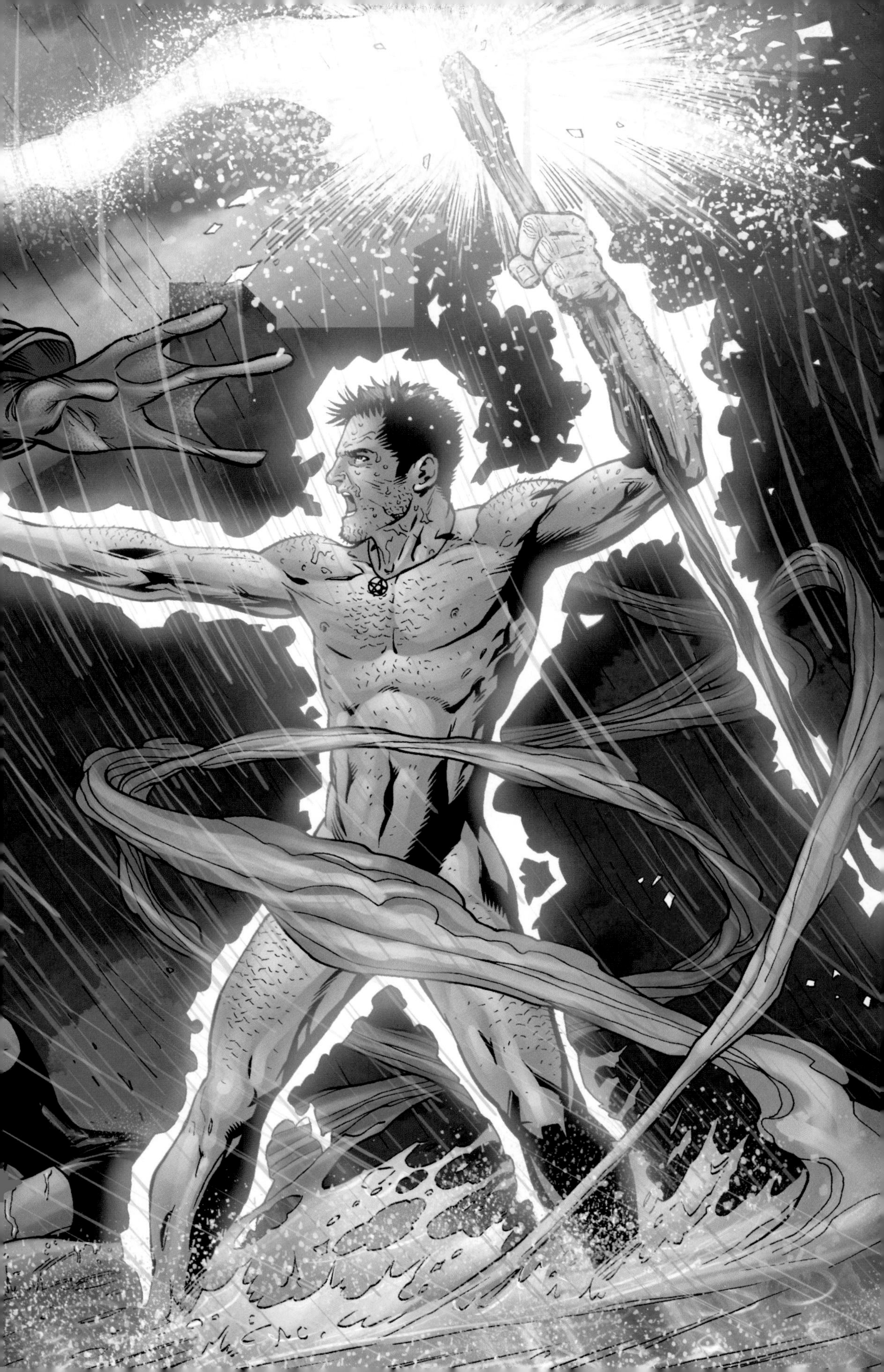

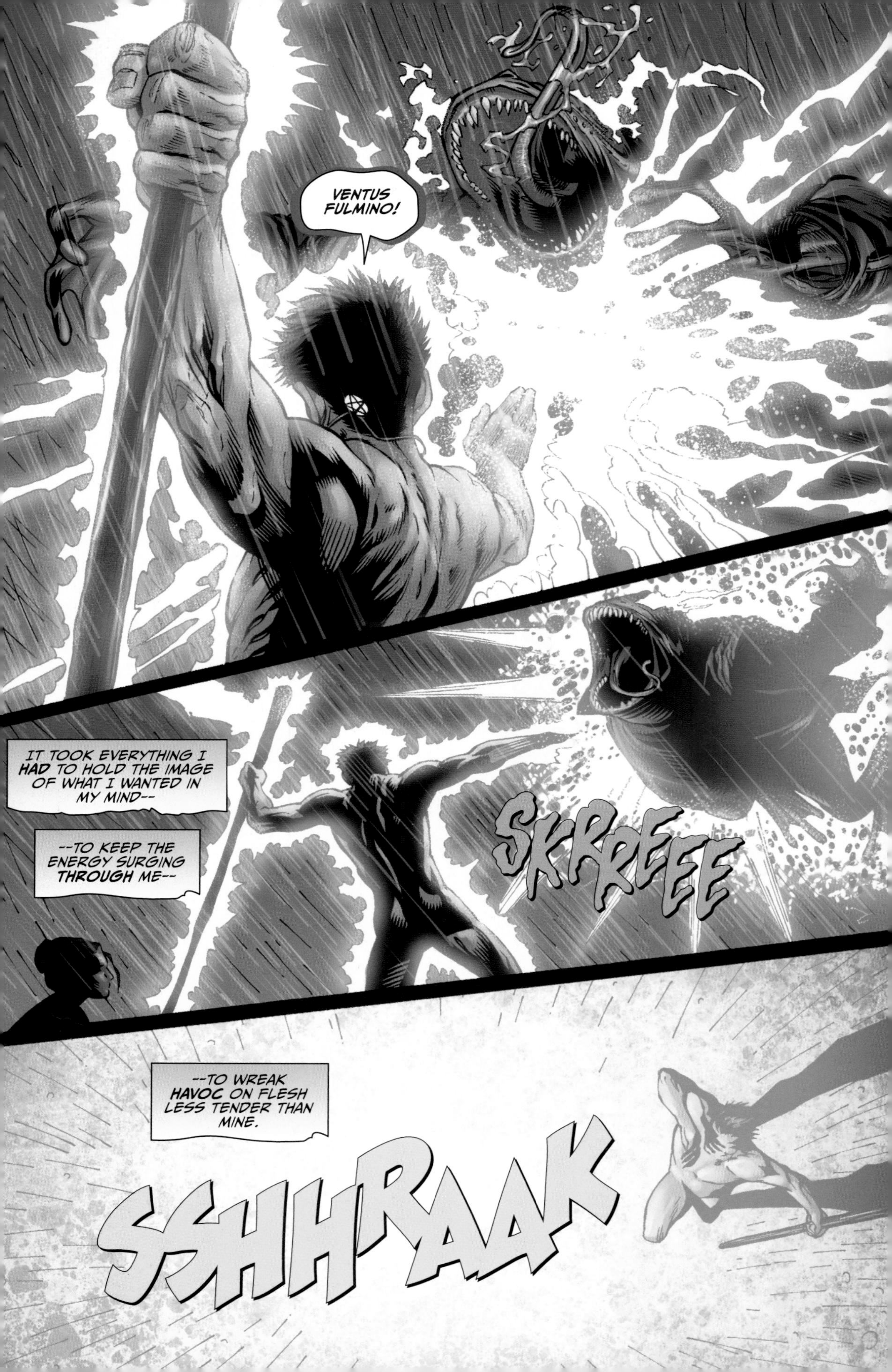
VENTUS FULMINO!
IT TOOK EVERYTHING I HAD TO HOLD THE IMAGE OF WHAT I WANTED IN MY MIND--
--TO KEEP THE ENERGY SURGING THROUGH ME--
SKRREEEE
--TO WREAK HAVOC ON FLESH LESS TENDER THAN MINE.
SSHHRAAK

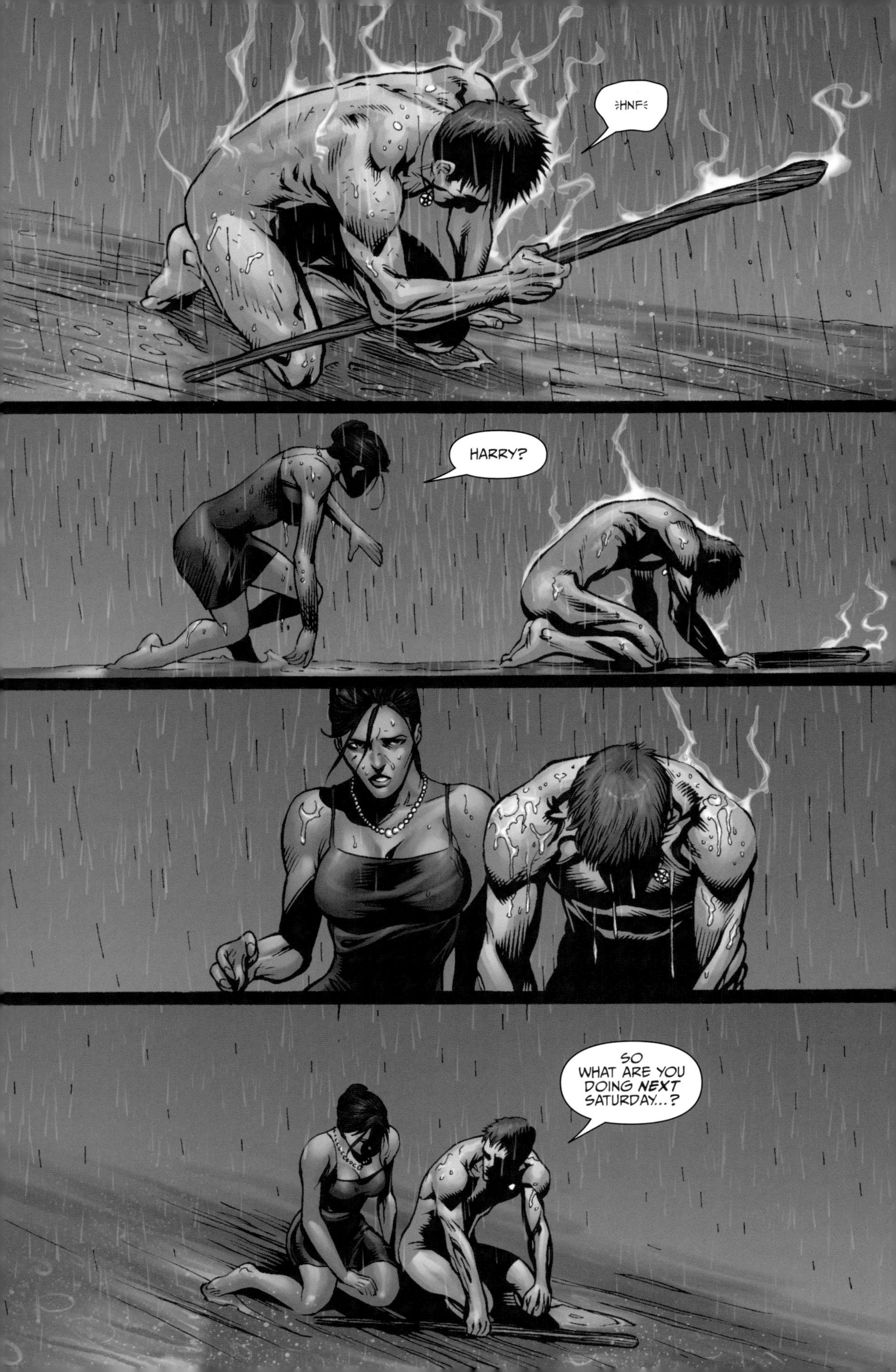

HNF
HARRY?
SO WHAT ARE YOU DOING ***NEXT*** SATURDAY...?

RESTORATION OF FAITH

PREQUEL CHAPTER

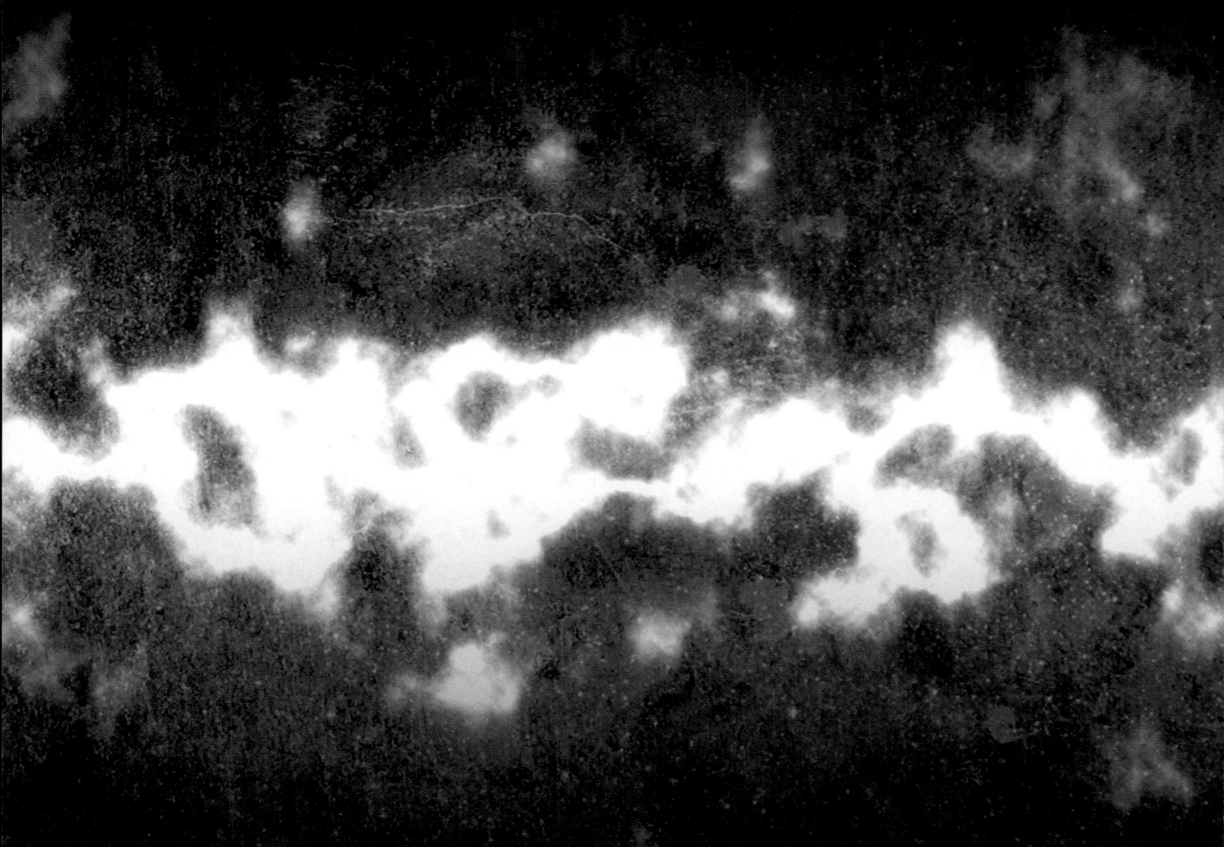

written by **JIM BUTCHER**
adapted by **GRANT ALTER**
art by **KEVIN MELLON**
colors by **KIERAN OATS**
lettering by **BILL TORTOLINI**

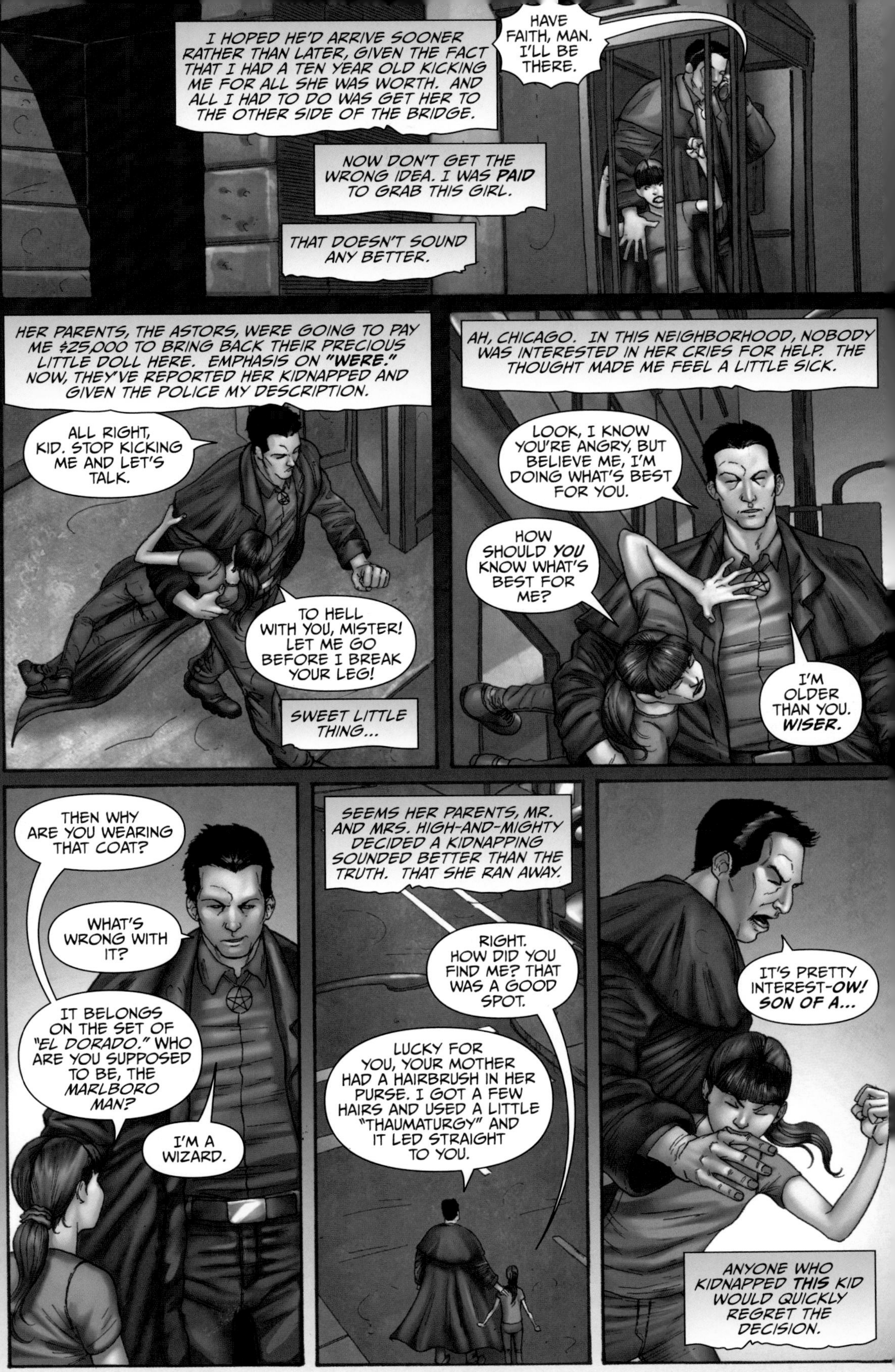
I HOPED HE'D ARRIVE SOONER RATHER THAN LATER, GIVEN THE FACT THAT I HAD A TEN YEAR OLD KICKING ME FOR ALL SHE WAS WORTH. AND ALL I HAD TO DO WAS GET HER TO THE OTHER SIDE OF THE BRIDGE.
HAVE FAITH, MAN. I'LL BE THERE.
NOW DON'T GET THE WRONG IDEA. I WAS **PAID** TO GRAB THIS GIRL.
THAT DOESN'T SOUND ANY BETTER.
HER PARENTS, THE ASTORS, WERE GOING TO PAY ME $25,000 TO BRING BACK THEIR PRECIOUS LITTLE DOLL HERE. EMPHASIS ON **"WERE."** NOW, THEY'VE REPORTED HER KIDNAPPED AND GIVEN THE POLICE MY DESCRIPTION.
ALL RIGHT, KID. STOP KICKING ME AND LET'S TALK.
TO HELL WITH YOU, MISTER! LET ME GO BEFORE I BREAK YOUR LEG!
SWEET LITTLE THING...
AH, CHICAGO. IN THIS NEIGHBORHOOD, NOBODY WAS INTERESTED IN HER CRIES FOR HELP. THE THOUGHT MADE ME FEEL A LITTLE SICK.
LOOK, I KNOW YOU'RE ANGRY, BUT BELIEVE ME, I'M DOING WHAT'S BEST FOR YOU.
HOW SHOULD ***YOU*** KNOW WHAT'S BEST FOR ME?
I'M OLDER THAN YOU. ***WISER.***
THEN WHY ARE YOU WEARING THAT COAT?
WHAT'S WRONG WITH IT?
IT BELONGS ON THE SET OF "EL DORADO." WHO ARE YOU SUPPOSED TO BE, THE *MARLBORO MAN?*
I'M A WIZARD.
SEEMS HER PARENTS, MR. AND MRS. HIGH-AND-MIGHTY DECIDED A KIDNAPPING SOUNDED BETTER THAN THE TRUTH. THAT SHE RAN AWAY.
RIGHT. HOW DID YOU FIND ME? THAT WAS A GOOD SPOT.
LUCKY FOR YOU, YOUR MOTHER HAD A HAIRBRUSH IN HER PURSE. I GOT A FEW HAIRS AND USED A LITTLE "THAUMATURGY" AND IT LED STRAIGHT TO YOU.
IT'S PRETTY INTEREST-***OW! SON OF A...***
ANYONE WHO KIDNAPPED **THIS** KID WOULD QUICKLY REGRET THE DECISION.

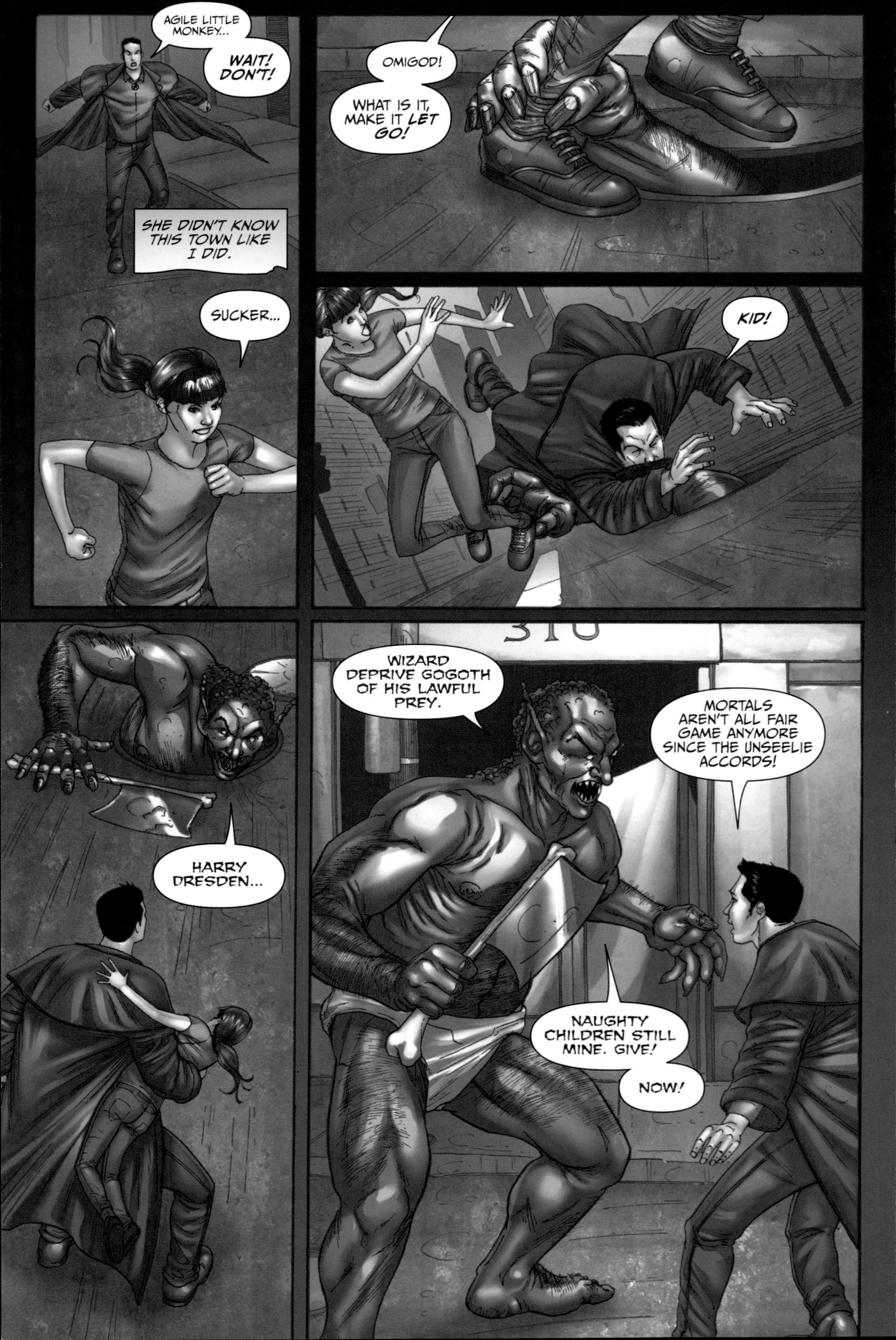

AGILE LITTLE MONKEY...
WAIT! DON'T!
OMIGOD!
WHAT IS IT, MAKE IT LET GO!
SHE DIDN'T KNOW THIS TOWN LIKE I DID.
SUCKER...
KID!
HARRY DRESDEN...
310
WIZARD DEPRIVE GOGOTH OF HIS LAWFUL PREY.
MORTALS AREN'T ALL FAIR GAME ANYMORE SINCE THE UNSEELIE ACCORDS!
NAUGHTY CHILDREN STILL MINE. GIVE!
NOW!

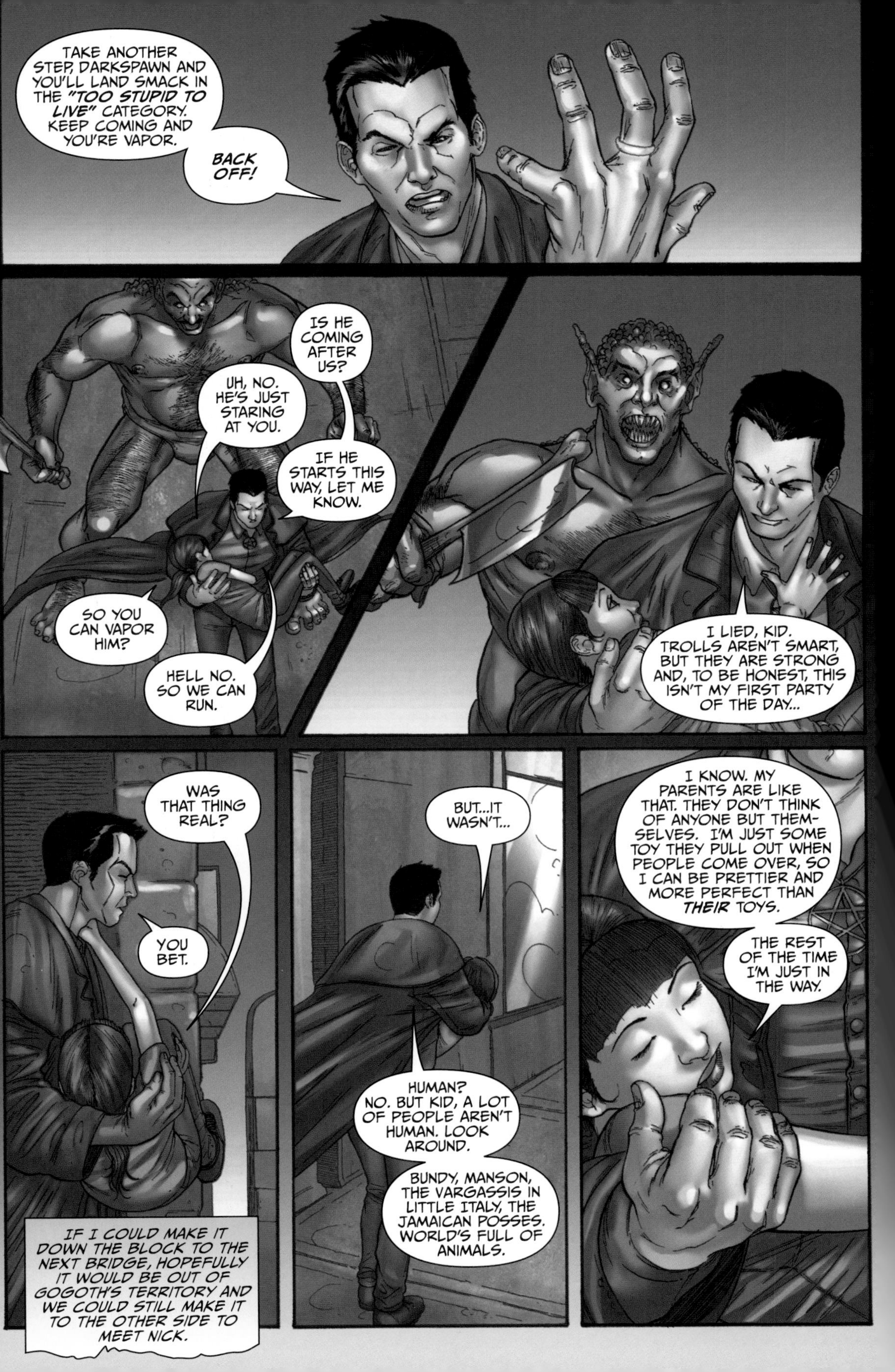
TAKE ANOTHER STEP, DARKSPAWN AND YOU'LL LAND SMACK IN THE "TOO STUPID TO LIVE" CATEGORY. KEEP COMING AND YOU'RE VAPOR.
BACK OFF!
IS HE COMING AFTER US?
UH, NO. HE'S JUST STARING AT YOU.
IF HE STARTS THIS WAY, LET ME KNOW.
SO YOU CAN VAPOR HIM?
HELL NO. SO WE CAN RUN.
I LIED, KID. TROLLS AREN'T SMART, BUT THEY ARE STRONG AND, TO BE HONEST, THIS ISN'T MY FIRST PARTY OF THE DAY...
WAS THAT THING REAL?
YOU BET.
IF I COULD MAKE IT DOWN THE BLOCK TO THE NEXT BRIDGE, HOPEFULLY IT WOULD BE OUT OF GOGOTH'S TERRITORY AND WE COULD STILL MAKE IT TO THE OTHER SIDE TO MEET NICK.
BUT...IT WASN'T...
HUMAN? NO. BUT KID, A LOT OF PEOPLE AREN'T HUMAN. LOOK AROUND.
BUNDY, MANSON, THE VARGASSIS IN LITTLE ITALY, THE JAMAICAN POSSES. WORLD'S FULL OF ANIMALS.
I KNOW. MY PARENTS ARE LIKE THAT. THEY DON'T THINK OF ANYONE BUT THEM-SELVES. I'M JUST SOME TOY THEY PULL OUT WHEN PEOPLE COME OVER, SO I CAN BE PRETTIER AND MORE PERFECT THAN THEIR TOYS.
THE REST OF THE TIME I'M JUST IN THE WAY.

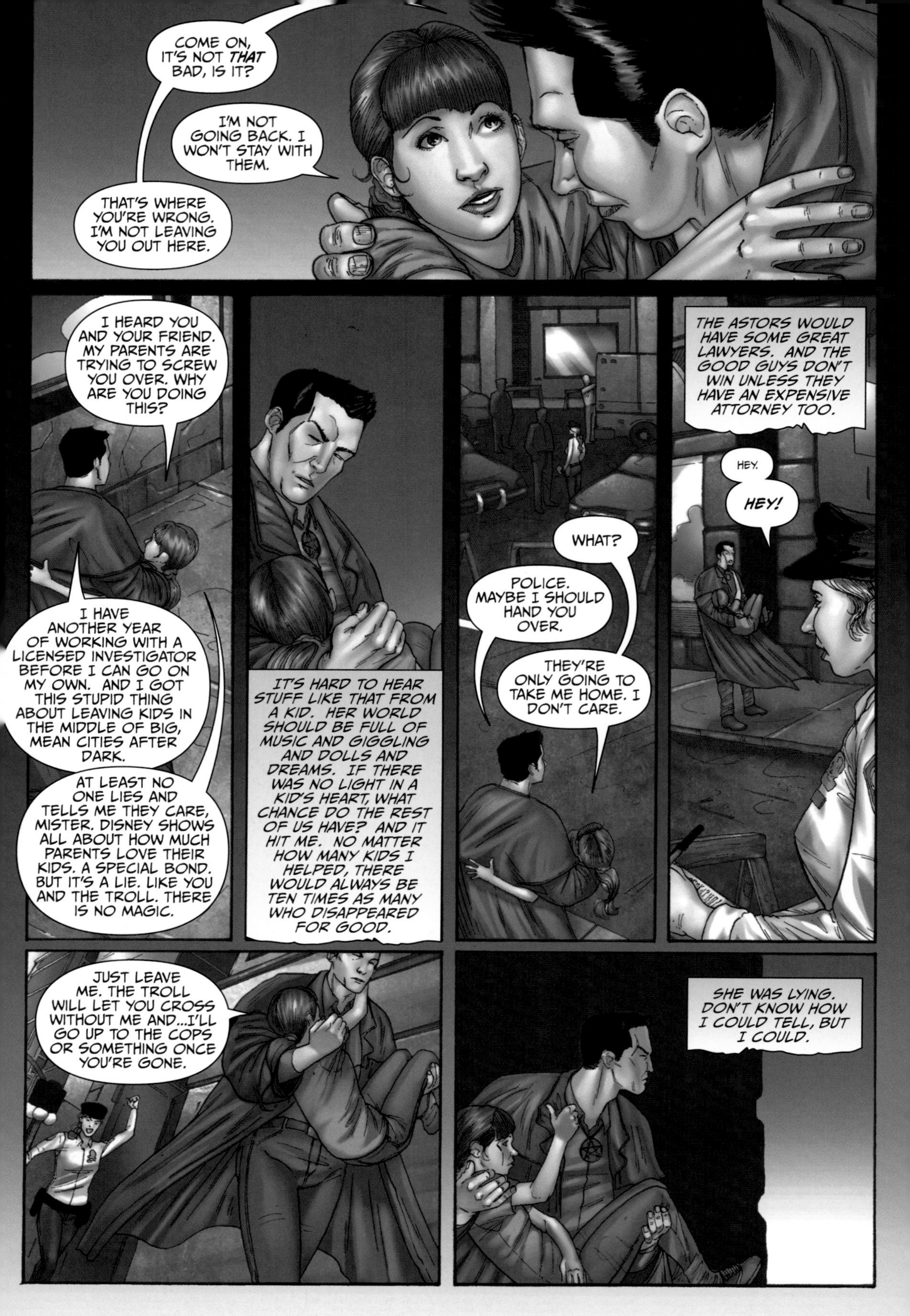
COME ON, IT'S NOT *THAT* BAD, IS IT?
I'M NOT GOING BACK. I WON'T STAY WITH THEM.
THAT'S WHERE YOU'RE WRONG. I'M NOT LEAVING YOU OUT HERE.
I HEARD YOU AND YOUR FRIEND. MY PARENTS ARE TRYING TO SCREW YOU OVER. WHY ARE YOU DOING THIS?
I HAVE ANOTHER YEAR OF WORKING WITH A LICENSED INVESTIGATOR BEFORE I CAN GO ON MY OWN. AND I GOT THIS STUPID THING ABOUT LEAVING KIDS IN THE MIDDLE OF BIG, MEAN CITIES AFTER DARK.
AT LEAST NO ONE LIES AND TELLS ME THEY CARE, MISTER. DISNEY SHOWS ALL ABOUT HOW MUCH PARENTS LOVE THEIR KIDS. A SPECIAL BOND. BUT IT'S A LIE. LIKE YOU AND THE TROLL. THERE IS NO MAGIC.
IT'S HARD TO HEAR STUFF LIKE THAT FROM A KID. HER WORLD SHOULD BE FULL OF MUSIC AND GIGGLING AND DOLLS AND DREAMS. IF THERE WAS NO LIGHT IN A KID'S HEART, WHAT CHANCE DO THE REST OF US HAVE? AND IT HIT ME. NO MATTER HOW MANY KIDS I HELPED, THERE WOULD ALWAYS BE TEN TIMES AS MANY WHO DISAPPEARED FOR GOOD.
WHAT?
POLICE. MAYBE I SHOULD HAND YOU OVER.
THEY'RE ONLY GOING TO TAKE ME HOME. I DON'T CARE.
THE ASTORS WOULD HAVE SOME GREAT LAWYERS. AND THE GOOD GUYS DON'T WIN UNLESS THEY HAVE AN EXPENSIVE ATTORNEY TOO.
HEY.
HEY!
JUST LEAVE ME. THE TROLL WILL LET YOU CROSS WITHOUT ME AND...I'LL GO UP TO THE COPS OR SOMETHING ONCE YOU'RE GONE.
SHE WAS LYING. DON'T KNOW HOW I COULD TELL, BUT I COULD.

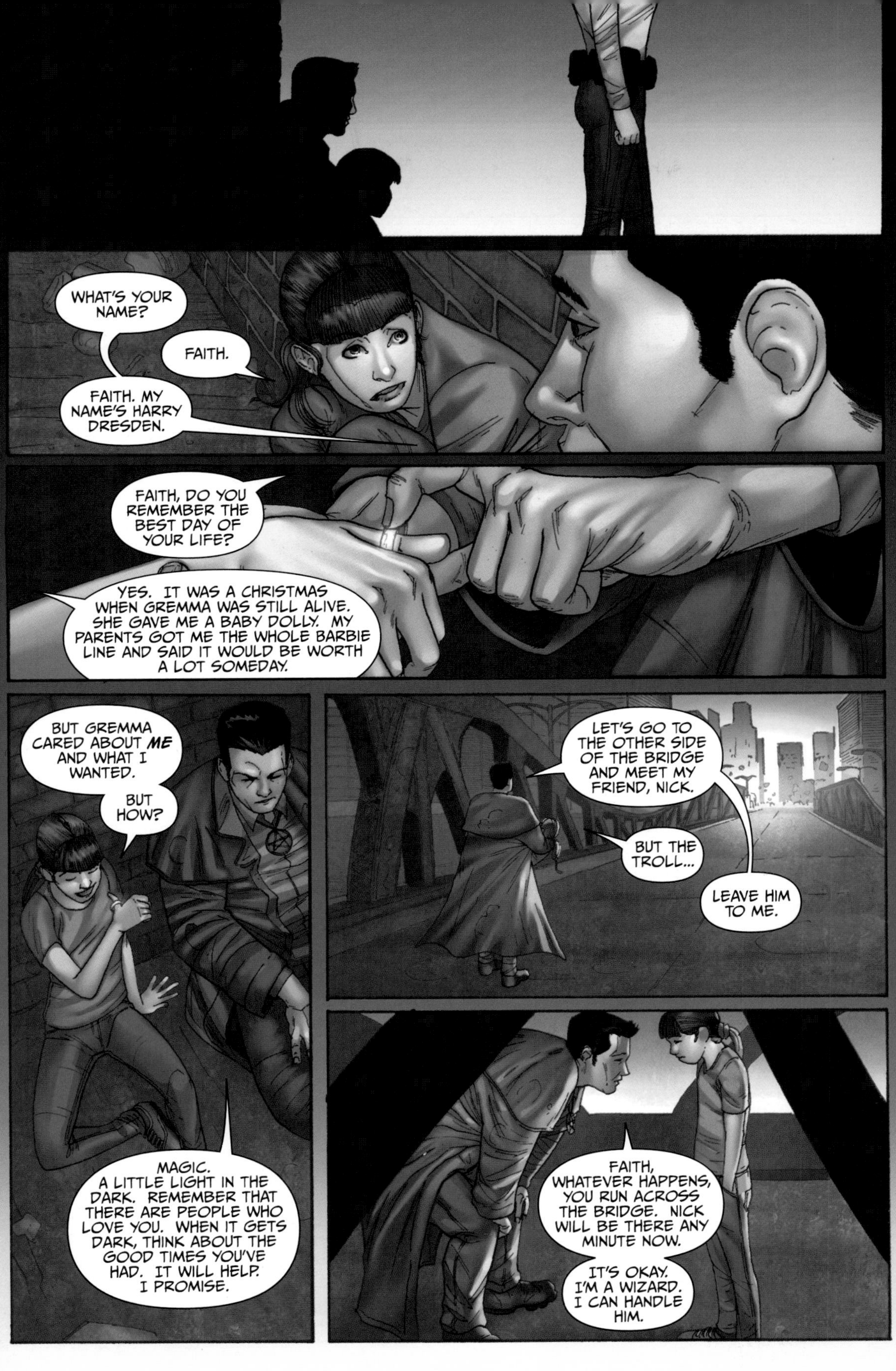
WHAT'S YOUR NAME?
FAITH.
FAITH. MY NAME'S HARRY DRESDEN.
FAITH, DO YOU REMEMBER THE BEST DAY OF YOUR LIFE?
YES. IT WAS A CHRISTMAS WHEN GREMMA WAS STILL ALIVE. SHE GAVE ME A BABY DOLLY. MY PARENTS GOT ME THE WHOLE BARBIE LINE AND SAID IT WOULD BE WORTH A LOT SOMEDAY.
BUT GREMMA CARED ABOUT ***ME*** AND WHAT I WANTED.
BUT HOW?
MAGIC. A LITTLE LIGHT IN THE DARK. REMEMBER THAT THERE ARE PEOPLE WHO LOVE YOU. WHEN IT GETS DARK, THINK ABOUT THE GOOD TIMES YOU'VE HAD. IT WILL HELP. I PROMISE.
LET'S GO TO THE OTHER SIDE OF THE BRIDGE AND MEET MY FRIEND, NICK.
BUT THE TROLL...
LEAVE HIM TO ME.
FAITH, WHATEVER HAPPENS, YOU RUN ACROSS THE BRIDGE. NICK WILL BE THERE ANY MINUTE NOW.
IT'S OKAY. I'M A WIZARD. I CAN HANDLE HIM.

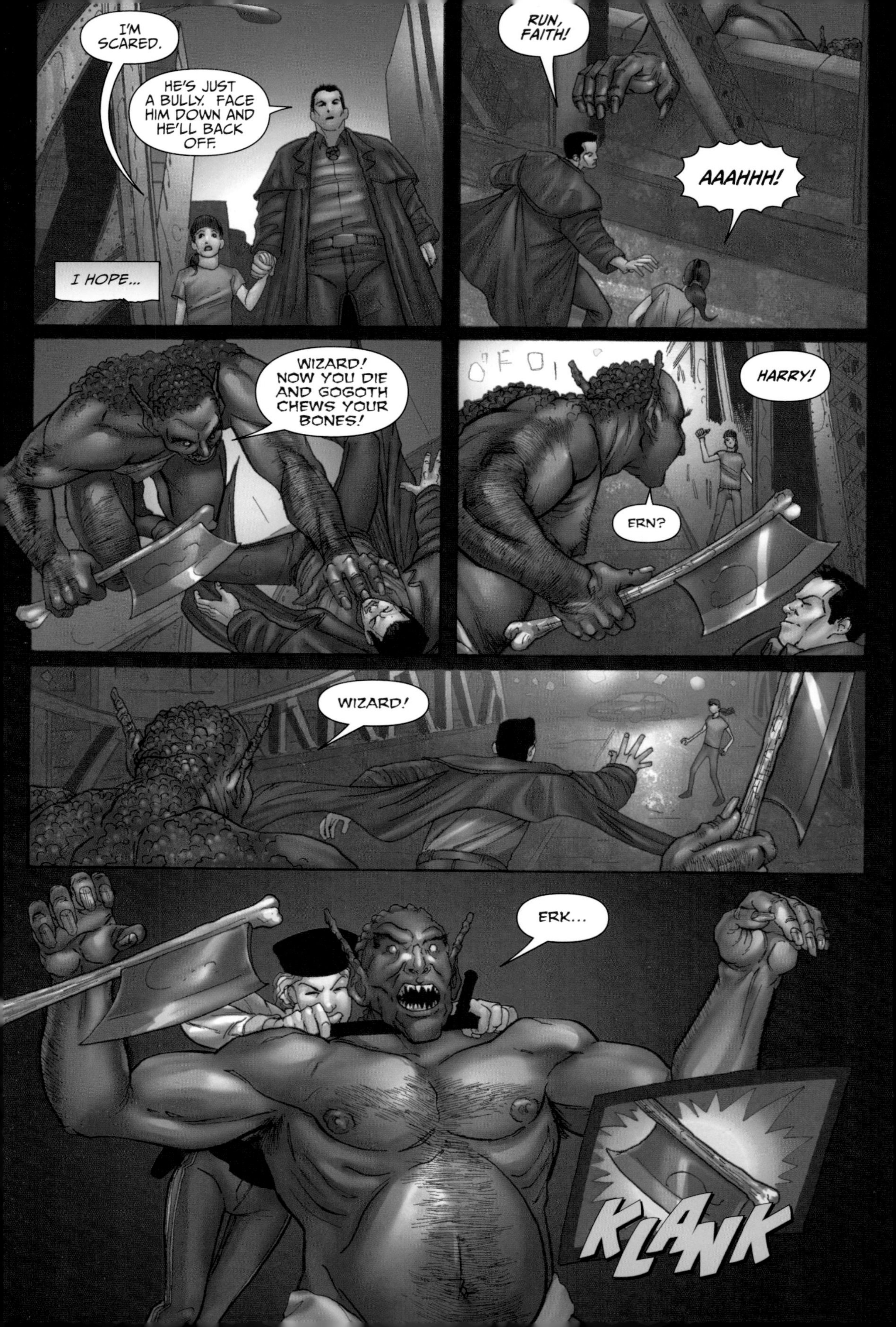
I'M SCARED.
HE'S JUST A BULLY. FACE HIM DOWN AND HE'LL BACK OFF.
I HOPE...
RUN, FAITH!
AAAHHH!
WIZARD! NOW YOU DIE AND GOGOTH CHEWS YOUR BONES!
HARRY!
ERN?
WIZARD!
ERK...
KLANK

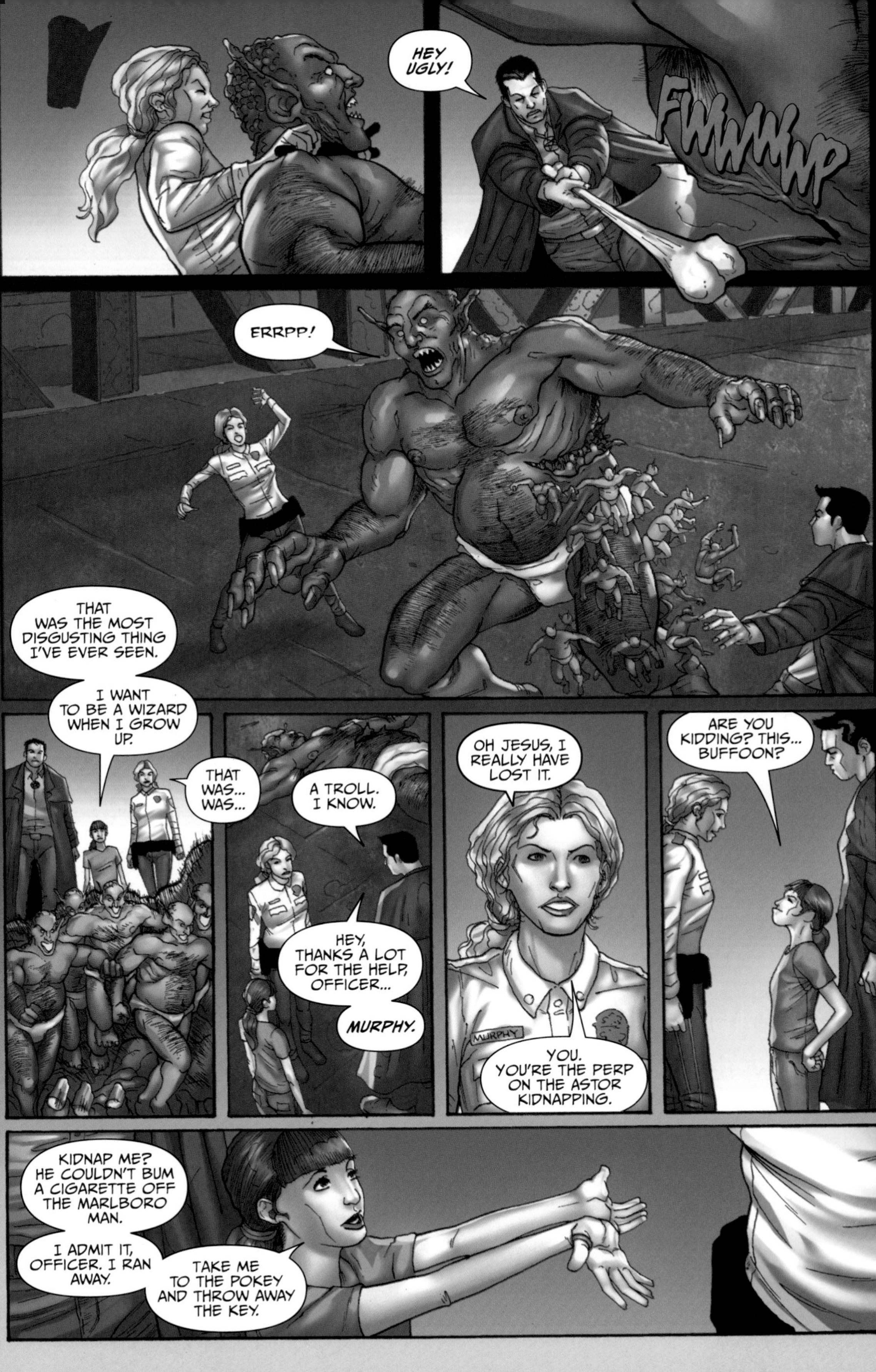
HEY UGLY!
FWWWWP
ERRPP!
THAT WAS THE MOST DISGUSTING THING I'VE EVER SEEN.
I WANT TO BE A WIZARD WHEN I GROW UP.
THAT WAS... WAS...
A TROLL. I KNOW.
HEY, THANKS A LOT FOR THE HELP, OFFICER...
MURPHY.
OH JESUS, I REALLY HAVE LOST IT.
MURPHY
YOU. YOU'RE THE PERP ON THE ASTOR KIDNAPPING.
ARE YOU KIDDING? THIS... BUFFOON?
KIDNAP ME? HE COULDN'T BUM A CIGARETTE OFF THE MARLBORO MAN.
I ADMIT IT, OFFICER. I RAN AWAY.
TAKE ME TO THE POKEY AND THROW AWAY THE KEY.

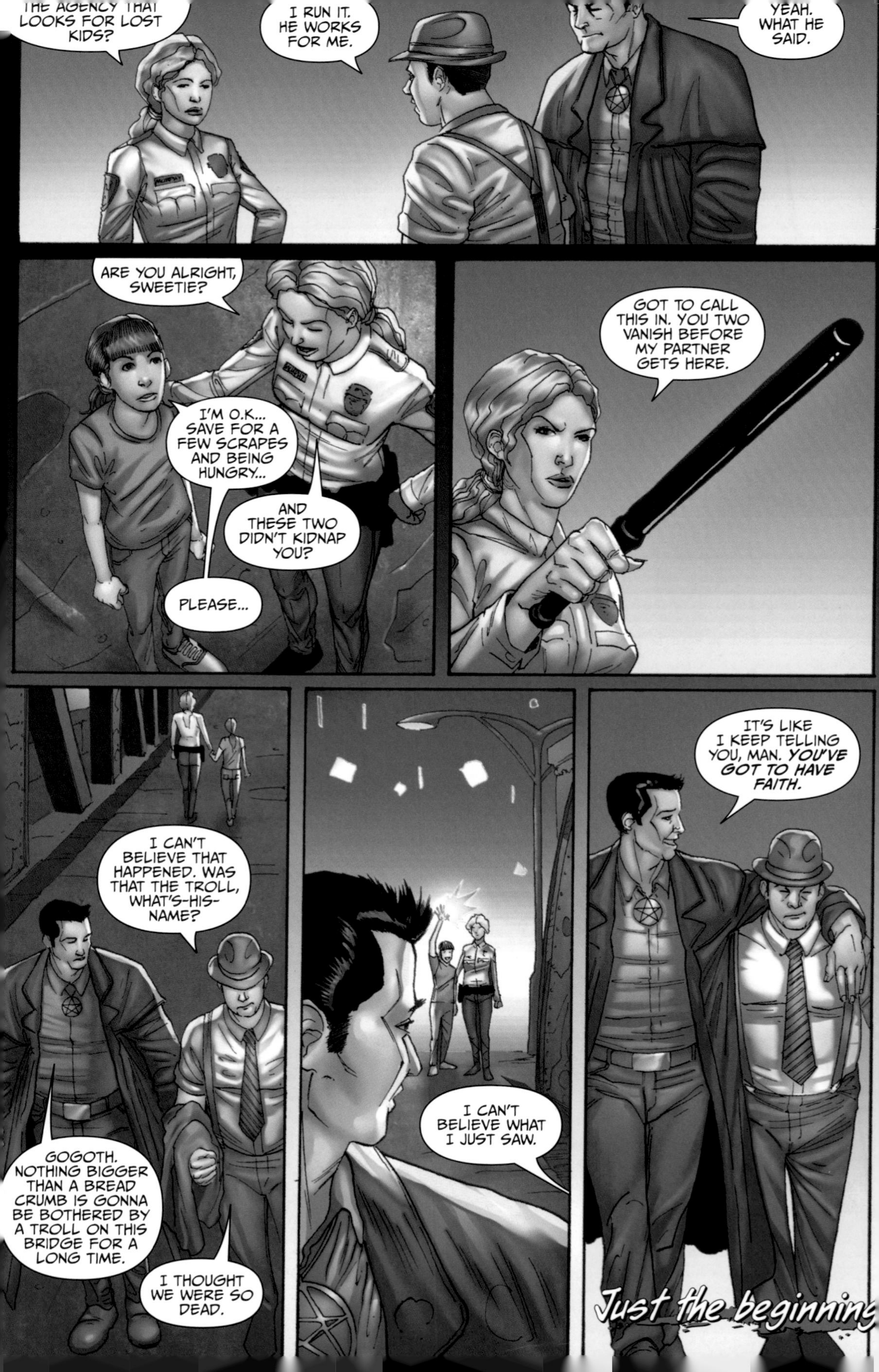
THE AGENCY THAT LOOKS FOR LOST KIDS?
I RUN IT. HE WORKS FOR ME.
YEAH. WHAT HE SAID.
ARE YOU ALRIGHT, SWEETIE?
I'M O.K... SAVE FOR A FEW SCRAPES AND BEING HUNGRY...
AND THESE TWO DIDN'T KIDNAP YOU?
PLEASE...
GOT TO CALL THIS IN. YOU TWO VANISH BEFORE MY PARTNER GETS HERE.
I CAN'T BELIEVE THAT HAPPENED. WAS THAT THE TROLL, WHAT'S-HIS-NAME?
GOGOTH. NOTHING BIGGER THAN A BREAD CRUMB IS GONNA BE BOTHERED BY A TROLL ON THIS BRIDGE FOR A LONG TIME.
I THOUGHT WE WERE SO DEAD.
I CAN'T BELIEVE WHAT I JUST SAW.
IT'S LIKE I KEEP TELLING YOU, MAN. YOU'VE GOT TO HAVE FAITH.
Just the beginning

COVER GALLERY

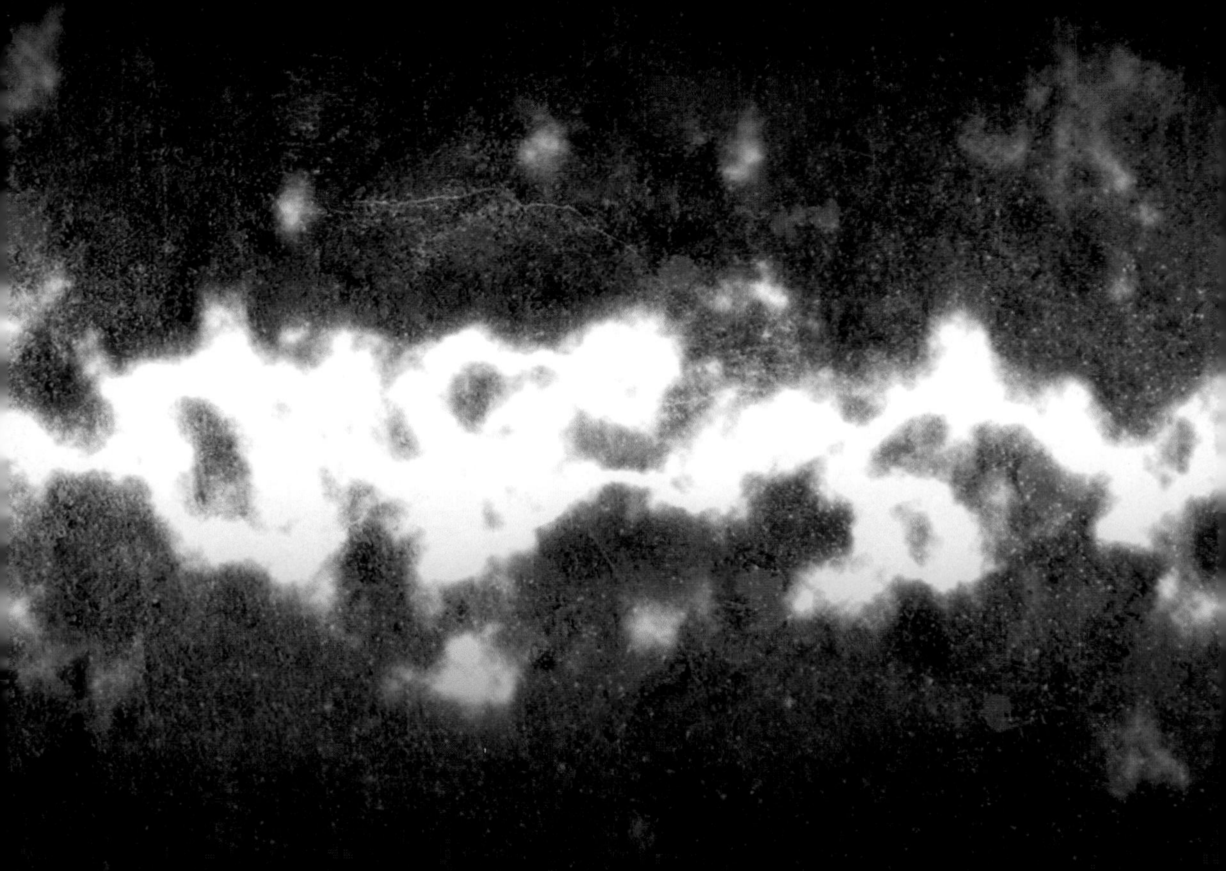

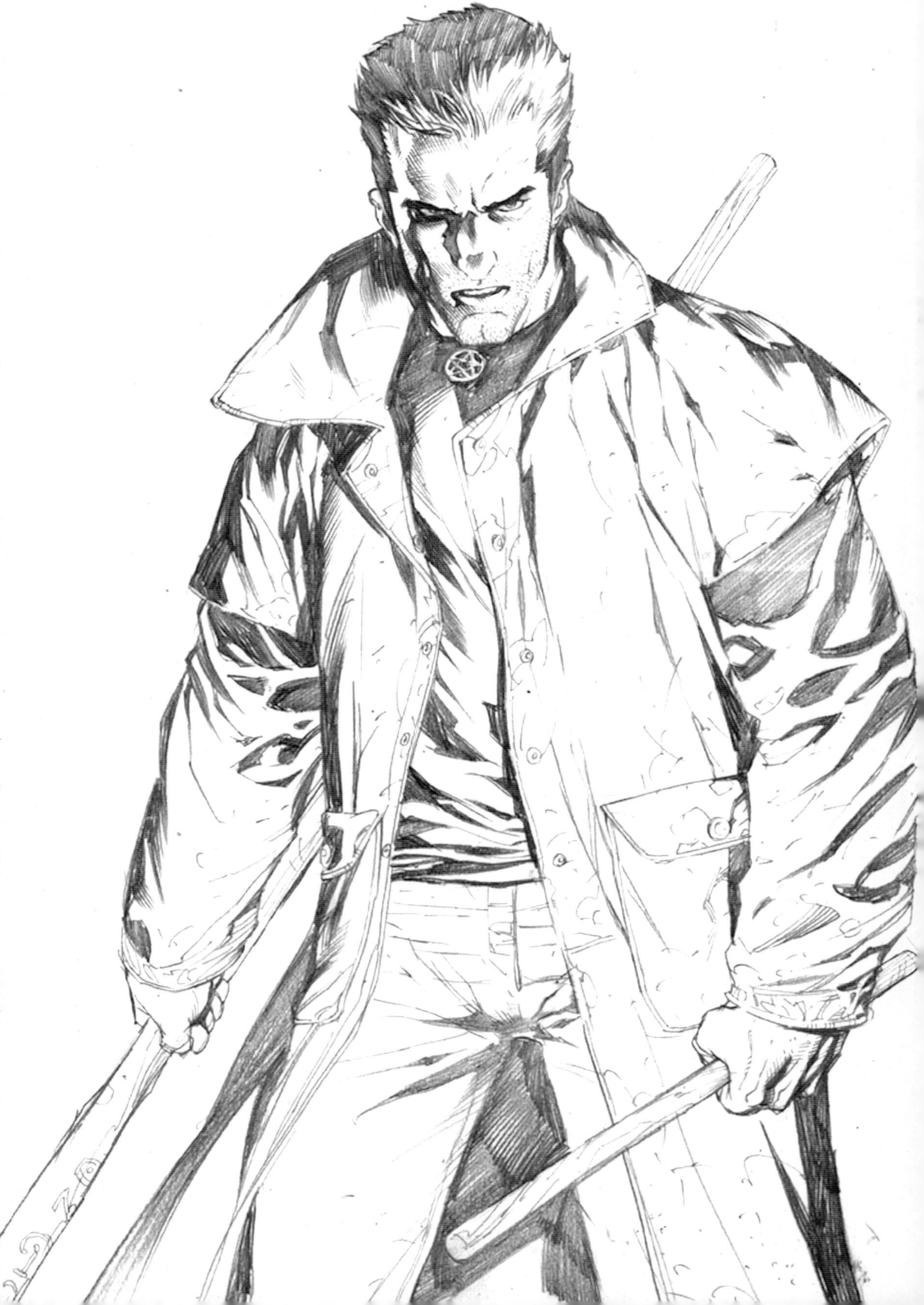

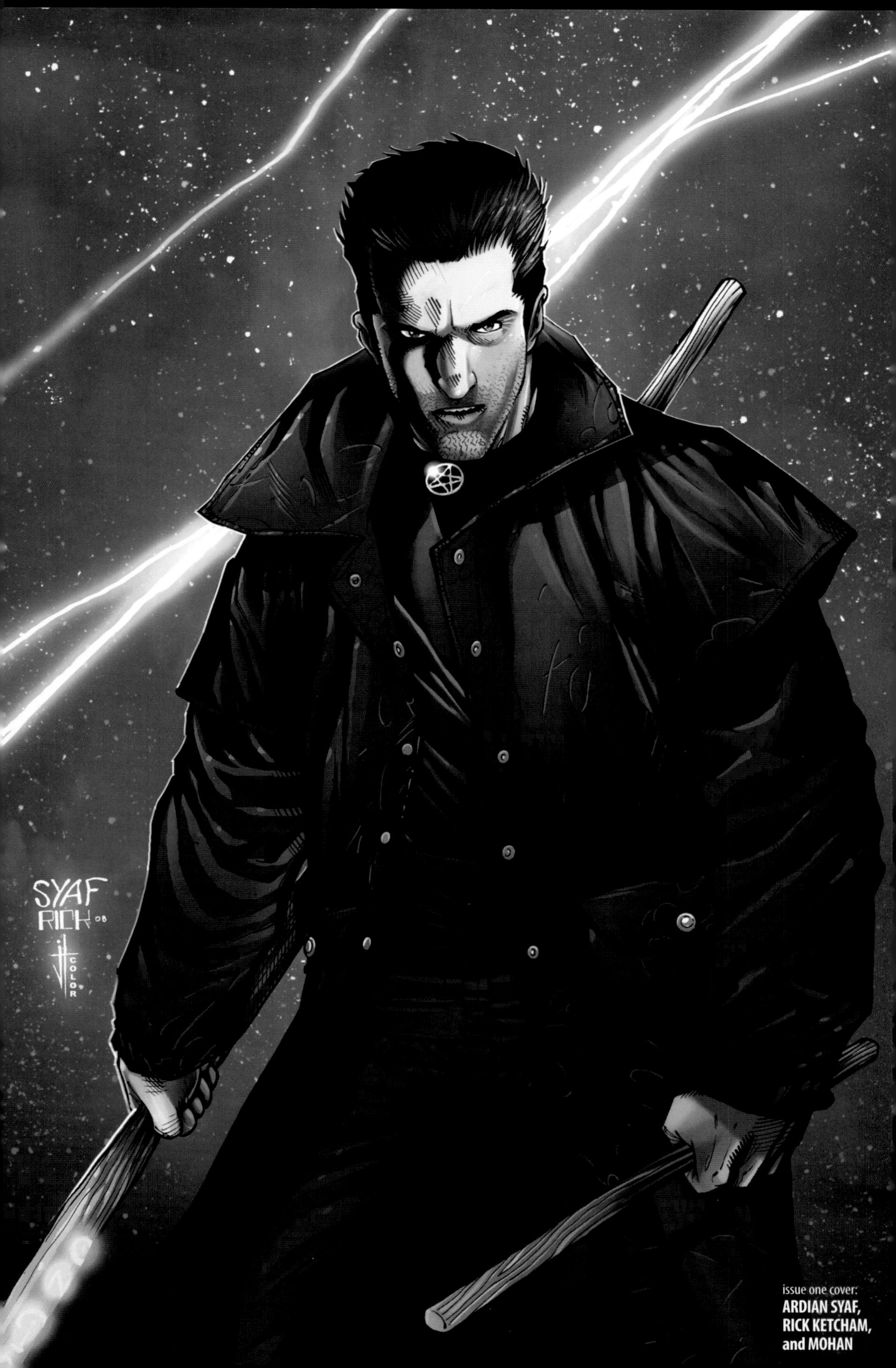
SYAF
RICK ·08
COLOR

issue one cover:
ARDIAN SYAF,
RICK KETCHAM,
and MOHAN

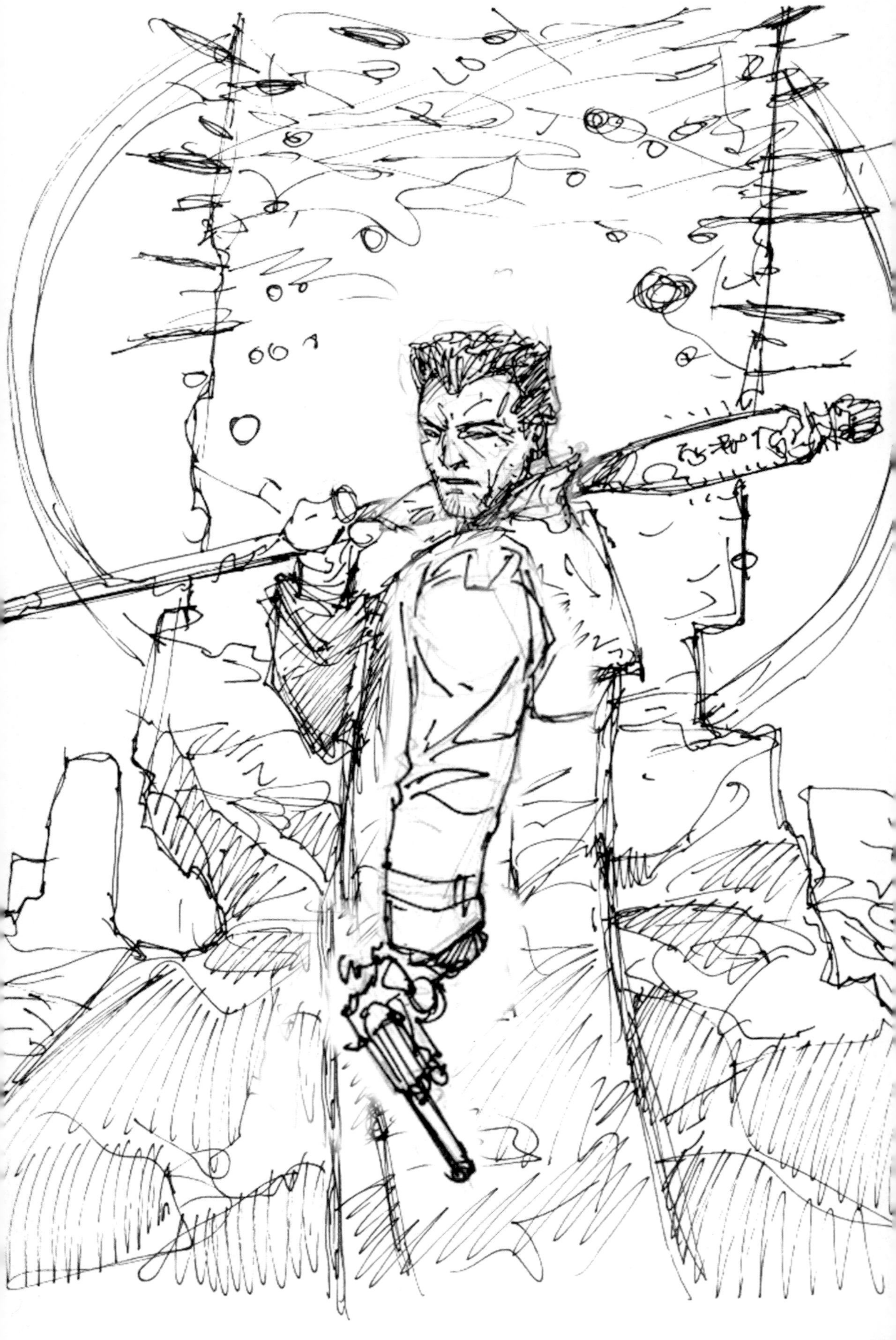

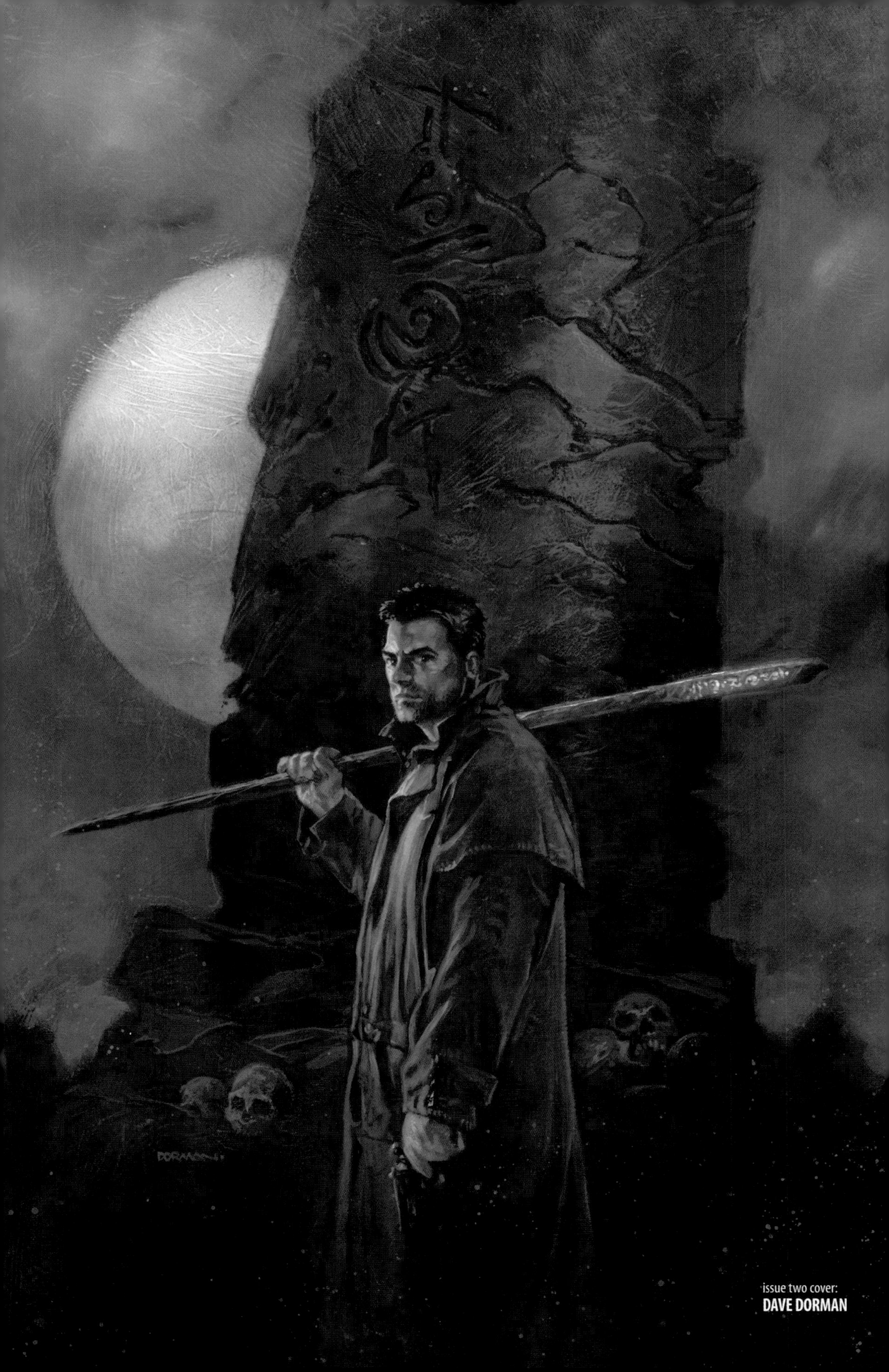
DORMAN

issue two cover:
DAVE DORMAN

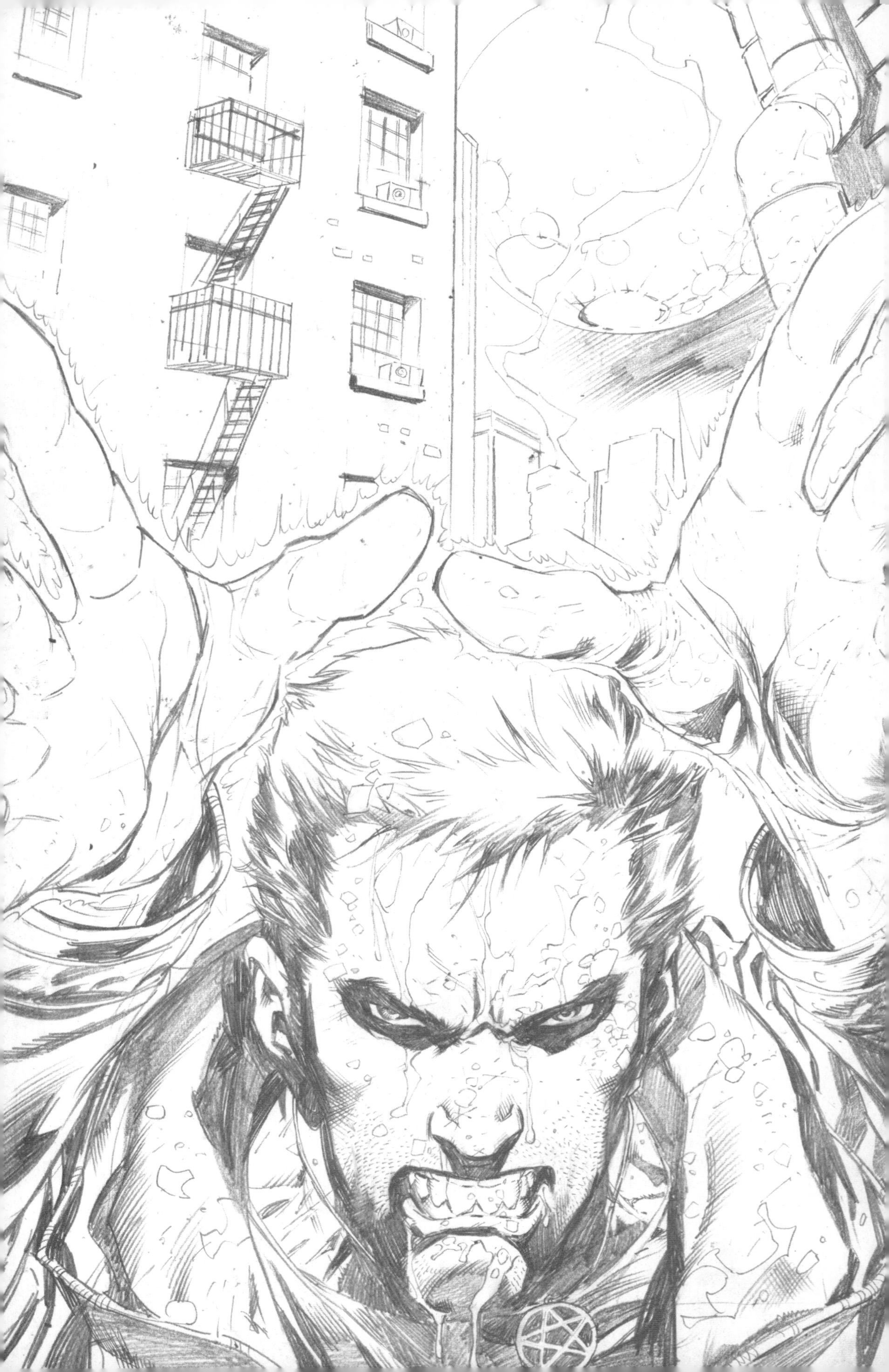

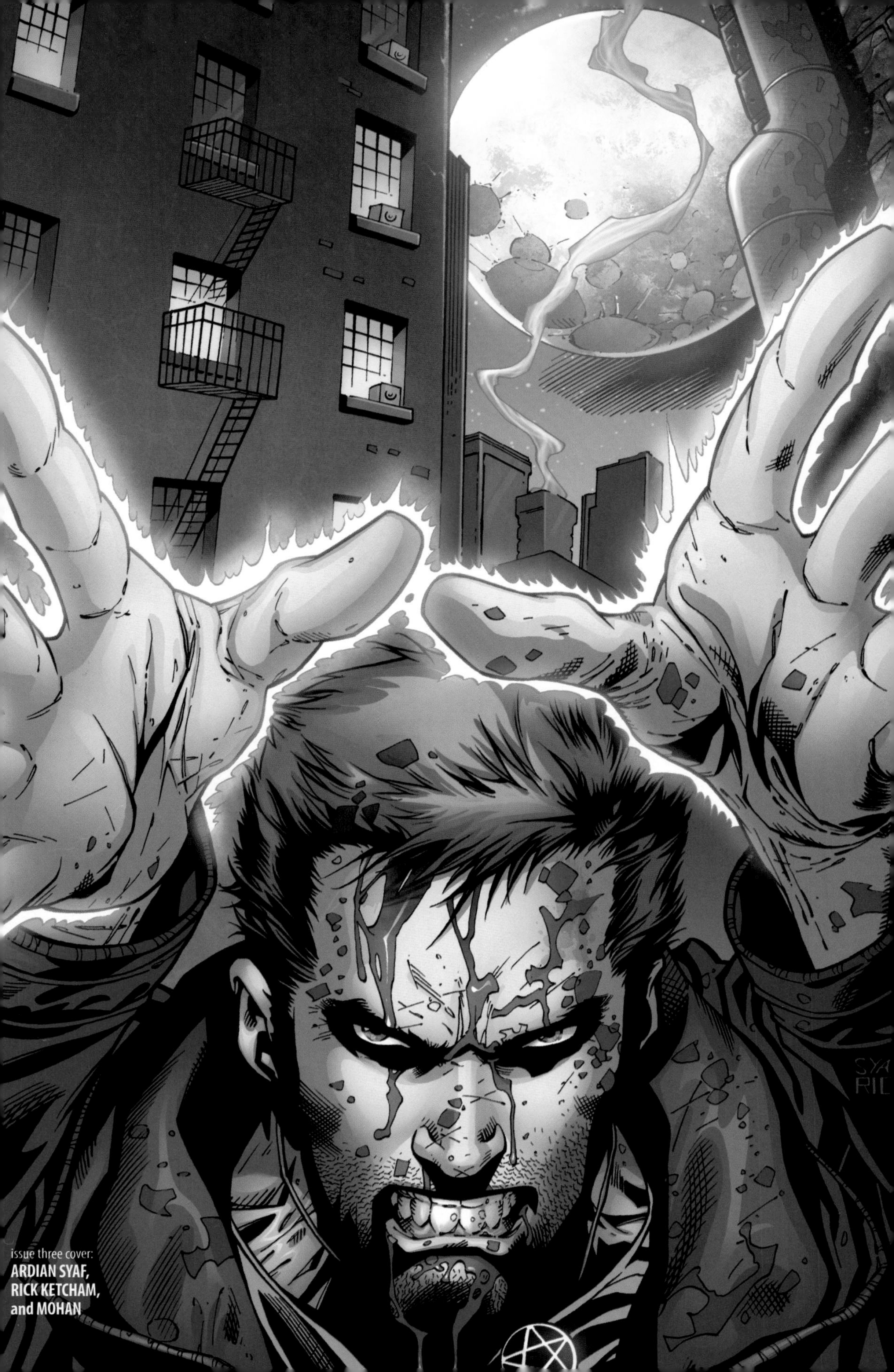

issue three cover:
ARDIAN SYAF,
RICK KETCHAM,
and MOHAN

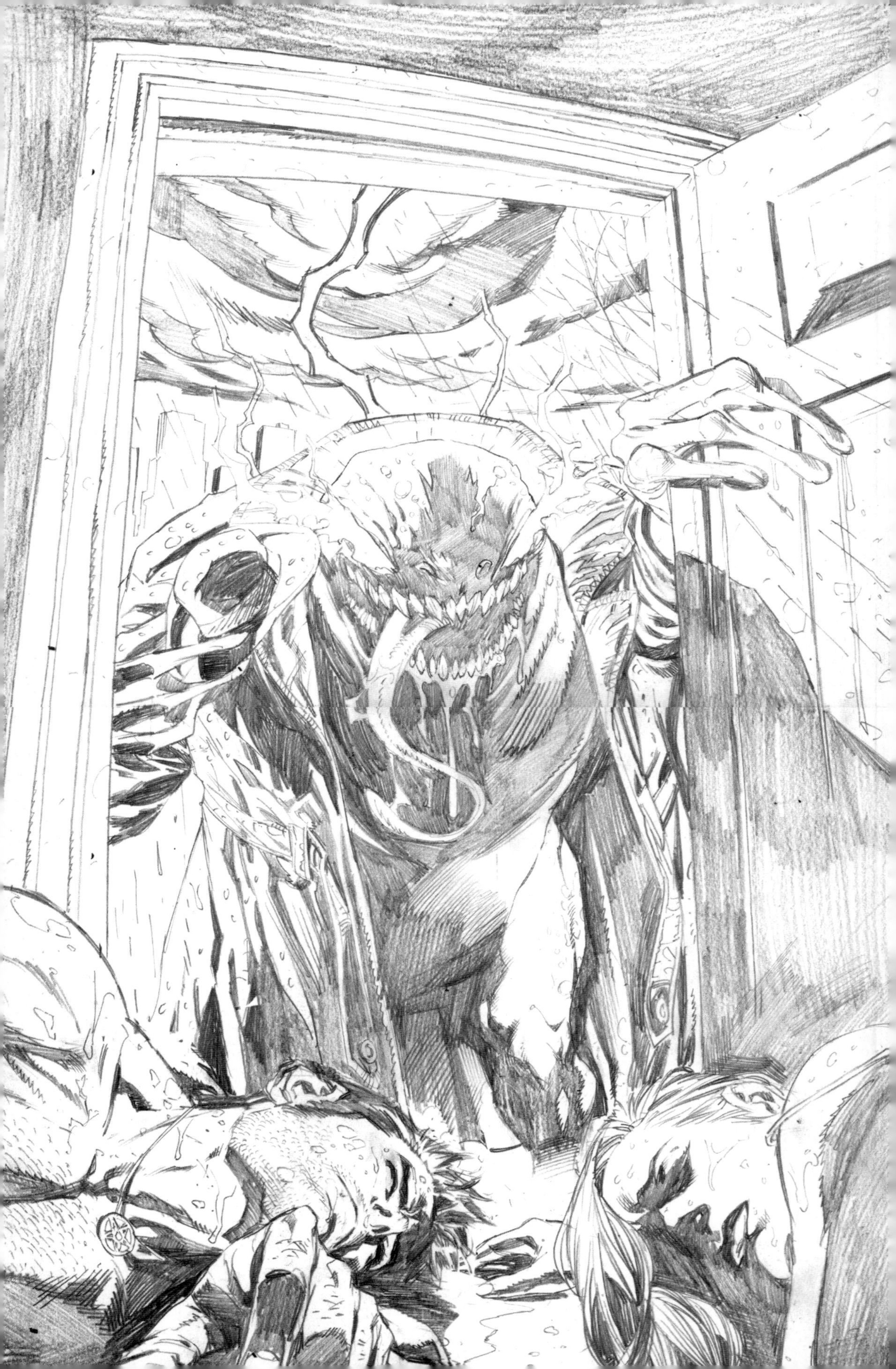

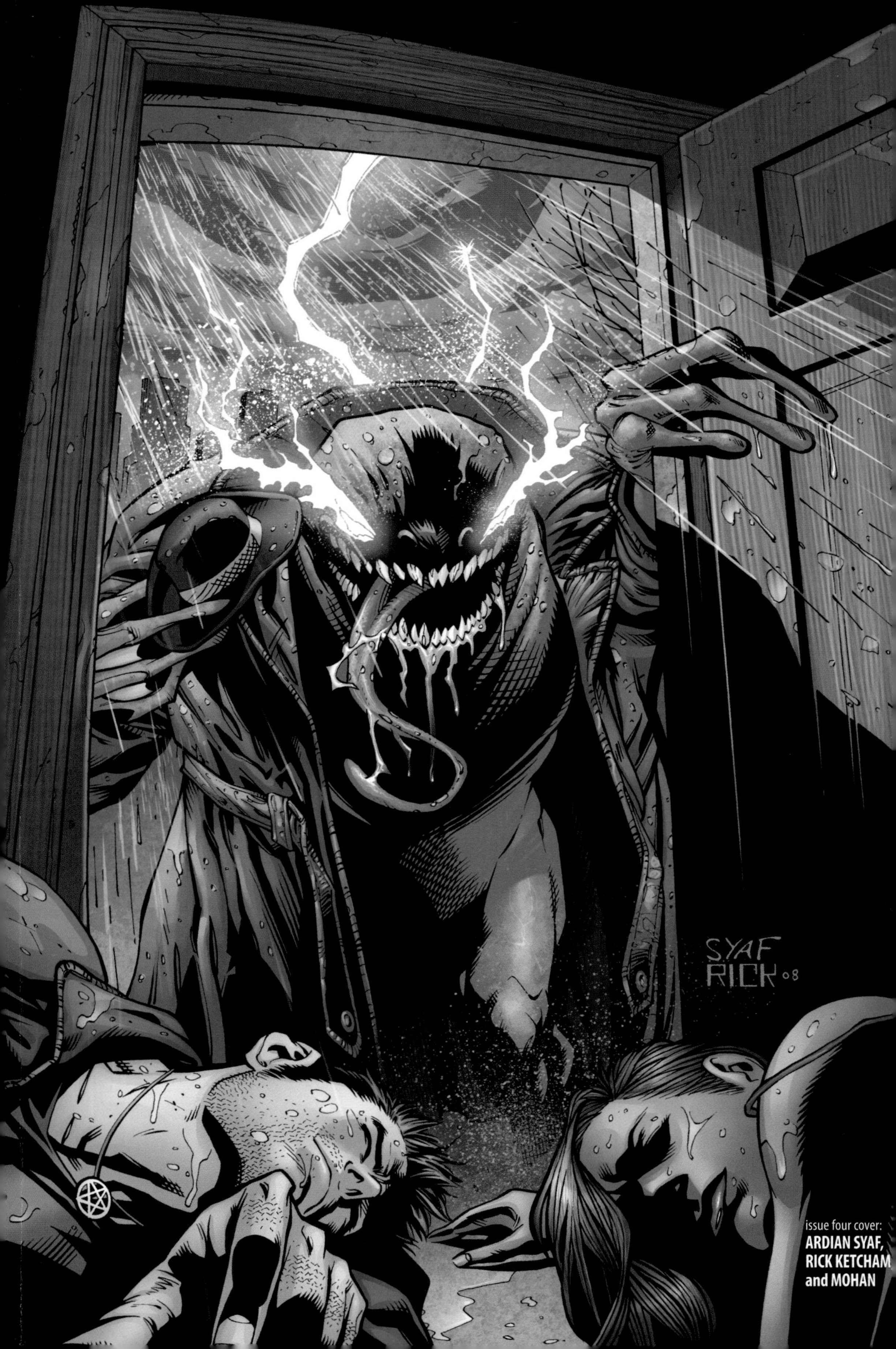
SYAF
RICK 08

issue four cover:
ARDIAN SYAF,
RICK KETCHAM
and MOHAN

JIM BUTCHER'S

THE DRESDEN FILES

STORM FRONT

VOLUME ONE: THE GATHERING STORM